THEOLOGY GOES TO THE MOVIES

Theology Goes to the Movies is an introduction to understanding theology through film. Clive Marsh, an experienced teacher in the field, uses a range of contemporary films including *Touching the Void, Bruce Almighty, Notting Hill, 21 Grams, Legally Blonde* and *The Piano* to explain key theological concepts such as ideas of God, the church, eschatology, redemption, humanity and spirit.

Starting from the premise that film-watching is a religion-like activity, the book explores the ways in which films require the viewer to engage at many levels (cognitive, affective, aesthetic and ethical) and argues that the social practice of cinema-going has a religious dimension. This stimulating and entertaining book shows how theology through film can be a method of reading the dialogue between film and Western culture, as well as a relevant and contemporary practical theology.

Clive Marsh teaches in the Department of Theology at the University of Nottingham and is also Secretary of the Faith and Order Committee of the Methodist Church. He is a well-respected writer and teacher, and his previous books include *Cinema and Sentiment: Film's Challenge to Theology* and *Explorations in Theology and Film*.

THEOLOGY GOES TO THE MOVIES

An introduction to critical Christian thinking

Clive Marsh

Routledge
Taylor & Francis Group

LONDON AND NEW YORK

First published 2007
by Routledge
2 Park Square, Milton Park, Abingdon, Oxon OX14 4RN

Simultaneously published in the USA and Canada
by Routledge
270 Madison Ave, New York, NY 10016

*Routledge is an imprint of the Taylor & Francis Group, an
informa business*

© 2007 Clive Marsh

Typeset in Joanna and Bell Gothic by Taylor & Francis Books
Printed and bound in Great Britain by Antony Rowe Ltd,
Chippenham, Wiltshire

British Library Cataloguing in Publication Data
A catalogue record for this book is available from the British
Library

Library of Congress Cataloging in Publication Data
Marsh, Clive.
  Theology goes to the movies : an introduction to critical
Christian thinking / Clive Marsh.
     p. cm.
  Includes indexes.
  1. Motion pictures--Religious aspects--Christianity. I. Title.
  PN1995.5.M27 2007
  791.43'6823--dc22
                                    2006026516

ISBN10: 0-415-38011-1 (hbk)
ISBN10: 0-415-38012-X (pbk)
ISBN10: 0-203-08883-2 (ebk)

ISBN13: 978-0-415-38011-9 (hbk)
ISBN13: 978-0-415-38012-6 (pbk)
ISBN13: 978-0-203-08883-8 (ebk)

CONTENTS

Acknowledgements   *ix*

Introduction   1

How to use this book   5

PART I
Contextualizing theology in a media age   9

1. Theology in a chaotic climate   11

    What is 'theology'? 11
    The chaotic Western climate 14
    Four features of contemporary Western cultural life 15
    Theology's critical task 19

2. Doing theology in a media age   21

    The challenge of media culture 21
    Some consequences for theology as a discipline 24
    Types of theology 27

CONTENTS

3. Theology and the Christian religion   32

    Theology as a church activity 32
    Four aspects of religion 34
    Theology as a communal, human practice 39

PART II
A systematic theology through film   41

    Introduction   43

4. God   47

    Films 49
      Bruce Almighty 49
      The Passion of the Christ 49
      The Truman Show 50
    Viewing experiences 50
    Connecting questions and issues 53
    Explorations: images and traditions; power and freedom 53
    Working conclusions 57
    For further study 58

5. Human being   60

    Films 60
      Koyaanisqatsi 60
      Eternal Sunshine of the Spotless Mind 61
      Do the Right Thing 61
      Notting Hill 62
    Viewing experiences 63
    Connecting questions and issues 66
    Explorations: gift and gratitude; individual and social sin;
        memory and identity; love and Trinity 67
    Working conclusions 76
    For further study 77

6. Spirit   79

    Films 80
      Amadeus 80
      Touching the Void 80
      Legally Blonde 81
    Viewing experiences 81

Connecting questions and issues 83
*Explorations: gifts and skills; re-creation; God's presence
    in the world 85*
Working conclusions 90
For further study 91

7. Redemption   93

Films 95
  Crimes and Misdemeanors 95
  21 Grams 96
  The Last Temptation of Christ 96
  Cries and Whispers 97
Viewing experiences 98
Connecting questions and issues 102
Explorations: evil; guilt; joy; participation in Christ 103
Working conclusions 105
For further study 107

8. Sacraments   109

Films 110
  The Piano 110
  Babette's Feast 110
  Don't Look Now 111
Viewing experiences 112
Connecting questions and issues 114
Explorations: sacramentality; baptism; Holy Communion 115
Working conclusions 122
For further study 122

9. Church   124

Films 125
  Eat Drink Man Woman 125
  Brassed Off 126
  The Magdalene Sisters 126
Viewing experiences 127
Connecting questions and issues 130
*Explorations: unity; holiness; catholicity; apostolicity;
    church as 'base group' 131*
Working conclusions 138
For further study 139

CONTENTS

10. The end   141

Films 141
  Truly Madly Deeply 141
  Jesus of Montreal 142
  Field of Dreams 142
Viewing experiences 143
Connecting questions and issues 145
Explorations: after-life; judgment; Kingdom of God; vision 147
Working conclusions 154
For further study 155

11. A Christological postscript   157

PART III
Christian theology in practice   159

12. Theology and life   161

But life's not like that! 161
The systematic character of Christian theology 163
'Theology through film' as 'theology of/from/through culture' 166
Theology through film as practical theology 168

13. Theology and God   170

Why 'God' matters 170
Realism and non-realism 171
A spectrum of theism 174
And finally . . . 176

Notes   177
Index   189

ACKNOWLEDGEMENTS

This book has been simmering away for about fifteen years, so there are lots of people who should be thanked. I have long since lost count of the conversations I have had with people that began with others saying: 'Hey, have you seen . . . ?' (and usually, I hadn't). All those conversations have fed into this book. I began teaching theology through film in Sheffield, at the Church Army Training College, where I taught Christian doctrine in the 1990s. That was an important starting point. After a lull in my theology and film activity, things took a fresh turn, though, as I began to process in my own thinking some of the reactions to *Explorations in Theology and Film* (Blackwell 1997), which I had co-edited with Gaye Ortiz. Many invitations followed on from *Explorations,* at that stage mostly to lead sessions in church educational settings. These provided opportunities to take things further during the late 1990s. I wish to thank all those colleges, courses, dioceses, circuits and churches that gave me the chance to try things out. The discussions I eavesdropped on, and the feedback I received, during those study days and training sessions were invaluable.

The most immediate prompt for this present book, however, came from Hugh Goddard, then Head of the Department of Theology (now Theology and Religious Studies) in the University of Nottingham. The invitation from Hugh to teach an undergraduate module 'Theology through Film' was too good to resist. This book has emerged from that teaching experience. I therefore thank the Department for hosting the module, and the three groups of students I have worked with during 2003–06. The 'explorations' contained in Part II of this text (and much else besides) reflect the conversations with, and ideas stimulated by, the seventy or so people who have taken the module.

Lesley Riddle at Routledge talked through the idea for the book and gave very useful guidance at significant points in its preparation. Gemma Dunn has been very patient in waiting for the final manuscript. I thank them both. In addition, John Lyden provided a very thorough and extremely useful reader's response to the full draft manuscript. Though I haven't made all the changes John would have liked (!), I have been able to make crucial adjustments to the text on the basis of his comments, and also in response to the comments made by a second, anonymous reviewer. I am grateful to both. The book has a better structure than it might have done as a result of comments made by three anonymous reviewers at proposal stage. I rarely feel that the anonymity which publishers rightly maintain in the reviewing process should be broken. But I do feel it here, as the production of this book has seemed even more collaborative than normal. So, to the anonymous contributors: thank you.

During the past nine months I have discussed my work on theology and film at the Fuller Theological Seminary, University College Chester, Regent's Park College Oxford and at the University of Uppsala. All of those occasions have helped me sharpen up or refine points in the text. I am grateful to all those who arranged for my visits and made me welcome, in particular Rob Johnston and Cathy Barsotti, Eric Christianson, Nick Wood, Anthony Clarke, Carl Reinhold Brakenhielm, Gunnel Cederlöf and Ulrika Persson-Fischier.

On a more personal note, I have enjoyed a number of conversations over the years with Jonathan Kerry and Charlotte Haines Lyon. Jonathan keeps me in touch with films I should have seen. Charlotte has actually done the film research I knew needed doing (and which has informed everything I have done over the past couple of years). I look forward to the day when analysis of the significant data she has brought together finds published form.

Clive Marsh
August 2006

INTRODUCTION

IN A RECENT INTRODUCTION TO CHRISTIAN THEOLOGY, Tyron Inbody writes candidly about the major changes in the make-up of the groups of students he has taught over his four-decade teaching career. Not only do his students now come with little grounding in Bible and tradition. The absence of a background in 'the humanities' generally is apparent. Then comes this telling statement: 'The one caveat is that most students are familiar with and responsive to popular culture, especially as conveyed by the electronic media, such as movies and television.'[1] In other words, students are not dumber than they used to be. Nor have they less knowledge – be knowledge defined as 'knowing that' or 'knowing how'. It is simply the case that *what* they know and *what they know how to do* has changed markedly in recent decades.

This observation made about theology and religious studies in the USA squares directly with my own perception of what has been happening in the UK. It might be possible to count on greater knowledge of Bible and tradition in theological college and course (seminary) contexts than can be assumed in the university sector – though even this is disputable. But even here, the limited knowledge acquired is contained within a much broader range of media and the arts (music, film, TV). Also, students of theology in either seminary or university contexts may not have discovered how best to use the Bible and tradition in the context of daily living. This is significant both for the task of reflecting theologically on what life throws up and for the challenge of addressing questions which media and the arts lay before us as part of culture. Further, how the critique and re-expression of the Christian tradition is to occur in an ordered and comprehensive way (systematic theology) might not be in view for students at all. The notion of re-working a 'doctrinal tradition' or a 'dogmatic theology' for a particular church tradition (denomination) may therefore be a very distant and alien prospect.

This book is written with that context of learning in mind. It is written with a university/liberal arts college context in mind. Its main purpose is to introduce Christian theology to those of Christian faith, of a different faith or of none to the themes and practices of (systematic) Christian theology. It undertakes its task mindful of Inbody's observation: most students now approach theological questions against a background of the stimulus of popular culture. In contemporary Western culture, in other words, theological interests and questions are always in part *shaped* by popular culture. There is no escaping this and it is not a situation to be regretted. It is simply the way things are. Some might want theology to 'correct' what popular culture does to people. Others might believe that theology's job is to disclose and highlight for public view the Christian ideas which remain embedded in popular culture. I support neither extreme position. Christian theological thinking has to do both tasks – critique and disclose – as well as doing more. It must construct a conversation with what is 'there' in culture so that the Christian theological tradition can both serve the present age, and be enabled to move forward, as evidence of its respect to the living God to whom it seeks to bear witness. This conversation is in many ways an imaginary one. The theological interpreter has to be something of a ventriloquist. Relatively few people in religious traditions sit down and discuss with purveyors of popular culture the theological implications (intended or not) of their work.[2] Yet the conversation is 'real' in the sense that religious believers are always reacting to what they see and experience around them. In the light of their faith tradition, they are adopting, rejecting or adapting what they encounter. Their appropriation of their faith tradition evolves. Even their faith tradition evolves (if very slowly) in the complex process of interaction. And those who profess no religion (whether they like it or not) are always interacting with religious practices and theological impulses which are implicit and explicit within cultural life. This book therefore makes public that complex process of ongoing interaction. It enables readers to

2

understand how Christian theology, as an example of a living religious tradition, is working in Western culture.

On this basis further groups of readers can be helped by the book's main purpose. Christians sceptical of the theological importance of media and culture or who view theology as rather static and 'contained' within a sealed box, impervious to the impact of broader culture upon it, can be challenged by its contents. For such readers, whether studying theology formally or not, this book can function as a primer in theology and culture. It can begin the process of requiring them to think more critically about how the content of Christian theology both maintains a consistent identity through time, yet also develops in constant interaction with the media and cultures in which it is embedded. In drawing attention to classic texts from the Christian past, the book notes that there have been discussions of theological topics within Christian history that have lasting value. But they cannot simply be lifted from the past and understood 'cold'. Assessing how films begin conversations for contemporary viewers enables a context to be created for making sense of such seemingly distant texts. Those texts themselves, however, invite critical consideration, in a process of dialogue that extends well beyond this book. It is this process of 'critical Christian thinking' to which Christian readers are invited.

Beyond that main theological intent, the book has a secondary purpose: to illuminate for film-watchers the fact that every act of film-watching is complex, occurring in a context of multiple, sometimes competing world-views.[3] It recognizes that all viewers watch films whilst inhabiting particular thought-worlds (cognitive frameworks, schemas) and whilst relating to particular communities of practice (families, friendships, political groups, religious groups). Without respect for this fact, film-watching remains entertaining, but what films are sometimes actually doing to people is left insufficiently examined.[4] The book is thus an extended case-study in contemporary meaning-making. It examines one media-cultural practice (film-watching) with respect to one world-view (that of Christian theology) as a window into the complex way in which people's approaches to human living are shaped today.

This is, then, a book about Christian theology, primarily for theology and religious studies courses. It does not pretend that the films studied simply deliver Christian meanings on a plate. In presenting its material it seeks to do justice to the films as films, and to the way that film as an art form 'works'. But it is not a film studies text. Readers expecting to find extensive film-critical analyses of the works considered will be disappointed. Ultimately this book grapples with what films can do to and for ordinary viewers.

In its treatment of Christian theology, the book makes no attempt to convey a particular denominational tradition (though, for the record, I happen to be Methodist and draw heavily, though not exclusively, on Protestant resources). But it does try to be thematically comprehensive. In other words, it tries to show the main themes you would expect to cover in doing justice to the beliefs and ideas of Christianity. It simply 'gets at' these themes by a highly contemporary – and hopefully enjoyable and stimulating – route. In taking this path, it respects the vibrancy of theology as a discipline that is always connected to everyday life. For one of the great advantages of getting at the subject-matter of theology through film is that the student of theology can be reminded that theology is not simply a matter of studying ideas and beliefs. Films work primarily through the emotions, but draw also on viewers' ability to use their senses of sight and hearing in order to formulate an aesthetic response. Because of this, the asking of theological questions which results from film-watching can immediately become a more existential matter than might be possible from reading classic works of theology as 'dry texts'. Getting at theology through film, then, sharpens a student's sensitivity to the existential char-acter of the study of theology. To read theological texts in the light of watching films, and to use the texts in turn to ask questions of films, makes the dry texts come to life.

The book thus acknowledges fully who the students of theology now are: those who sit in lecture- and seminar-rooms across the world and may not have begun to examine the differences between salvation, liberation and atonement, but are interested in tackling them and have seen The Shawshank Redemption.

HOW TO USE THIS BOOK

THIS IS A WORK-BOOK FOR STUDENTS OF theology or religious studies, or anyone else who is interested, who want to find out and explore the ideas and beliefs that drive the Christian religion. It 'gets at' those ideas and beliefs, however, by an unusual route. In order to do justice to the fact that Christians 'live' their faith, it is important that those who want to understand Christianity find out how ideas and beliefs therefore work in practice. Christianity is more than a set of ideas. So its theology cannot simply be learned by reading books about beliefs.

This book therefore finds a place in contemporary cultural life where Christian theology comes to life, that is, where consideration of its ideas and beliefs is evoked by virtue of the way that people of all faiths and none consume popular culture. This is always in part because of what is explicit or implicit in the films themselves. But the discussions of film which form the heart of this book also result from respect for the proven ways in which films 'work' on people. The theological reflection undertaken is thus offered as a contribution to the examination of the 'negotiations' which occur as people consume films as media products.

I would not recommend reading this straight through as a text-book from which one can simply extract a Christian theology. It is not written with that purpose. For one thing, the theology offered is not comprehensive enough to do justice to the breadth, depth and diversity of the Christian tradition. For another, it would not respect the films under consideration. How, then, should one use it? I suggest four ways.

Method 1

This method will appeal to avid cinema-goers and to those who may be a little suspicious of what this book is going to contain. By starting clearly with the films themselves, and with your own responses to them, you are then in a good position to be able to make an assessment of whether you think the films are being well used or abused in what follows.

- Check through the list of films being used. Remind yourself about all those you have already seen. Jot down notes about them. (What was it about? What themes or scenes have stuck in your mind? Did you enjoy it? Why/why not? Which characters stand out? Did you identify with anyone? Why? In what way?)
- Make a list of the films you've not seen. Set yourself a programme for watching, and then go to the DVD/video rental shop (or check the cut-price sales at a local store – sometimes this can be as cheap as renting) and start viewing. (You may, of course, also want to watch again any films you've seen before, either to 'give them another chance' if you didn't 'get' or enjoy them the first time round, or because you simply want to see them again.)
- When you end up with a set of viewing notes for all 23 films, then you're ready to tackle the book. You can then follow the procedure suggested for each chapter in the other methods outlined below.

Method 2

This method will appeal to those who like to vary the kinds of tasks they undertake when studying. So you'll be mixing reading, film-watching and note-taking. It will also satisfy those who like to work through text-books in a systematic way.

- Read Part I. In that way you will become clear about some of the theo-retical background to the book.

- Watch the three films to be discussed in Chapter 4 if you haven't already seen them. Make notes along the lines suggested in Method 1 above.
- Then read Chapter 4. As you read, you'll be able to start assessing your own insights, and to start critically evaluating the material in the chapter. How is the conversation helping you become clear about Christian ideas?
- Follow up some/all of the suggested Further Reading.
- Conclude your consideration of the films, the material in the chapter (especially the Explorations section) and the Further Reading by composing some notes on the chapter's main theme.
- Follow this procedure for each of the Chapters 5 to 10. You will then have a set of notes on most of the main themes of Christian theology.
- Complete your reading of the book.

Method 3

This method will appeal to those who like to vary their study tasks, but don't like the thought that study should be undertaken in a linear fashion!

- Follow Method 2, but when you get to Part II, work through the chapters in any order you like. There are cross-references between chapters, but these can be picked up from different directions.

Method 4

This method will appeal to those with a strong sense of theology as a tradition of belief or thought. This may include Christian believers, or those who come to study Christianity as a belief system within the history of Western thought. One of the challenges of this book to both groups is to bring the texts to life, reminding them that theology is more than just words or thoughts.

- Read Part I. In that way you will become clear about some of the theoretical background to the book.
- Turn next to the Further Reading sections of each of the chapters in Part II. Follow up some/all of the readings suggested and make notes on what you read. In this way you will be beginning to construct a

basic sketch of some of the key debates and insights from the history of Christian thought.

- Turn back to Chapter 4, then follow the procedure for either Method 2 or Method 3.

General comment

It is worth mentioning with respect to all of the above methods that it will take time to get the most from this book. There are about fifty hours of film-viewing in the films alone. (This is as much, if not more, than the entire recommended class contact and preparation-time for a module in many institutions of Higher Education.) And then there's the Further Reading to be added to that. If that is skipped in its entirety, then the true task of theological reflection on film will not be able to materialize in its richest form.

I hope, though, that this is the kind of book that will not only provide substance for a taught module, but may accompany people throughout a whole theology course. It is, after all, offering a framework for thinking about the whole of Christian theology. And in seeking to introduce people to such systematic thinking in a stimulating (even entertaining) way, it is to be hoped that it makes theology enjoyable as well as life-enhancing.

So choose your method! And off you go . . .

Part I

CONTEXTUALIZING THEOLOGY IN A MEDIA AGE

Chapter 1

THEOLOGY IN A CHAOTIC CLIMATE

What is 'theology'?

THEOLOGY IS ULTIMATELY A PRACTICAL UNDERTAKING. GOD-TALK is meant to help people live. Whatever people make of 'God' – as concept and/or reality – the point of talk about God is to understand human life better and to decide on how to act in relation to an overarching theological framework for living. Some readers may admittedly balk at the suggestion that the point of God-talk is to help human beings. For is not that too pragmatic a procedure? Is not the point of God-talk to understand God better? True. Or, more critically, is not theology's job to serve the task of praising and worshipping God rather than understanding God? From a standpoint within a particular religious tradition that is surely true too. My point, though, is that once God-talkers believe they have grasped something of the meaning of God, this has inevitable consequences, both for them and others. God-talk is not undertaken in isolation from the practice of living. Or if it is, then it has lost its way. The very notion or name 'God' identifies a concept or reality with existential import for people using the word. Even to reject the term, or to argue for the dangers of its use, let alone its misuse, is existentially significant.

Theology would not exist without religion. Religious traditions see it as their specific responsibility for carrying theologies in society even if God-talk also happens outside of religions in the context of wider society. Religions carry different theologies from each other. Religion scholars and specialists in inter-faith encounter may be able to point to common ground between religions.[1] But the irreducibility of religions to a common core of human experience is now more commonly accepted than the view that appeal can be made to some basic spiritual impulse in the human being. That there is some such spiritual or religious impulse need not be disputed. But this does not produce 'religion' in any generic sense. Religions are contingent, particular, historical, culture-related and contextual, and the theologies that they carry are too. This does not mean that 'God' as understood within any particular religious tradition is nothing but the result of the impact of contingent factors. It means that these factors have to be acknowledged and highlighted whilst theological viewpoints are examined. Otherwise the reality about which one seeks to speak, God, may not be spoken of at all. Recognition of the radical contingency and pluralism of religions does not turn all theologians into relativists. It simply means that theology is hard work and that all who engaged in it have to be prepared to ask hard questions of their own contingency and context.

Religions also carry a diversity of theologies within themselves. This insight applies the recognition of the historical, culture-related character of all religions to a single religious tradition. Christianity is identifiably the same across the world in some respects (e.g. God is always understood in relation to the figure of Jesus Christ, and Christian communities are called 'churches'), but a variety of theologies exists within it. Admittedly, not all religions depend on the existence of a supreme being. Theravada Buddhism, for example, explicitly denies the existence of such a being. Even those traditions which are theistic (Hinduism, for example) do not speak of a theology in quite the same way as 'religions of the book' (Christianity, Judaism and Islam).

In the light of all this, theology could therefore immediately become something of a vague term which may or may not imply the existence of any ultimate, transcendent reality ('God') in relation to which human beings live their lives. It may be better to speak of the 'ideology' or 'philosophy' of a religious tradition. In this book I shall, however, speak of 'theology' both because I think it is still viable and necessary to continue to speak of God, and because the religion which provides my extended case-study, Christianity, still does so. Furthermore, Christianity still speaks in this way because most of those who practise it believe that 'God' names a reality in relation to which Christians believe that human beings live their lives. Distinguishing 'theology' from 'religion', whilst also keeping them close together, however, opens up the question of what theology as an analytical discipline is seeking to do with respect to religion as a practice and also where its subject-matter comes from. Does the material with which theology works come only from a religious tradition itself (from scriptures, creeds, classical writings, liturgies, sayings of religious leaders, accounts of religious experience)? Is theology but the explication (even if with some critical reflection) of what people in a religion believe and articulate?

Theology certainly does derive its subject-matter from the *practice* of religion. Because religion is not simply ideas and beliefs, but involves rituals and practices which shape, and are shaped by, ideas and beliefs, a religion's theology cannot simply read off from a religion's scriptures. At its fullest, therefore, theology has to work with symbols, rituals, gestures, ethical actions, art, and architecture, as well as texts and the history of people.

But the task of theology is more complex still. Religions exist within culture, and are themselves cultures. Theology's subject-matter thus in part results also from the ways in which religions interact with the wider cultures in which they are located. Direct engagement with themes and symbols of religious traditions appears throughout culture outside of 'official' religious locations. Mel Gibson's *The Passion of the Christ* and Martin Scorsese's *Kundun* are examples of such explorations in film. Furthermore, believers within a tradition practise their religion within a context of constant interaction with world-views and outlooks different from their own. This applies to official leaders within a religious tradition as well as so-called 'ordinary believers'. However much a religion may entail the 'handing-on' of a clearly identifiable Great Tradition, history shows that changes do happen to that 'Great Tradition' in the process. Identifiable continuity contains within it discontinuity as a result of the interactions which constantly occur between a religion's adherents and those of other traditions and outlooks within any given culture.

Theology, then, is a critical discipline that makes the attempt to study God in this context. It recognizes it would have no work to do without religions. But it does not simply expound a religion's ideas from within. However much attention to the internal authorities within a given religious tradition may dominate its work, theology recognizes that religions are more than ideas. It will therefore always be in the task of teasing out ideas and beliefs from both religious traditions and practices and from the results of its participants' interactions with wider culture. Theology will need to be particular, for although it is addressing an aspect of what may prove true of all human beings, God will inevitably be spoken about in limited ways, using specific cultural forms. In undertaking a limited task, theology at its best is, however, always conscious of the broader cultural context – that of religious and many other pluralisms – within which theology is done, and which is likely to affect how it is done and the conclusions it may reach.

The chaotic Western climate

So much for the first stage of clarifying what theology is and what it must do. But much more must be said about the cultural context in the West in which the discipline is practised. For if more and more people are studying religion and theology who do not begin from a standpoint of commitment to a religious tradition, then what sense is to be made of how such students experience the world? In this section, then, I shall characterize the culture and the experience of that culture which contemporary students of theology and religion report.

All students of theology and religious studies will have had some contact with religion. That 'contact' takes less and less the form of a religious upbringing. Though some bring to their studies past or present experience of belonging to a religious community, this is less the case than for much of the modern period. Furthermore it is much more likely that those who do have religious commitment offer a cross-section of religious backgrounds. Groups studying Christian theology may therefore comprise a wide range of participants of whom only a minority brings Christian commitment. 'Contact with religion' may therefore take a variety of forms: through participation in religious practices associated with rites of passage, through friends of varying religious traditions in the context of education, or through media coverage of religion.

The aspect of media coverage is particularly significant for those with limited personal contact with religiously committed people.[2] Religion may appear reactionary, conservative, misguided or dangerous due to particular slants in the coverage. Attention to prominent religious leaders, often at times of state occasions or in crisis, may lend an air of authority, but figureheads may appear quaint and dated. In the UK, for example, Christian leaders can easily be made to look out of touch.

'Religion' and 'terror' have also often appeared closely allied across media coverage of religion in recent years as a result of the 9/11 attacks on the World Trade Center, the July 2005 bombs on the London Underground and Western involvement in Iraq. This alliance is not lost on critics of religion *per se*.[3] Western media coverage of religion is not uniform, but some of the more nuanced reporting on religion needs documentary rather than news time, and therefore shows outside of primetime. It is therefore not surprising to find students choosing religion and theology classes *because* religion is clearly important – it makes people do seemingly insane things, but there is puzzlement and suspicion as to how and why. Students then have the chance to examine what religions are, and begin to look at history, ideas, society and what it means to be human. But at the same time, it may all appear just plain baffling. Furthermore, if all religions are viewed 'from the outside' (adopting what it often called a 'religious studies perspective'), then the existential dimension of religious faith and theology, which this present book seeks to address, may be missed altogether.

It is crucial that opportunity be given to students, as they begin their study of religion or theology, critically to assess their actual encounters with religion, either in their own experience or through their observations of people known to them and through media reports. My own experience in the classroom shows that students are wrestling with all sorts of hesitations, puzzlements and fears, as well as commitments past and present (mixed up with family stories) for and against religion. Without giving the impression that any class on religion or theology becomes a therapy session, some opening up of what theological study involves will be needed.[4]

But characterization of what students in the West face when preparing to study religion and theology needs more than acknowledgement of how they themselves have experienced religion. The chaotic climate in which we all find ourselves in the West needs further mapping. It is fashionable to speak of 'fragmented culture' or 'postmodern times'. There is no need in this book to debate whether or not something major has or has not been lost from the past (be that Christendom, or a more unified culture based on some other foundation). Nor do we need to find a definitive label to describe our present situation. Our task is to characterize it accurately so that we see, by the book's end, how theology is to work within it. What, then, does Western culture look like from within?[5]

Four features of contemporary Western cultural life

There is no single account of reality that receives wholesale support. Many accounts compete to offer the most plausible understanding of, or framework within which to live, human life (religions among them but also modern rationality too), but none has overall cultural dominance. The assumed dominance of Christianity ('Christendom') has gone in the West. Pluralism is a fact. Western pluralist culture is often termed 'postmodern'. This means that the West has moved beyond a 'modern' (Enlightenment) phase in which it was assumed that a single form of rationality could be used by all, to reach a single truth, and a universal account of what it means to be human. Modernity constructed on such lines has proven to be a thinly veiled form of Western, colonialist, Christianity-driven imperialism. Christianity need not be assumed, as a result of this critique, to be fundamentally corrupt, misguided or untrue. But it has to ask questions of itself and be more open than it has often been to the questioning of others.

In a postmodern context, religions are part of what is often called a 'market-place' of belief systems and world-views which vie for people's attention. Talk of a 'market-place' implies that people are free to choose. In practice, of course, the situation is more complex. People are 'born into' sets of cultural assumptions (through family, education, nation) which they adopt without realizing, and must then choose to stay within, or to opt out of. In the West, it could be argued that global capitalism, issuing in a consumerism that is more than just a way of shopping but also a way of life, is the dominant world-view. I am not so sure. Some of the critiques of global capitalism overlook the fact that people have to consume in order to live, and underplay the great variety of ways in which people discover and construct meaning. It is, however, true that the alliance between postmodernism, pluralism, capitalism and the demand for choice affects thinking about how people come by, and inhabit, religious traditions. In so far as people are invited to 'shop around' for a religion or a spirituality, as if religions are like shampoos, then consumerism has affected faith.[6]

However, though there may be no dominant *account* of reality, there are, second *practices* that are recognized to make up a human life. These include family, friendships, sexual activity, work, leisure, sport, charitable action and political commitment. Religious commitment overlaps with many of these human practices. At a time of considerable uncertainty as to whether there is, or can be, any overarching way of making sense of human life (i.e. there can be no 'meta-narrative' which enables people to make sense of it all), it is participation in such practices which *are* the meaning of life. Rather than trying to make sense of the complex and bewildering pluralism of Western society, it may be deemed better simply to launch oneself more intensely into the business of living. Coherence may not be possible. Actions one undertakes may not fit within a logical framework of living. Perhaps, indeed, the quest to find or create such meaning is itself misguided, assuming a hidden, prior meaning that simply does not exist.

At its most extreme, such a course of action may lead to selfish hedonism. But it need not. Many of the basic practices listed would inevitably take a person beyond themselves in a more altruistic direction. It is not possible to be a good family-member or friend without bearing the needs of others in mind. Political activity is rarely wholly selfish. My point is that a bewildering pluralism can actually contribute to a refusal to reflect, because it simply seems such a hard thing to do. This book recognizes this and picks one cultural practice out of list – from the 'leisure' section – and subjects it to sustained critique. The book acknowledges that whether people go to the cinema for intellectual stimulus or not, film-watching is the kind of activity which is a location in life in which critical reflection is often provoked.[7] It is thus a practice that stimulates reflection without being intended as such. This, however, is how philosophical and theological reflection often occurs: in response to the practice of living.

Third, the bewilderment of pluralism is coped with in part through closer attention to local identity. Identities still need to be found and shaped. Human beings need to find some way of working out who they are, where they fit in to the society and culture of which they are a part and where they think they are heading. But in a postmodern context of multiple, sometimes conflicting, world-views, discerning and choosing from available value-systems is a hard task. Furthermore, the global reach of media means that borders seem to carry little meaning. Claims that we are all 'citizens of the world' can easily be made.

Of course, such claims are too grand. Passports are still needed for border-crossing. The world is at the feet only of the wealthy who have the money to travel. Globalization has, then, joined forces with the opposition to claims for universality and led people to place much greater emphasis upon the local and the particular. This emphasis takes many forms.

Awareness of one's national identity is one form. In the UK, there has been considerable investigation of 'citizenship' and 'Britishness' as a result. The cultivation of a new pride in being British on the part of people of quite different backgrounds is a noteworthy feature of recent British culture. In contrast to an implicitly racist form of nationalism that looks nostalgically, and mistakenly, to a past (English) history of dominant white culture, this new sense of Britishness notes the diversity present in British culture. The attempt is being made to respect the particular within a new fashioning of national identity.[8]

A second aspect of the emphasis upon the local and the particular is thus the acceptance of ethnic and religious diversity inevitably present in any modern state. Respect for diversity can clearly not simply be a reluctant acceptance that 'this is the way things are' (as if the loss of Christendom is something to be bemoaned). Positive respect takes the form of seeking to value the particularity of different cultures. Respect for particular cultures (including religious cultures) thus becomes part of the effect of the opposition to universality.

Fourth, support for organized Christianity in much of the Western world is in steep decline. This is of especial importance to the subject-matter of this present book. For why keep on trying to work with a tradition which fewer and fewer people seem to be supporting explicitly? Admittedly there are differences between Europe and North America here. Processes of secularization have taken different forms. In the USA, Christian affiliation remains a more standard cultural practice than throughout much of Europe, despite the stark separation of church and state. Conservative Christians, furthermore, exert a major influence in political life in the USA. That said, there is no need to doubt the evidence of secularization across the West. It is well documented over a long period.[9] If conservative Christianity remains a cultural force in the USA, it can be argued that this merely highlights the particular form of American secularization: Christians are expected to be lobbying from the outside, however 'mainstream' they may appear to be. They are peculiar, counter-cultural voices, sounded from the private/privatized world of religion. As far as the understanding of theology espoused in this book is concerned, however, Christianity is to be looked towards as a critical, public voice in any context where discussions about meaning, value and purpose occur.

Here is not the place to examine fully the arguments about Christianity's future in the West or further afield. This present book simply acknowledges that Christianity still exists, as both religion and theological system, shapes the lives of a great many people throughout the world and remains influential in many cultures. For that reason alone, then, it is worthy of study. The fact that, alongside Judaism especially, its symbols and beliefs feed into many of the films which are watched across the Western world merely confirms how inextricably linked religion and culture are, and how influential Christianity remains, even if numerical support may be weakening at present. To explore the content of Christian theology in relation to film, then, is to examine a way in which Christianity functions culturally. If this present book also becomes a work of Christian apologetics, then so be it. But although I write as a Christian theologian, my purpose, as will be clear throughout, is not primarily to defend Christianity's contents. My purpose is to disclose their meaning and comprehensibility at a time in Western culture when the existential significance of Christianity is little grasped or frequently misunderstood.

Theology's critical task

Theology takes its place as a discipline in the thick of the four features of contemporary, chaotic, pluralistic Western culture just identified. Theologies will always themselves be religion-specific. There can only be Christian, or Jewish or Muslim theologies. There is no 'global theology'. Even though the conviction may be maintained that there is one God, conflicting truth-claims exist about how that one God is to be spoken to and about. Theology is thus itself caught up in the turn to the local and particular, and the resistance to metanarratives.

But whatever tradition a theology emerges from, it has a critical role to play in two senses. First, theology has a responsibility to the tradition it seeks to understand and interpret. For example, a Christian theology – whether engaged in for religious purposes or not – has the task of testing the coherence and adequacy of Christian ideas and beliefs. Christian theology therefore keeps close to Christian religious practice. But its task is not simply to articulate that practice. It must critique it. And it must be clear on what basis the critique is offered. (Is it from an outsider who is basically critical of Christianity *per se*? Is it from an insider who may be less critical than she should be about Christian practice itself? Is it from outsiders or insiders sympathetic to what Christianity believes and seeks to do, but who have noted some significant problems?)

Second, theology has a critical task beyond a religious tradition itself. One of the greatest problems of the postmodern context in which we now find ourselves in the West is that the opposition to universals and the turn to the local conspire together to produce a situation in which *any* form of critical analysis is difficult. If there are no agreed standards of universal rationality, and all local forms of self-expression and identity-creation are deemed acceptable and equally valid, then there are no generally accepted criteria for the critical evaluation of respective truth-claims. In religious studies and theology, this means that readers of tea-leaves may be deemed as insightful as the profoundest of Hindu mystics, or the work of biblical interpreters as useful for society as statements made by those who claim to see UFOs.

Any truth-claim is subject to critique, of course. But to say that all must be subject to criticism is not the same as saying that every claim is of equal worth before and after being subject to critique. The fact that criteria can be established *at all* for distinguishing the relative merits of different claims to truth indicates that despite the absence of universal valid criteria of rationality applicable in all cases, to all forms of human knowledge, there are nevertheless tests that can be applied. In the case of religion, proven worth in enabling people to live purposeful lives and the impact of religious faith on altruistic behaviour are two criteria that come into play.

Religions and theologies cannot, then, be left in ghettos. If the emphasis upon the local and the particular comes to mean that different world-views do not speak to each other or critically compare each other's truth-claims, then humanity globally is in a very dangerous situation. 'Live and let live' is a positive reading of pluralism. Terrorism is the negative flip-side: the unwillingness to accept pluralism, or to be so threatened by the bewilderment it creates, that it cannot be faced. Pluralism is best lived with, however, when peaceful, mutual critique occurs. It is both a very difficult yet also very creative place to be in (as anyone involved in inter-faith dialogue testifies). But it is a vital place to be.

This book does not venture so far. But it does invite readers who are also viewers (film-watchers) – especially those not within the Christian tradition – to enter in a fresh, creative way into the theological world-view which is Christianity. In this way, film-watching becomes an engaging enjoyable pastime which also enables viewers to reflect further on what they have seen, and on what such reflection might mean for them as people. If this reflection happens for readers, as I hope it will, then film will continue to do what it often does best: it opens viewers up to other worlds.

Chapter 2

DOING THEOLOGY IN A MEDIA AGE

The challenge of media culture

IN THE OPENING CHAPTER I SOUGHT TO characterize the contemporary Western cultural context in which theology is undertaken. I made the briefest of references to the role of the media in Western culture. I pointed out how for some students of religion and theology today their main point of contact with religion is through media reports on religion from around the world. As much of this reporting is of cases where religion is tangled up with conflict, it is not surprising that some students approach their studies with some trepidation. For they may undertake their study fully aware of what a destructive phenomenon religion can be.

In this second chapter I offer a different take on the relationship between media and religion. For there is a second perspective on the relationship that receives too little attention in courses of study across the West. This second perspective links with the observations made in the opening chapter about the interplay between religions and cultures, i.e. that theology's content evolves as a result of the constant interaction between participants in a religious tradition and the wider cultures of which they are a part. But it takes those observations to a new level in its respect for the media domination of contemporary Western culture. The chapter is in some ways a slight detour on the journey from Chapter 1 to the content of Part II. It is, however, important that contemporary students of Christianity grasp something of this chapter's content with respect to how Christianity as a religion is actually working in the West today. Some readers may, though, wish to skip the chapter at this stage (or at least the section 'Types of Theology') and return to it once they have worked through Part II.

Stewart M. Hoover's *Religion in the Media Age* is a major progress report on ongoing research undertaken by scholars at the University of Colorado into the way in which patterns of consumption of media affect how religions work.[1] It is one of a number of studies written across media-related disciplines that reflect the shift of focus that has been under way from production (of media 'texts' or works of art), to text, to receiver. In the same way that in the humanities there has been a shift from the writer (original author), to the text to the reader (resulting in 'reader-response' approaches to interpretation of texts), so also in media and film studies, increasing attention has been paid to how people *use* media in their daily lives. Hoover's study reflects this shift and confirms its importance for the study of religion. His book provides multiple examples of the different ways in which people use media in the construction of their religious lives. Whatever evaluations one may have been tempted to make about the media, it has become increasingly clear that 'The realms of "religion" and "media" can no longer easily be separated . . . '.[2] Indeed, 'They occupy the same spaces, serve many of the same purposes, and invigorate the same practices in late modernity.'[3]

This is a significant conclusion in a number of ways. First, it pinpoints in a stark contemporary form what has always been true of religions and theology: that their rituals, practices, ideas and beliefs interweave with the products of the culture of which they are a part. Second, it indicates that people who do not profess a religious tradition nevertheless make their meaning in similar ways to those who do. For what Hoover's research shows is the complex way in which Western citizens access and make use of a 'package' of various forms of media (e.g. TV, Internet, music, film). For the religiously inclined this includes the explicit consumption of religious resources. But meaning-making is not different in kind for those not so inclined. What differs is the identity of the resources accessed.

Third, it must be noted how individualized these patterns of meaning-making have become. One of Hoover's emphases is that people make meaning through construction of 'coherent narratives of themselves as active participants in their social and cultural surrounds'.[4] The vast expansion of the range and sophistication of media technologies, and the way in which people access such technologies, means that people pick and choose what helps them. Religious groups might not welcome this individualizing development, for it is a challenge to the coherence of religious traditions. People may simply pick up from a religious tradition 'what helps me' regardless of whether what is selected is understood according to the insights of that religion. Furthermore, the likely absence of reference to a community of faith (with all the attendant issues of membership and authority) will concern religious traditions that have a strong sense of belonging and commitment. Nevertheless, this development is occurring. It may simply indicate more clearly what has long happened with respect to religions: people have often 'picked and mixed', even if they were not supposed to. And it may also be a pointer to ways in which religious traditions themselves are changing.

Fourth, this de facto role of media in the construction of meaning invites a more positive evaluation of the media than they often receive in the disciplines of theology and religious studies. The longstanding opposition to 'mass media' which religious groups have often shown may of course continue.[5] Indeed, this opposition may only be exacerbated by the observation just made about the individualizing of meaning-making. Alternatively, the recognition that meaning-making happens by a complex process of consumption of media products (and has perhaps always done) may give pause for thought. If, for example, liturgies are less effective in enabling people to 'learn' a religious faith than is sometimes assumed (e.g. by being less connected with daily life than leaders of such worship assume), then other means of 'inhabiting a theological tradition' may need to be found. The discoveries about meaning-making which studies of the relationship between media and religion disclose, therefore, may have widespread significance.

Film fits into the 'package' of available media that people access in order to make meaning even though they do not feature prominently in Hoover's research. They are, of course, both an art and a form of media. They therefore have the advantage and disadvantage of being classifiable as both 'high' and 'popular' culture. Some films count as art. Most (in the world of theology and religious studies, at least) are deemed 'mere entertainment'. Perhaps Hoover's study may at least lead to a re-assessment of the attention that will need to be given to film as part of the re-think called for about how meaning-making is occurring in Western culture.

Some consequences for theology as a discipline

Hoover's research shows, then, that no-one is detached from the practice of consumption, and the task of meaning-making. But what does this mean for the contemporary student of Christian theology in the West? Three points need making. First, *studying Christian theology does not require a student to be a Christian believer.* Hoover's research indicates that issues about participation, belonging, empathy and the sheer capacity to grasp what it means to 'be committed' to any particular point of view arise in a media-dominated culture. There is, however, an obvious difference between undertaking study from within the Christian faith and when the Christian religion is considered from the outside. There are advantages and disadvantages for believers and non-believers. Believers may find it easier to tease out the theological implications of Christian practices (Holy Communion, for example) through regular participation in them. They will know words from prayers or liturgies. But their commitment to a specific form of Christianity may, of course, prevent them from looking sympathetically at other forms of Christianity, or from being able to imagine what Christianity looks like from the outside.

Those studying Christian theology from outside the Christian tradition – either as believers in another religious tradition, or from a position of agnosticism or atheism – may well be helped by the relatively detached stance. It is likely to prove easier to look at a range of Christian viewpoints in the course of examining theological themes prominent in Christianity. The assumption of 'objectivity' which may accompany this relative detachment is, however, misleading.

All people have ideological commitments, working philosophical assumptions, myths that they live by and communities that they belong to, whether or not these are acknowledged or clearly articulated. All of these shape, and are shaped by, life experience and the encounter with the diverse products and practices which make up a society's complex culture. The detachment of a non-religious observer of Christianity, or of someone of another religious tradition, does not then lead to interpreters having no commitments. Theological enquiry thus becomes an imaginative exercise of what living within a theological tradition *would* be like. And if such study is to carry any existential import for the interpreter, then it will also include the making of critical comparisons with their own world-view.[6]

As Hoover's research shows, the religiously committed are themselves actively engaged in the consumption of various forms of media as part of the construction of their faith identity. But they do this in a manner that is not different in kind from the non-believer. Hoover's research thus shows that 'insider' and 'outsider' perspectives and appeals to 'objectivity' may be less clear-cut than often assumed. A teacher of theology can thus show through the way in which a form of the media (e.g. film) is being consumed how its theological use by religious believers corresponds to other forms of philosophical and ideological use.[7]

Christian belief is not, then, a requirement for the study of Christian theology. It can both help and hinder. But lack of Christian commitment does not inevitably lead to critical detachment. The value for all students of theological engagement with examples of popular culture, when undertaken with full awareness of patterns of media consumption, is that the workings of theology within culture become clear. In using this book, then, students are able to see what the Christian theological tradition as a 'system' contains. They are also enabled to see how it comes into play in the cognitive processing of life experience, through the way in which responses to films become built into theological reflection. Religious commitment is not required to see all of this at work. Whether a person then chooses to inhabit the theological world-view espoused is another matter, and lies beyond the book's remit.

Second, *Christian theology is not simply the 'thought' or 'belief system' of the Christian religion.* This is an emphasis that reverberates throughout this present book. Study of Christianity's history and practices highlights the beliefs and ideas by which Christianity lives, and the way in which those ideas and beliefs have developed through time. But theology is not reducible to whatever ideas and beliefs are disclosed and scrutinized. Ideas and beliefs are embodied in *practices*. Christian theology therefore lives in the form of its life as a religion (and thus as a collection of religious communities) and through the actions of individual Christians. Ways have to be found to do justice to this insight. The study of Christianity as a set of practices has to be part of the theologian's work.

This insight is relevant to the approach adopted in this book in two ways. First, the development of a theology is recognized to be an active process. A person's theological outlook may not come as a result of a conscious, cognitive programme of study. For a religiously committed person, a theological position results from their participation in a range of religious practices (e.g. prayer, worship, singing or chanting, charitable acts). In the light of the observations made about how people make meaning in a technological media-dominated age, still more is clear. The notion of a theological position being reached, or a tradition learned, by passive reception, or by straightforward accessing of written texts, may be wide of the mark. This has huge implications for theology's handling of scriptures and liturgies. The reading or hearing of scripture (within or outside formal worship) and participation in a liturgy are not passive practices. However, whether the inhabiting of a religious tradition is seen as an active practice by those who do not already inhabit such a tradition is a moot point. The *apparent* passivity of involvement in a religious tradition may, in other words, fare badly in contrast with the active meaning-making encouraged by the consumption of media products.

Second, by scrutinizing the way in which film is consumed in contemporary Western culture, and bringing those patterns of consumption alongside study of how theological reflection occurs, a challenge is issued to theology itself. Film works primarily through the emotions, even whilst also working on the senses. It has the capacity as a medium to get viewers experientially involved in the subject-matter of the narratives it presents. In considering film and theology together, the discipline of theology is reminded that it is itself a multi-dimensional discipline. If theology is acknowledged to be more than just ideas and beliefs, then the work of the theologian will relate to a range of practices and life experiences. Theology must see itself as a discipline that takes account of the affective, aesthetic and ethical aspects of being human, as well as the cognitive.[8] And all of these aspects of being human occur in embodied form. We feel, sense and act, as well as think, as embodied beings. If theology overlooks one aspect of this in attempting to do its work, then theology's task is distorted. The easiest mistake a theologian can make is to turn theology into a cognitive discipline that fails to respect that even thinking is done within and by *people*. As we shall see, the practising of theology through reflection on film provides an opportunity for the theologian to respect that theology is not just about beliefs, but also how those beliefs are felt and lived.

Third, *the theologian is committed to interpreting the traces of Christianity that are displaced elsewhere within Western culture*. Theological exploration must investigate the assumptions and meanings behind religious practice. But it will also have to investigate where those meanings surface in culture at large. Christian insights, or traces of residual Christianity, appear throughout Western society. The cultural dominance of Christianity throughout the culture of the North West during the last two millennia has inevitably led to Christianity being the primary religious tradition which culture 'plays off against' positively and negatively. At a time of declining explicit support for organized Christianity it cannot but be of interest to the theologian to know whether Christian theology is being *displaced* (and thus appearing in society outside of identifiable Christian communities) or *replaced* (by other religious traditions or substitutes for religion, such as sport or entertainment).[9]

The apparent decline of support, and thus of influence, itself begs questions of Christianity's capacity to remain persuasive. Christian theology can therefore not overlook the question of where, in Western culture today, meaning is actually being sought.[10] But the Christian theologian is not engaged in the task of picking up the scraps left behind after the party is over. As Part II of this book will make clear, the exercise of undertaking Christian theology through film is not a quest for residual traces of a spent cultural force. It is a demonstration of how a living tradition continues to interact with what human enquirers (who make and watch films) cannot do without, and the kinds of resources which human beings need to do their reflecting on life. The shaping of the experiences of film-watching and the reflective processes which are begun within a theological framework reveals itself to be a legitimate and fruitful way of processing the film-watching experience. Doing the theological task in this way makes theology pedagogically interesting. It also invites readers to reflect on the cultural function of religious themes and symbols.

Types of theology

The theological engagement with culture undertaken in this book will not receive the support of all Christian theologians. There are different ways of doing theology, only some of which are prepared to take such a positive stance towards culture beyond the church that it becomes part of theology's resource material. Ten years ago I sought to map the different approaches to culture in three main ways:

- theology against culture
- theology immersed in culture
- theology in critical dialogue with culture.[11]

The procedure adopted in this present book continues to espouse the view that theology re-works and re-states its content in constant, critical dialogue with the cultures in which it is located. For this view to hold, there remains a sense of a 'given': a theological tradition out of which Christian theologians critically compare what churches are saying with readings of reality which do not derive directly from Christian (or even religious) sources. That 'given' is itself always moving. It is not hopelessly fluid, otherwise there would be no identifiable thing which could be labelled 'Christianity'. It is this recognition which prevented, and prevents, my being able to support a view that theology is wholly immersed in the culture of which it is a part.

Having said that, with hindsight I can see that I need to acknowledge more the sense in which theology is undeniably immersed in culture. And it is this sense of immersion that this book takes up and runs with. Religiously committed people are always immersed in culture. The question for them as people is whether, in order to maintain a religious identity, the distinction between theology and culture has to be so sharply made that it appears as though theology is in constant conflict with culture. Is it really necessary so to separate 'church' from 'world' in order to maintain a theological perspective on life and thereby to be able to 'live theologically'? To suggest this would end up with the first of three options (theology against culture). The evidence from the study of religion and media being adduced by Hoover's research team suggests that such a stark dichotomy is not only ill-advised, it is simply not possible to make. The way in which religious faith is formulated really is a process of constant, critical dialogue with culture.

How does this inform an understanding of how theology works, given that people will do theology in different ways? What 'types' of theology exist given that theology has now to be done in a highly technological, media age? In his 1999 study *Spiritual Marketplace: Baby Boomers and the Remaking of American Religion*, Wade Clark Roof offers a five-fold typology of approaches to religion in American society.[12] Hoover makes use of this typology in *Religion in the Media Age*, noting how each different approach correlates with a different use of media culture.[13] I want to take the application process a stage further, noting how each of the approaches relates not only to patterns of media-consumption but also to types of theology.

The five 'religious sensibilities' identified by Roof are:

- Born-again Christians
- Mainstream believers
- Metaphysical believers and seekers
- Dogmatists
- Secularists

Born-again Christians place great emphasis on personal (individual) salvation. For them, 'membership or participation in conventional churches is less important than their experience of faith'.[14] Their pattern of media-consumption is, however, less overtly critical of non-Christian culture than might have been supposed. Thus, though they do consume Christian resources (music, videos, books,etc.), and work hard to evaluate the media products emerging from the culture around them, they participate in the generally assumed practices of American cultural life (TV, radio, movies, Internet). This group is, however, aware that it is somewhat detached from where it perceives mainstream culture to be.

Mainstream believers think of themselves as 'mainstream'. They inhabit traditions which would have been regarded as normative forms of religion (not only Christianity) in mid-twentieth-century America. History and a clear tradition of faith and practice are important to this group. It would be expected that this group exhibit a critical view of much mass media. There is some evidence of this. However, mainstreamers are just as 'embedded in media' as other groups. The difference is simply that mainstreamers see their convictions as the norm, that is, as holding to basic values according to which it will be clear what is acceptable and unacceptable in the media.

Metaphysical believers and seekers consciously detach themselves from tradition. They favour 'spirituality' over 'religion', as the latter implies restriction. They may belong to a group, but the emphasis is likely to be on individual exploration. This group makes extensive use of modern media, knowing that 'searching' means that what is spiritually enriching may be found in many places. Any technology that therefore assists the search is to be welcomed. The group is, however, suspicious of the cultural impact of some forms of media (especially TV).

Dogmatists are the group who most adhere to the rituals of religion, and 'their social networks tend to revolve around their places of worship'.[15] It is here, rather than amongst the born-again Christians, that heavy control or 'church advice' as to what is or is not acceptable to consume comes into play. This applies across Christian traditions, for example the group includes both Roman Catholics and Evangelical Protestants. That said, dogmatists remain media-consumers. At issue is merely what is consumed within a 'hierarchy of media' (e.g. reading better than watching TV), and who decides.[16]

Finally, *secularists* are those who have distanced themselves from all interest in religion or spirituality, and are 'a-religious or ir-religious rather than anti-religious'.[17] These tend to be high-income, highly educated people with ready access to many forms of media. They tend to display a critical view of 'popular media' (e.g. TV) but, through not being linked with specific religious traditions, display a wide range of lenses through which their accessing and consumption of the arts and media occurs (e.g. art and film criticism).

Hoover's comments and reflections on the empirical findings from study of media consumption by the above groups are instructive in a number of respects. Here I can focus on only three that are especially relevant for the purposes of this book. First, it is clear that all groups perceive the media as creating a *common culture*. Whatever stance people adopt towards religion, participation in the media is accepted as an intrinsic part of contemporary human living. Second, there is *widespread resistance to the notion that people are being controlled by media*. 'We do not want to think of ourselves as subject to the influence of media (or – interestingly – of clerical or institutional religious authority, either).'[18] There is a strong sense that people think they know what they are doing as media-consumers. Third, there is a clear element of *playfulness* in the way that people use media. People 'think of the media as something that they simply "do." Their mode of practice in this "doing" seems to follow its own logics, not the sort of cognitive, deliberative course that we might have wanted or expected.'[19]

The identification of the five 'sensibilities' and the three observations just made prove highly instructive for understanding how theology works in relation to film. First, some comments on the five-fold typology. It obviously comes from a US context and not all the categories would be directly applicable elsewhere. In the UK, for example, the born-again Christians would not be categorizable in quite the same way as a group distinct from the type of believer who might fit equally well within the dogmatist group. Nevertheless the different patterns of religiosity and media-consumption would be identifiable in other places.

In terms of the relation between media consumption and theology, it is clear that some surprising alliances result. The born-again Christians, the metaphysical believers and the secularists are similar, for example, in so far as they are engaged in individual searches for meaning. They may access, or appeal to, theological resources within that quest (even if secularists might do so incidentally or accidentally). But the question of the origin or authority of any source consumed from the media is of less concern than it is for the other two groups. In terms of film, then, using theological resources in order better to understand what film may be doing to and for them as people turns theology into a 'resource' in their personal quests for meaning.

Mainstream believers and dogmatists, by contrast, carry a much greater sense that *theology is itself a tradition*. Their patterns of media consumption are thus located within a sense that a cultural legacy must be preserved and passed on (mainstream believers) or that, whatever happens, a religious tradition must be maintained (dogmatists). Despite their extensive consumption of the media, then, the normativity of tradition remains paramount. Theological engagement with film, therefore, must in some way serve the task of continuing a legacy of civil, communal living.

Taking up the three observations made by Hoover, more becomes apparent which is of consequence for this book. First, Hoover's insight about common culture highlights the fact that whatever different approaches to religion people adopt, media culture is a shared space in which meaning is being worked out (and where real ideological conflict happens). The theological discussion of film is thus one of the many important conversations occurring in that shared space. Second, the sense that people have of not being passive indicates the extent to which people believe themselves actively engaged in their own meaning-making. This means that there is greater openness to the making of theological meaning being more active that it is often assumed to be. Participation in theology is not being viewed as the passive learning of a tradition, or a passive form of participation in a religious community. In a media age, the sense that doing theology is an active process should be an easy conclusion to draw.[20] Third, the playfulness that Hoover observed in the way in which people consume media deserves the greatest respect. Both this and the previous point cohere directly with the findings of (as yet unpublished) research in which I was involved myself in the UK in 2004, which indicates that when people watch films they rarely go deliberately to be educated.[21] The attention which Hoover rightly gives throughout his study to the *cognitive effects* of media consumption should, however, not lead us to overemphasize the play element. People may, for example, indeed go to 'escape'. But they often keep on going precisely because much more happens to them (which is cognitively satisfying, ethically stretching, intellectually stimulating) as well as entertaining.

This present book pitches into the middle of the media world that Hoover is describing. Its contribution, I suggest, is to show how theological reflection emerges today in relation to the Christian tradition inside and outside churches across the range of ways in which people consume the media. If I were to suggest one great hope for this book, it is this: that it demonstrates and represents appropriately how the concerns of both tendencies identified in Roof's analysis of religious sensibility (one towards more individualized meaning-making, the other emphasizing communal tradition) take effect in theology. Film-watchers are sometimes being provoked to do theology. And whether aware of it or not, they are leaning on longstanding theological traditions as they do so.

Chapter 3

THEOLOGY AND THE CHRISTIAN RELIGION

Theology as a church activity

S O FAR I HAVE LAID OUT THE context within which theology is currently undertaken. I have showed that meaning-making happens in the midst of people's complex negotiations with many forms of media. In Part II I shall illustrate this with respect to a number of worked examples drawn from people's consumption of film. It will become clear that for any theological dialogue with film to happen, a framework needs to be provided. That framework is maintained not in the abstract but as a living tradition. It is carried through history by a body of people (the church). However rigid or flexible that living tradition is deemed to be, inside or outside the church, and whatever judgments are made about its relevance or usefulness for church or society, it only exists because there is a community of people who embody it. Whatever patterns of meaning-making are occurring, then, there remains a sense that whether people do or do not count themselves 'in' within an active religious community, the persistence of theological traditions depends on the existence of such communities.

The focus of this book is on theology as a reflective practice. The primary setting for which it is written is a university or liberal arts college context. Its purpose is to demonstrate how theological thinking happens.

In order to do that, it is necessary to emphasize the systematic character of theology as a body of knowledge. As we shall see in Part III, however, it is ultimately the practical nature of theology which is most apparent when attention is paid to the way that the body of knowledge is made use of in the task of critical reflection upon life (and upon the watching of films).

But does this mean that one needs, after all, to be part of a church in order to do theology? Will Part II inevitably imply that in order to appreciate how theology works existentially it is necessary, after all, to situate oneself inside a community of faith? Two responses are possible. First, it remains true that theology can be engaged in by anyone interested in knowing and understanding how theological traditions inform life. The point made in Chapter 2 is still valid ('studying Christian theology does not require a student to be a Christian believer.'[1]). However, it is important to recognize the role that the church plays in enabling Christian theology to happen at all. A second response is therefore necessary. Students of theology do not need explicitly to locate themselves within the community of faith. But they do need to do three things. They need to place themselves imaginatively inside the Christian framework of thinking in order to gain the best possible grasp of what the Christian theological tradition offers and how it works. Second, they need to respect the sociopolitical and ethical significance of the church as it carries, and wrestles with, the Christian tradition in all its diversity. Third, they need to consider carefully, if they are not members of the church, what 'communities of practice' they in fact belong to which correspond to the church in their own lives, so that they see clearly how their thinking takes place. I shall pick up each of these three points in turn.

Understanding how theology is done in Christianity requires an imaginative act of seeing the church from the inside. This means respecting the fact that theology is *lived*. Doctrines of creation, redemption, the Kingdom of God, and so on, can all be respected as theological concepts or ideas. But unless a theological interpreter begins to understand what these concepts mean for believing individuals, they will have been misunderstood. In this sense, then, Christian theology has to be grasped 'from the inside', from the perspective of one who has chosen to live within the theological framework which the church carries. It is this practical, existential approach which will become apparent throughout Part II.

Second, because the capacity to undertake any theology at all depends on religions to carry traditions with them, then it is essential that the church receive respect for what it achieves in society. All human beings live in, and out of, a variety of different groups (family, work teams, friendships, in leisure contexts, in political life). Religious groups feature within this range of groups. The most meaningful of these groups can be considered 'communities of practice'. These are the primary communities in and through which we explore the values and insights that mean most to us. They shape who we are.[2] Churches function as communities of practice for many people. Recognizing this is to acknowledge the decisive social and political role that Christianity plays in society. Viewing the church as a whole as a collection of communities of practice thus enables a student of theology to see clearly not only how theology is carried, but also the social contexts within which theological traditions 'work' for believers. For theology to be a reflective practice, the question arises as to the social or institutional context within which such a practice might be sustainable.[3]

This leads directly to the third point. Whether or not readers of this book are Christian believers or actively engaged in church life, they will nevertheless be involved in some 'communities of practice' in and through which they test and explore the stories and values that they live by. As a result of using this book a reader is compelled to ask: if I do not reflect on life within a theological framework, what frameworks *do* I use? Where do I get those frameworks from? And by which groups that I am part of are they supported?

Christian theology is, then, clearly a work of the church. There would be no Christian theology without it, and all Christian theology, wherever it is undertaken, relates to the church in some way. It is churches that carry the traditions out of which this book, and the reflective process it has promoted, is possible. But this simply acknowledges that Christianity is functioning like any religion. So what more can be usefully learned from this about how theology is done?

Four aspects of religion

Religion may, of course, have nothing to do with 'God'. A religion may not necessarily be theistic. Buddhism is the most obvious example from amongst mainstream religions which contains forms where belief in God is not presupposed. Religious practice is not an end in itself; there is growth and development to a new dimension of living. But this development is not dependent upon the existence of a transcendent being. It is true, of course, that in everyday usage, the term 'religion' is usually associated with belief systems in which reference to God or the divine is assumed. But as already noted, though an association is commonly made between the term 'religion' and 'existence of God/the divine', in the West, the cultural practices which normally come under the heading of 'religion' are in serious decline. It is also clear that what religions address (meaning, purpose, how to live, the nature of reality) are simply displaced into other activities.

In considering how Christianity functions in this context, this section will do two things. I shall demonstrate briefly how cinema can be argued to function in a 'religion-like' way in contemporary Western culture.[4] I shall do this by showing under four headings how Christianity exhibits all the main features one might expect of a religion, thus functioning as the carrier of a theological tradition in society. I shall then show how cinema-going imitates these features. These headings are different ways of looking at religion, four aspects of the way that religions work, and what a religion needs in order to function: myth, ritual, community and spirituality.

Religions depend on *myths*. This notoriously difficult term has now been replaced in much discussion of Christianity by the term 'narrative'. This is understandable because of the negative connotations that myth often carries. Myth in the sense I am using it here simply means 'authoritative, symbolic story'. Any religion carries with it a story or set of stories which it invites (and expects) its adherents to inhabit. The stories are held to be true in the sense that they accurately characterize what reality is, and what life is like. This may not mean, however, that their truth resides in histor-ical facticity alone. In the case of Christianity, then, for example, it may or may not be historically true that Jesus of Nazareth walked on water. (It is highly unlikely.) But the narrative of him having done so (e.g. Mark 6.47–52) carries persuasive, religious power: his functioning as God (and being considered as one with God) means that this is the kind of thing he 'must have' been able to do. Presenting his equality with God is best done in narrative form than as an abstract statement. Myths are thus crucial in reli-gion because they both form the communities who attach significance to them, and provide a framework through which life is structured and found meaningful in those communities.

Cinema-going is religion-like in that it has recognized how powerful stories are, and the extent to which human beings need them to refer to (and live within) in order to make meaning. Furthermore, though the reading and hearing of stories can have the same function, the dramatic visual and aural form in which films present stories (akin to the dramatic form which worship can often take) makes the accessing and using of narratives more compelling. Clearly, cinema is unlike religion in so far as one is not presented with a single story or set of stories at the cinema.

Multiple world-views and ideologies are explicit and implicit in the films which cinema-goers watch. This is part of the fun of cinema-going. It is also an illustration of the extent to which a contemporary Western person is confronted with a diversity of options. The pluralism of the cinema is different from the relative uniformity of a religious tradition.[5]

Readers will nevertheless be reminded of this religion-like aspect of the cinema in Part II. An experiential link will be forged with what religions achieve through the way in which the impact of films upon viewers, and their processing of the experience of watching, is similar to how people use narratives within religion. Religions enable people to live with an overarching story or set of stories. In this way, life has more chance of seeming, or becoming, coherent. This aspect of a religion only becomes problematic when interpreted in a fundamentalist way, so that the myth or set of myths is deemed immune from criticism and must be inhabited slavishly. Even though Christian fundamentalists exist, such a rigid approach to the Christian story is inappropriate. Both the fluidity of the theological use of the Christian story in systematic theology and the recognition of how the myth is always being re-worked in a broad cultural climate counter such fundamentalism. The myth is not meant to be absolutized in this way. Normativity is not the same as absolutism.

Second, religions use *rituals*. Rituals can even be called 'enacted myths'. Religious people come to inhabit the myths and stories that they live through participation in dramatized versions of them.[6] Rituals are important because of their regularity, their structure, their familiarity and thus the way that they order human life.

Again, the practice of cinema-going reveals itself to function in a religion-like way. The regularity of cinema-going can itself be ritualistic: for example, a person chooses to go weekly in order to be entertained, or follows the same habits whenever they attend. A cinema-goer may rarely articulate the ritual practice in terms of ritualistic exposure to stimulating narrative. But empirical evidence shows that this is precisely what cinema-goers receive from their supposedly 'escapist' activities. Cinema engages both hearing and sight. It functions as a 'whole body' experience because of the emotions it rouses and the sheer physicality of the event of watching (emotions are embodied, surroundsound can make bodies shudder). It thus makes encounter with whatever narratives are presented on screen a more compelling and memorable occasion. Cinema is, though, different from a religion in so far as it is not a single myth being enacted. Furthermore, though no cinema audience is passive, the level of participation of an audience is often quite different from a religious congregation.

The latter is usually expected to contribute (to sing, chant, or participate in responsive prayers, for example), as well as sit and listen.

Ritual consolidates a religion's narrative world (its myths). In Christianity, then, worship and structured devotional life, both of which are life-shaping, are the main means by which a person comes to inhabit the Christian story. The content of theology as a body of knowledge can, to some extent, be learned. But if theology is to be lived, and the Christian story is to be inhabited, then regular encounter with the story is needed. If this encounter takes multi-sensual and non-cognitive, as well as cognitive, forms, then the story is inhabited more effectively. This is what worship and devotion achieve.

Third, religions create *communities*. However much emphasis might be paid to what an individual religious believer believes and does, a religious community is not simply a collection of individual believers. Traditions and myths are made use of by individuals, but need groups to carry them in society. Religions depend on the groups that carry a religion's myths cele-brating, reflecting on and re-telling the traditions ritually and communally.

Cinema is a communal experience. People may attend alone, or go in small groups. But watching a film in a large group at a cinema offers something more than watching at home, even with a high quality home cinema package. People receive something from others (contagious laughter, shared gasps of shock). The communal experience adds a further dimension to the film-watching experience. Unlike religion, of course, the communal dimension of cinema demands little commitment. Season-tickets may be a bargain but are not a life-commitment, and make no demands beyond the cinema. Unless you go to the cinema with friends, indeed, you are not likely to know who you sit next to. So the 'communal' aspect of cinema-going does have clear limits.

Christianity is a social religion. The church is called 'the body of Christ'. Most Christians around the world share bread and wine as symbols of their allegiance to Christ and to each other. It is expected that a Christian will have some sense of belonging, and commitment, to an actual group of people. This is admittedly under challenge on many fronts. Vastly changing patterns of social mobility mean that 'belonging' has taken on different meanings. I may live, work and have my main friendships in three different places, and so any sense of Christian attachment may be difficult to work out. I may also want to access Christian ideas and beliefs because I find them helpful and meaningful and want them to inform my life, but not feel any need to link up with others. The Internet has contributed to this individualizing of faith. These observations connect with what was noted in Chapter 2 above. It could be argued that Part II of this book will contribute to the cultivation of an individualistic approach to Christian faith through the way it promotes theological reflection. It is thereby contributing to the breakdown of the essentially communal nature of Christian faith.

My own view is that it is much too early to judge precisely what impact the technological revolution is having on the social character of Christianity across the Western world. I agree that virtual communities cannot replace embodied ones. But I also think that Christianity needs to take a hard look at some of the embodied forms its communities take. There may be new, as yet unenvisaged, communal forms which Christianity needs to take. This is not about the church's survival. It is about asking how the myths and rituals are best carried and celebrated communally for the benefit of society as a whole.

Finally, religion takes the form of *spirituality*. In the present cultural climate this constitutes the most contested heading discussed here. This is because religion is often rejected in *favour of* spirituality, as if the two can be separated. Spirituality is considered an individual matter about which individuals can make their own choices. Religion, by contrast, is deemed as restrictive. I want to argue, however, that the present favouring of spirituality over religion is simply an expression of the individualizing of religious choice. 'Spirituality' admittedly sometimes comes to mean little more than 'disciplined exercise' when the term is used. Where it is used to relate to personal development in a fuller sense, however, it is referring to the development of a person's inner life. This being so, it is misguided to detach a concern for spirituality from religion. Not all spiritualities are religious. But religion cannot do without spirituality (because they are very much concerned about the development of the inner life). And in practice, there is so much overlap between the two. Many contemporary spiritualities, indeed, turn out to be rediscoveries of spiritual traditions from the past.

Cinema-going feeds the inner life. By the way it stirs emotion, tests the senses, invites viewers into narratives, makes people laugh, cry, shout, gasp, it helps people live more fully. It does not, however, 'train the emotions' in any particular way as some religious traditions might want to. It cultivates no particular spiritual tradition. It offers no guarantee of some kind of connectedness with a 'transcendent other'. A sense of transcendence may occur for some viewers in the cinema. But it is not an inevitable part of cinema-going.

In Christianity, spirituality could be regarded as the process, both individual and communal, of making Christian tradition fully your own. It is a danger to understand spirituality individualistically, for it feeds off the myths, rituals and communal experiences of which the Christian religion is comprised. There is no solitary Christianity. Nor is there any 'content-less' spirituality. The cultivation of a rich inner life (through prayer and reflection) is always accompanied by attention to the theology which Christianity carries with it.[7] This fourth aspect of religion, as understood in relation to Christianity, thus draws attention to how theology is 'owned' and used in a person's life. Spirituality marks the focal point of a person's inhabiting of a theological tradition. In other words, the reader is invited to reflect on how the theological tradition worked with throughout Part II actually informs a person's practice.

Theology as a communal, human practice

This chapter has sought to show that theology, like any discipline that illumines human life, depends on forms of communal life to do its work. Inevitably, theology in its Christian form works most directly for those who consciously stand within the Christian tradition and seek to live in a Christian way. This book demonstrates that Christian theology can, however, be accessed and made use of in other communal settings, for example in the academic community. It is necessary to note that for this to happen, churches are depended upon by other communities. Wherever Christian theology is interacted with and made use of, the work of the church, the primary community in which Christian theology is carried, is inevitably prominent. This does not, however, mean that the church always controls theology's content. It has a responsibility to be the guardian of what it believes to be orthodox Christian faith — thereby preserving the identity of Christianity. But doctrine evolves. The interaction between theology and culture, noted throughout this book, reflects the theological conviction that Christian theology keeps on finding out new things about God as a result of God's continuing participation in creation. Much as it would like to control the content of theology, then, the church ultimately cannot. Christian theology, in whatever social context it is done, therefore needs the church. But the content of theology is constantly being worked out, in effect, in the interplay between different communities of practice. In other words, academy, church and any other group which draws on theology as a resource (e.g. in healthcare, community work, psychology, politics) all need each other. Theology is a profoundly collaborative discipline, to which many communities contribute. Society depends on their interaction.

PART II

A SYSTEMATIC THEOLOGY THROUGH FILM

INTRODUCTION

E ACH CHAPTER IN THIS MAIN PART OF the book follows a similar format. Each has six sections and it is recommended that, except for those readers who want to get ahead with the 'Further Reading' first, each of these sections is worked through in sequence. A comment is, however, worth making on each of the six sections.

Films

This section offers a brief summary of the plot of each of the films considered in the chapter. Note is also taken of any specific feature of the film worth highlighting for the task in hand.

Viewing experiences

This section offers comment on aspects of the films' reception. Account is thus taken, where known, of how ordinary viewers of the films have responded to them, in addition to what film critics have said. This section is not based directly on new empirical studies undertaken for this work.

But the material included here draws on much more than how the present author reacted or guesses other people may react/have reacted to the films. Nearly all of the films used in this part of the book have been used in teaching and therefore actual student responses have informed this part of the work.

Connecting questions and issues

This section provides a bridge between consideration of what the films can do to and for viewers and the theological reflections that then follow. Theological reflection can take off in many directions in response to the impact that films have, the emotions and insights they provoke and the questions they raise. This book only scratches the surface of what the films considered can do. In this section, a list of the many theology-related questions that arise is presented. Very few of these questions can be taken up in any depth. In every case, therefore, the list of questions spill over beyond what it is possible to address, and invites the reader to carry on thinking beyond the chapter, and beyond the reading of the book as a whole.

Explorations

This section picks up some of the listed questions and investigates how theological reflection undertaken within the framework of the beliefs and ideas of Christian thought can inform a viewer's thought-processes. The attempt is made to conduct a genuine conversation between film and theological tradition, so that the film highlights an aspect of theology's content or workings, and theological traditions in turn amplify and illuminate reflections provoked by the film and its reception.

Working conclusions

This is a 'taking stock' section. An attempt is made to summarize briefly the results of the chapter's enquiries. Readers are invited to check their own reflections against what is presented here, and to identify lingering questions of their own before they turn to the final section of each chapter.

For further study

This section provides pointers to classic passages and texts from the Bible and the history of Christian thought which relate to the questions taken up, and the explorations conducted, throughout the chapter. This is in no way meant to be an exhaustive or definitive list of sources. Nor is the list meant to suggest that 'here are the answers' to the questions which may still linger for the reader. All of the texts – biblical and from the history of Christian thought alike – are meant to draw readers' attention to discussions which have proved influential, or in some way encapsulate key Christian insights. Whether readers see, for example, the biblical texts as always most authoritative will always depend on other factors than those being discussed directly in this book. Or if readers find themselves privileging specific texts from Christian history (e.g. early Christian Fathers or Reformers), this may result simply from the denominational tradition in which they stand. Reflection on such matters is to be commended as part of further response and use of this book. But as it stands, the 'For further study' section is simply intended to help readers approach the texts in a way which makes them 'live'.

The further reading is meant to be *illuminated* by the film-watching and the reading of the chapter. It is for this reason that it is best left to the end. Texts from two centuries which may have seemed dry or incomprehensible if read 'cold' can come to life when read against the background of contemporary questions, formulated in a way which connects with the reader's experience. Similarly, the question of the continuing adequacy of the insights and viewpoints offered in these texts can be posed in the light of the contemporary exploration of the theological themes explored.

The suggested reading is drawn mostly from well-known collections of classic theological writings ('Readers'). The main ones used are the following:

Gillian T. W. Ahlgren (ed.), *The Human Person and the Church*, Maryknoll: Orbis 1999

Peter C. Hodgson and Robert H. King (eds), *Readings in Christian Theology*, Philadelphia: Fortress Press (= London: SPCK) 1985

Alister E. McGrath (ed.), *The Christian Theology Reader* (2nd edn), Oxford: Blackwell 2001

William Madges (ed.), *God and the World*, Maryknoll: Orbis 1999

William C. Placher (ed.), *Readings in the History of Christian Theology* (2 vols), Philadelphia: The Westminster Press 1988

Some of the suggested readings are also drawn from:

John H. Leith (ed.), *Creeds of the Churches: A Reader in Christian Doctrine from the Bible to the Present,* Richmond: John Knox Press 1973
Ann Loades (ed.), *Feminist Theology: A Reader,* London: SPCK 1990 (= Louisville: Westminster John Knox 1990)
Gesa E. Thiessen (ed.), *Theological Aesthetics,* London: SCM Press 2004
Susan B. Thistlethwaite and Mary P. Engel (eds), *Lift Every Voice: Constructing Christian Theologies from the Underside* (2nd edn), Maryknoll: Orbis 1998

Useful companion volumes of essays on the various theological themes explored throughout Part II include:

Peter C. Hodgson and Robert H. King (eds), *Christian Theology: An Introduction to its Traditions and Tasks,* Philadelphia: Fortress Press 1982 (= London: SPCK 1983)
Alister E. McGrath, *Christian Theology: An Introduction* (3rd edn), Oxford: Blackwell 2001
William C. Placher (ed.), *Essentials of Christian Theology,* Louisville: Westminster John Knox Press 2003

In reading the texts, especially those from the history of Christian thought, some readers might come across unfamiliar concepts or technical terms. It will be worth making a note of these, and pursuing them further either by consulting a glossary (as can be found, for example, in McGrath's *Christian Theology: An Introduction* or Placher's *Essentials of Christian Theology*). Readers could pursue their interest in such terms and concepts further by consulting dictionaries of theology such as:

J. Bowden, *Concise Dictionary of Theology,* Philadelphia: Trinity Press International 1991
M. J. Erickson, *The Concise Dictionary of Theology,* Grand Rapids: Baker Book House 1994
S. Grenz, D. Guretzki and C. F. Nordling, *Pocket Dictionary of Theological Terms,* Downers Grove: IVP 1999
G. O'Collins and E. G. Farrugia, *A Concise Dictionary of Theology,* Mahwah: Paulist Press 1991
A. Richardson and J. Bowden (eds), *A New Dictionary of Christian Theology,* London: SCM Press 1983 (= *The Westminster Dictionary of Theology,* Philadelphia: Westminster John Knox Press 1983)
D. F. Wright and S. B. Ferguson (eds), *New Dictionary of Theology,* Leicester and Downers Grove: IVP 1988

Readers will need to be aware that all such dictionaries work out their definitions out of, and in relation to, particular Christian traditions (e.g. evangelical, catholic, liberal). But part of the excitement of theological study is the discovery and exploration of differences and tensions between traditions. Readers are therefore encouraged to move on from establishing basic, working definitions of concepts to the exploration of different definitions.

Chapter 4

GOD

T HEOLOGY BEGINS WITH GOD. THERE WOULD BE no justifiable God-talk were it not believed that it makes sense to use the term 'God' in human speech, and that there are traditions of God-talk to which one can relate, and within which one can live one's life. Most who refer to God believe that the word 'God' refers to a reality beyond the thought and experience of the speaker. 'God' names a reality within which one lives, moves and has one's being. Religious traditions are therefore seeking to present in speech a reality to which adherents relate in their daily lives.

God-talk can happen without there being a God (atheists believe this is what happens anyway). But most who use God-talk of any kind believe that human beings are trying to get to grips with a reality which, whilst 'wholly other', must nevertheless be grasped in linguistic form so that that reality may be talked about at all. God's 'wholly otherness' would be uncommunicable without being turned into images, verbal or otherwise. If people are to grasp hold of any sense of God, then there has to be some tradition about the reality of God upon which people can draw in order to come to an understanding of what is being talked about. Only on that basis do people have a chance to test out their experience of human life and work out whether or not they believe that living life 'in relation to God' is either possible or desirable.

The reality of God and concepts of God are not, of course, to be equated. All verbal or visual images of God are at one stage removed from God's reality. God is being 'pictured' in words or images. The reality being pictured remains mysterious, though is usually assumed to be good: the source of all goodness indeed, the goal of creation as well as its originator, supreme benevolence, the ultimate and most just judge of all. But such precision is what has yet to be disclosed, and differences exist across religious traditions. The mysterious reality – God – is not at the beck and call of religious efforts to describe God. But the gap between God as reality and God as described in human images is an important one to respect. The belief that God is, and that God wills what is good for the world, still leaves much open about how humans grasp God and what God wills for the world, and how they fashion the world accordingly. That is the task that theology plays within religious traditions, and within the wider societies of which religions are a part.

All seven chapters in this second part of the book are about grasping hold of a Christian doctrine of God. But there is still a specific task of identifying 'concepts of God' as they appear in society. For it is not immediately apparent to those outside of a religious tradition that, say, notions of human being, heaven, or redemption necessarily have anything to do with God. So we begin in this chapter with concepts of God as they appear in film. In the process of examining a small sample of Western filmic portrayals of God in critical comparison with Christian understandings of God it will be possible to identify some parameters within which all the discussion in this part of the book takes place.

God has been portrayed in a number of different ways in film. From the dramatic actions of God in The Ten Commandments, through the white-haired old man of Oh, God, to God as a woman in Dogma, the images have varied as have the genres of films in which God has 'appeared'. From revered off-screen character (silent or otherwise) to figure of fun (rarely irreverently presented), God has not surprisingly proved a difficult role to play, and still more difficult to cast. Of course, the Christian conviction that when people have to do with Jesus Christ they are dealing with God leads to the reminder that Jesus-films are portrayals of God too. Though true up to a point, even Christians know that the incarnation of God in the person of Jesus Christ does not mean that the whole of God is revealed. Despite Jesus-films, then, there is still an issue about how God is portrayed on screen. Mention of Jesus-films does, however, highlight the fact that for Christians the figure of Jesus Christ is central in theology and religious practice. Even if a Jesus-film is not a direct image of God, then how God is being imaged is contained within a portrayal of Jesus.

In this opening chapter of Part II, I have opted to explore a recent humorous portrayal of God in film – Morgan Freeman's 'God' in *Bruce Almighty* – and a topical and controversial Jesus-film – Mel Gibson's *The Passion of the Christ*. Alongside these two portrayals I shall refer also to *The Truman Show* in which a God-like figure appears, the overall impact of whom within the film's narrative raises telling questions about what it means to live within a defined 'world' of thought or practice. In this way I am able to examine in general terms how images of God take shape at the cinema and also to begin addressing the question how concepts of God function in Christianity.

Films

Bruce Almighty (Tom Shadyac, 2003)

Bruce Almighty is a comedy in which Bruce Nolan (Jim Carrey) is a TV reporter who is given the opportunity to play the role of God whilst still living within his normal, everyday world. In response to a rant against God for what he perceives to be an unfair world, after Nolan has had a particularly bad day, God (Morgan Freeman) hands Bruce divine powers. There are just two caveats to his exercise of divine powers: he cannot let people know whose powers he possesses, and he cannot bypass people's exercise of free will.

The result, however, is that Bruce has the chance to put obstacles in the way of his competitors for positions in the TV company for which he works. Bruce's discovery is that the possession of such powers presents him with a frightening, stifling level of responsibility, and that even so, because he cannot make anyone love him, possession of such powers has limited value. Sobered through his encounter with God, he returns to his life appreciative of what he has and of the love of those around him.

The Passion of the Christ (Mel Gibson, 2004)

Much has already been written about this rather unusual film. Hugely successful in terms of viewing figures, *The Passion of the Christ* is a biblical epic in Latin and Aramaic that presents a meditation on the last twelve hours of the life of Jesus of Nazareth, portraying the crucifixion of Jesus with graphic realism. The broader context of the circumstances surrounding Jesus' death is supplied through a series of twelve flashbacks which provide some clue about his earlier life.[1] In the main, however, the focus is on the political intrigue between Jewish and Roman authorities which led to Jesus' conviction and execution and the horror of the acts of humiliation and crucifixion themselves. Notoriously, in the first box-office version of the film (2004) the flogging scene lasted twenty minutes.[2]

The Truman Show (Peter Weir, 1998)

The Truman Show is a satire on the power of the media, and specifically on the genre 'reality TV'. Again starring Jim Carrey, the film portrays the life of Truman Burbank, a figure who lives his life unaware that he is himself the subject of a reality TV show. All other characters who are part of his life are actors, even including his wife (Laura Linney). Burbank's life is lived within a huge TV studio. His every move is monitored and his life orchestrated by Christof (Ed Harris), a TV producer. When blunders begin to occur in the staging of Truman's life he begins to become suspicious. His dramatic discovery of the fabricated nature of his existence occurs when he undertakes a sea journey, survives a staged storm, and makes it to the edge of the TV studio to confront his 'creator'/producer.

Viewing experiences

These three recent films present explicit and implicit images of God in very different ways. Cognitively, the films present a playful, homely image of a God who supports people in their discovery of love (Bruce Almighty), a God entangled in some way in the violence of the world (The Passion of the Christ) and, implicitly, as a director-like figure who seeks to control people's every move (The Truman Show). Only in the case of the first film is the God-image fully explicit. And through portrayal of God by a black, male actor (Morgan Freeman), though a clear anthropomorphism, a basic stereotype of God-image (as an old, bearded white-man) is undermined. It is, however, not at all clear whether the viewer is intended to 'use' the image of God only as a means to focus on human love (for viewers 'know' that images of God are but stories). Alternatively, the playfulness exercised with the God image in the film can remind viewers that images of God are necessary in human life, though do undergo change. The film may receive either of these responses from viewers. *Bruce Almighty* thus opens up questions both about the function of images of God, and how they relate to any reality 'God'.

The Passion of the Christ offers an image of Christ within a portrayal of the story of Jesus. Without familiarity with the tradition, however, the viewer of this film can be at a great disadvantage. It could be argued that the image of God communicated by this film is that of a bloodthirsty God. Where reference to God and God's will is made explicit in the film, the focus is inevitably on God requiring this suffering from Jesus. The focus is, after all, upon the last hours of Jesus' life. Jesus wonders whether he can carry the weight of the sins of the world (and it is assumed that this is necessary, i.e. that God requires it). When carrying the cross, Jesus expresses his awareness that he is fulfilling the Father's will.

It is the stark presentation of the Passion Narrative (the final chapters in each of the four New Testament Gospels) in relative isolation from the rest of Jesus' life that creates this rather distorted image. In Christian terms, then, the image of God implied is incomplete. A Christian viewer inevitably receives a fuller view of God than a viewer dependent on the film itself (in which a truncated set of Christian convictions is displayed). Knowledge of more of the Christian Gospel narratives than just the endings – not to mention the content of the rest of the Christian Bible – is thus necessary to ensure that a Christian reading of the circumstances of Jesus' life, death and resurrection is grasped. As it stands, *The Passion of the Christ* purports to offer a Christian view of God, though conveys only a partial picture. It leaves a theologically interested viewer merely with a further question: why on earth would early Christians ever have thought that insight into a loving God could be gained through reflection on a crucifixion and its aftermath?

Christof, the director/producer of *The Truman Show*, need not, of course, be seen as a God-figure at all.[3] For the film is clearly about the way in which the boundary between reality and fantasy can be smudged by the way that communication media affects people's perceptions of what is. If seen as a God-figure, then, Christof represents a sinister, lurking, controlling hand. The media have become like a God because of the extent of their influencing of people's experiences and reactions. But if God is like this, the film implies, then this is not a figure who is to be welcomed within human experience.

Affective responses to the three films take us further in our consideration of the God-images they present. Viewers are likely to feel warm towards the God of *Bruce Almighty*. The film's humour makes us feel good. Morgan Freeman's God, as a supportive presence, helps both Bruce and viewers to develop as people. We are to learn the same lessons as Bruce. And yet we are given mixed messages. We are to leave the cinema also reminded that we are on our own. We may feel good, and feel supported in our endeavours (even by God) to 'be the miracle' (to be active in loving others, and not expect everything to be done for us). But God has disappeared back into the loft (back to heaven?) and has left the task of living to us. The pleasure of the humour viewers experience hides the symbolism of the isolation in which they are left.

In response to *The Passion of the Christ*, as many published reviews have indicated, disgust has mixed with moral outrage for many viewers. Whether Christian or not, viewers have reacted badly to the suggestion that any god would require the brutal execution of a human being in order for the divine will to be fulfilled. The film may be prefaced with words from the prophet Isaiah. It may well be presented as a theological meditation of the death of Jesus. But its affective impact upon many viewers is that grotesque brutality is somehow required by God. The numbing effect of the portrayal of the violence perpetrated against Jesus leads viewers who do not already inhabit a Christian theological thought-world to be immune to the potentially salvific message which such a death might eventually produce.

Christof need not be a God-figure. But the emotional impact of *The Truman Show* as a film can make him more of a God-figure than was intended by the makers of the film. Any form of viewer identification with Truman culminates in the possibility of Truman's liberation from his confinement in the constructed world of 'The Truman Show' as soon as he reaches the edge of the studio. Whether or not motifs such as control of the sea are explicitly acknowledged by viewers as features that link Christof with God the creator, the viewer is invited to share in an experience of breaking out from whatever confines or restricts. In the film, the creator cannot also be the liberator without also destroying the whole experiment. Allowing Truman his freedom from the reality TV show means the end of the show. Viewers of the show within the film are all rooting for Truman, urging him to break free (even though they know their voyeuristic fun will end too). Viewers of the film are encouraged to become anti-Christof. In so doing they are being invited to break out of whatever contains them, or shapes them against their will, or whatever makes them conform. The film thus promotes individual, existential liberation. It could also imply, for some viewers, that the only way that this is achievable is by opposition to all institutional contexts in which we live and move, or via the discovery that God and God-figures are ultimately not supportive of human freedom. Alternatively, it could mean that the media and institutional contexts within which we live must be exposed and critiqued. But at an affective level, despite its feelgood ending, the film can promote a constructive rage in the viewer: whatever constrains the viewer must be destroyed.

Connecting questions and issues

To enable the films' engagement with questions about God to be more fully explored, it is now necessary to distil from the above summaries of the film plots and themes and viewer responses to them a series of questions which will make theological discussion possible and fruitful.

- What more can be said about the images of God offered in and through the films?
- What is being done with these images?
- What 'reality value' are we expected, as viewers, to attach to the God portrayed in these images?
- What does it mean to 'have', to 'use', or to 'carry' an image of God?
- What do these films tell us, if anything, about a society's functioning and the transmission of images of God within it?
- What relationships and tensions are there between a culture's carrying of God-images and the religious traditions which claim primary responsibility for preserving and working with them?
- What is to be made of the distinction between the 'reality' and the 'image' of God in religions and societies? How do responses to these films help us, if at all, to address the question of realism and non-realism in discussing the meaning of the word 'God'?

The next section will work within a framework created by these questions.

Explorations: images and traditions; power and freedom

The fact that the subject of God is treated humorously in film is intriguing. It may suggest a lack of reverence. Or it may be a challenge to an inappropriate degree of reverence shown to the topic of God within cultures which have lost a sense of what it means to speak of God in a more matter-of-fact way, clearly related to everyday life. Whatever the intention behind Bruce Almighty, the film brings discussion of God into mainstream popular culture through the medium of comedy. Humour is, however, two-edged. Are God and religion being laughed at? Are they artistic devices to enable the film to handle the subject-matter of human love?

Bruce Almighty is a clever film in that by virtue of its having a clear 'moral' it proves accessible and enjoyable for those with little or no sympathy for the concept of God or religion. A key question of the film's reception and interpretation, however, is the extent to which its theological theme is essential to what viewers take from it. It is evidently essential to the plot. But does the film imply that for the miracle of human love to occur God is indispensable?

Certainly, in order to get the most from the film within its own terms, a viewer needs to bring a broad appreciation of theistic belief in order to grasp some of the jokes and allusions made. Some of these are common to most religious traditions. Others are specifically Jewish or Christian. The film assumes a basic appreciation of such motifs as God giving signs (via road-signs, billboards, TV adverts), God as light/source of light (God as an electrician fixing lights), God's being one ('I am the One') and God's hearing/answering prayers. More specifically, there is reference to the Exodus (Bruce 'parts the waves' in his soup bowl) and to walking on water (by both God and Bruce).

It is, however, unlikely that a viewer – if aware of such allusions – would take time or care to disentangle them all. A film like this works in a non-specific way, making jokes about allusions to 'the divine' ('the Almighty', 'the guy upstairs') in a general manner. Such generality, however, creates problems if it is then assumed that a film like this can somehow contribute to a culture's carrying of an image of God. For it offers a number of mixed messages about who and what God is supposed to be, and be about. In addition to the allusions already cited, the view that 'everything happens for a reason' is expressed by Grace (Jennifer Aniston), as if God is responsible for all things that occur. The departure of God back into his loft suggests deism rather than theism: human beings are left to their own devices by a God who has set creation up, but then ceased to interact with it. Furthermore, the lingering presence of the divine in the human realm is even given a Gnostic twist ('you have the divine spark'), in a way which suggests God's presence as only spiritual, as opposed to spiritual and material in the world.

Two central questions therefore emerge from this film and its reception. What is the value of the imagery of God for the viewer beyond the film?

What is to be made of the absence of specificity of the image/s of God presented? I shall return to these in the 'Working conclusions' section in due course.

The Passion of the Christ offers a very different range of theological issues and questions to the viewer. Here, the image of God is highly specific. From humour and the generalized image of 'the divine' of Bruce Almighty, we have turned to a specific form of Christianity and a particular interpretation of the doctrine of the atonement. This is a film about Jesus. As such, in any culture where it is recognized that in Christian understanding God-talk is undertaken with respect to the person of Jesus Christ, then the film presents an image of God. In this sense, the film reflects Christianity's inevitable Christocentrism. The film will surely, in time, be grouped within the emerging canon of 'Jesus-films'. Despite this, the film implies that it is primarily, or only, in the death of Jesus that God is at work.[4] By not doing very much to interpret the death of Jesus in the light of his life it presents a limited view of the Christian understanding of God.[5]

Gibson's Jesus may thus seem utterly orthodox. I suggest, however, that the film and its reception highlight two issues about the relationship between religious communities and the wider culture of which they are a part, and thus about the way in which concepts of God are carried culturally. First, the film and its reception indicate the sheer difficulty of offering a concept of God outside of the context of a living religious community. Religious communities seek to 'live' their understandings of God. This means that images and concepts of God are complex symbols that are hard to communicate.[6] The theological significance of the observation that The Passion of the Christ is only in a restricted sense a 'Jesus-film' (because it does not offer the viewer enough about the life of Jesus) may not be apparent to many viewers.[7]

Second, the distinction between religious communities and wider society is crucial. It may be possible to talk of societies 'carrying' a number of images of God. But unlike religious communities, societies do not choose to 'carry' specific images of God. They incorporate the pluralism of images which religions carry with them, and societies' members – whether they consider themselves religious or not – adopt, reject or adapt images and concepts of God in a complex variety of ways. Any exploration of a concept of God therefore has to take account of whose concept of God it is. To note that all God-concepts are tradition-related and community-specific does not then make them the inventions or projections of those communities. The observation merely respects the life-involving character of God-concepts. No-one can say 'I believe in God' in any meaningful way without this also connecting with who they relate to, what they think about themselves and the world, and about how they choose to live their lives. The distinction between society (as a whole) and religious traditions (in particular) thus indicates that any interpreter of God-concepts needs to be clear about which particular traditions are 'carried' (and 'lived within') by which particular communities. Only on the basis of such detailed examination, I suggest, is *The Passion of the Christ* and its reception comprehensible.[8]

The truncated nature of the image of God implied in *The Passion of the Christ* – its bloodthirsty God – does, however, find echoes in a very different form in *The Truman Show*. As already stated, Christof need not be seen directly as God-figure at all. He is God-like in so far as he runs the show (literally). But again, if the comparison with God is to be drawn then it is a limited comparison. It is God's omnipotence that is being either parodied or criticized. The importance of the way that *The Truman Show* works theologically as a film is, however, two-fold. First, its theological possibilities are implicit rather than explicit. The film therefore primarily does emotional work on viewers – enabling them to get inside Truman's story and the stories of the viewer of The Truman Show within the film. The possibility of a comparison between Christof and God can then be warmly received by a viewer who is anti-religion, or beyond it ('I am glad I do not live within such a world'). It can also be received appreciatively by a theist who does not believe in this dominant kind of God, a God who leaves little *de facto* freedom to God's creatures. It could, however, be a shock in its implications for a believer who draws the comparison and is then faced for the first time with the question of possible limits to God's omnipotence. Perhaps God cannot do everything (if creatures are in any sense 'free'). Furthermore, what are the implications for God's creatures if there is no escape from God?

With *The Truman Show* we have come full circle. We are back facing, in a significantly different way, some of the same basic issues about what it means to believe in God, and what God might be like, as were presented in *Bruce Almighty*. In the latter film, God is quite upfront in handing over his powers: Bruce could not tell people he was God and he could not undermine human freedom. (Problematically, of course, God and Bruce still seem able to 'do everything' when it comes to moving objects around, changing the weather and generally defying the laws of nature.) In *The Truman Show*, the expression of qualified omnipotence is more sinister. But the challenge for the viewer is more intense precisely because of the emotional commitment which the viewer is lured into making: it really does matter that God is not like Christof.

Working conclusions

This juxtaposition and brief discussion of three recent films demonstrate that the question of the nature of God is alive and well within popular Western culture. They do not pose in any direct way the question of God's existence, but they all accept that cultures contain within them images of God with which its people interact. Only one – *The Passion of the Christ* – makes explicit a direct link with a specific religious tradition, and I have suggested that the link it makes with Christianity is inadequate.

Nevertheless the films and their reception suggest that exploration of images of God remains culturally and existentially necessary. Examination of issues of omnipotence, dominance, freedom and the possibility of love and concern for others, what it is that human beings may need releasing from, and whether God requires suffering (e.g. that of Jesus) for such release to occur will be necessary within such theological exploration. The examination of such topics is not, however, ultimately possible in any generalized way. Concepts of God are tradition-specific and community-related. There can be comparative theological studies across religion.[9] Philosophers may also continue to speak of a 'concept of God' in a general-ized sense. But religious belief deals with God in more specific ways because of the ritual practices of which it is comprised and the ethical conduct that flows from them. Images of God can, in Western culture, be explored through many different religious channels, for all major religious traditions are part of Western culture. From here on I shall be examining in more detail a Christian view of God, through the component parts of a Christian systematic theology. This is partly because there is much residual Christian thought lurking throughout popular culture (and you have to have some hooks to link onto – theological exploration never occurs in a vacuum). But it is also because a choice has to made about a tradition on which to major, and within which to work.[10]

It will take six further chapters for this book even to begin to address some of the specifically Christian forms of questions about God. By begin-ning to address such questions 'through film', the film-watcher/reader will, however, already be developing a 'whole person approach' to the task of theology (relating to body, mind and spirit). The enjoyment and chal-lenge of watching/experiencing and responding to film becomes theological exploration in which emotions and aesthetic responses play a crucial part alongside thinking. From here on, the book invites the film-watching student of theology constantly to ask: and has Christian theology insights to offer the process of my response to and reception of this film?

And likewise: does this film, and my response to and reception of it draw out anything specific from, or question or sharpen any aspect of, Christian tradition?

For further study

Before more films are watched and discussed, however, it is vital that the history of Christian theology be allowed its say. The following texts would be useful in introducing readers to some of the major treatments in Christian history of the basic questions about who and what 'God' is.

From the Bible, the following are worth exploring:

Genesis 1.1–2.3 One of the accounts of God with which the Bible opens.

Exodus 3 The account of God's appearance to Moses, where the divine name 'I am who I am' is revealed to Moses.

Exodus 19–20 The account of the giving of the Ten Commandments on Mount Sinai.

Psalm 33 A psalm which gives expression to the way in which God is held to watch over the earth.

Jonah This short book from the Hebrew Bible/Old Testament is intriguing because of the way it shows God having a change of mind (to Jonah's annoyance) in order to be merciful.

Colossians 1.15–20 Often thought to have been an early Christian hymn (then included within this letter to the church in Colossae), this passage speaks about Christ but indicates how Christians have always done their God-talk by speaking about Christ.

I John 4.7–21 One of the clearest passages in the New Testament about God's nature as love.

The following texts from later Christian history will help readers think further how human beings speak of God, about aspects of God's relation to the world, and some of the different ways of understanding the death of Christ which have been offered in Christian history.

Anselm and Abelard (late eleventh century) offer two views on the death of Christ (in McGrath, pp. 340–3). Anselm offers a 'satisfaction' theory of atonement, according to which the death of Christ pays the necessary price for human sin. Abelard sees that Christ has died 'for us', but wants to put greater stress upon the way in which God, in Christ, invites people to loving action in response to Christ's death.

Calvin, 'God's Providence Governs All' in Hodgson and King, pp. 123–8. This is a classic sixteenth-century statement on the sovereignty of God, and expresses the view that lies behind Grace's statement in *Bruce Almighty* ('everything happens for a reason'). God is here portrayed not simply as having created the world, but as continuing to direct its course in some detail.

Hegel, 'Without the World God is not God' (in Hodgson and King, pp. 132–6). This text from a famous nineteenth-century philosopher-theologian opens up the thorny question of whether, having created the world, God is in some sense dependent on it.

'Karl Barth on Revelation as God's Self-Disclosure' (= *Church Dogmatics* 1/1 [1932, E.T. 1976]), pp. 191, 193–94; in McGrath, pp. 138–40; longer extract in Hodgson and King, pp. 97–101). This extract from a seminal work by one of the most influential of twentieth-century theologians argues for the priority of God's self-revelation in all thinking about God.

Moltmann, 'On the Suffering of God' (in McGrath, pp. 117–20). This highly influential twentieth-century text probes the question of what was happening to God at the point of Jesus' crucifixion. It therefore focuses on many of the issues left unclear or unresolved by *The Passion of the Christ*.

James Cone, 'God is Black' (in Thistlethwaite and Engel, pp. 101–14). These reflections by a leading black theologian offer a critique of much theological thinking in showing how images of God and human experience interrelate.

Chapter 5

HUMAN BEING

F ROM DISCUSSION OF WHO AND WHAT GOD is and how God relates to the world, we turn to the created order itself. Who and what are human beings and what is their place within the created order as a whole? Why call the world we know 'the created order' at all? In this chapter I juxtapose four very different films in order to enable the reader to examine the doctrines of creation and human being.

Films

Koyaanisqatsi (*Godfrey Reggio, 1983*)

Koyaanisqatsi has been variously described as 'a rather pointless, very beautiful, and finally rather boring experience' and 'perhaps the most powerful film about nature ever'.[1] It is an evocative, dialogue-less, film which juxtaposes striking visual images of nature, space and human beauty with the sometimes ugly aspects of human habitation: smoky cities, heavy industry and car-filled freeways. 'Koyaanisqatsi' means 'a state of life that calls for another way of living' or 'life out of balance' in Hopi, a Native American language. The film's purpose is thus to reflect back to the viewer what is happening to the world, and what role human beings are playing in damaging it. Despite its visual and aural beauty as a film (Philip Glass's music enhances the viewing experience), its message appears bleak. But the contrast between its apparent narrative purpose (the world was beautiful but human beings are destroying it) and the experience of viewing will be worth examining further in due course.

Eternal Sunshine of the Spotless Mind (Michel Gondry, 2004)

The second film to be looked at focuses on human beings. It is a love story and a humorous but by no means formulaic romantic comedy. Joel (Jim Carrey) and Clementine (Kate Winslet) have been in a relationship before. When they meet at the start of the film, however, neither we nor they know this. We discover that they have had their memories of each other erased. The film tracks the ups and downs of the relationships between two quite different people: shy and withdrawn Joel, and lively, demanding Clementine. Using clever dialogue, trickery with time, and striking camerawork, Gondry and scriptwriter Charlie Kaufman take the viewer through their meetings, their fallings out, their parting, their memory-erasure (complete with Joel's regrets and struggles to prevent it happening) before leaving us and them back where they started: meeting again on Valentine's Day.

Do the Right Thing (Spike Lee, 1989)

This influential and challenging film by Spike Lee tackles race relations head-on. Using a (hot) day in the life of a Brooklyn street, and focusing on the owners and customers of a pizzeria ('Sal's Famous'), Lee – who wrote, directed and acted in the film – draws out the complexity of urban race relations in a powerful way. Lee plays Mookie, a pizza delivery man whose links with all the main characters through his work form a focal point of the plot. Sal's pizzeria is run by an Italian immigrant and his two sons, is frequented by many people from the predominantly black neighbourhood and is located opposite a grocery store run by a Korean couple. The pizzeria is thus a concrete site of the encounter of ethnicities and cultures. The plot revolves around the tensions between the various groups, and the diverse ideological outlooks of different individuals and groups. A particular emphasis in the film is the tension within the black community between the different ways of Martin Luther King and Malcom X with respect to whether or not violence should ever be contemplated when one encounters injustice. However, the film skilfully presents many aspects of the way that ethnic difference both creates a rich cultural mix, and also produces a social context in which great demands are placed on the human capacity to handle such difference. Though fully representative of a black perspective, Lee has successfully made a film which makes it clear that all the characters are ambiguous (none wholly good, none wholly bad) and that no single ethnic group deserves special favour.

Notting Hill (*Roger Michell, 1999*)

In stark contrast to *Do the Right Thing* the films of Richard Curtis present a very different view of urban life. They deal mostly with the lives of white, affluent English city dwellers (all three considered here are London-based). They all deal with the making and breaking of relationships and risk presenting near caricatures in the stereotypical characters used. They trade off some stock British/American contrasts. They are for the most part fantasies, comedies with clever plots and some nice twists. I want to read *Notting Hill* in the context of the three main films in which Richard Curtis has thus far been involved (i.e. alongside *Four Weddings and a Funeral* and *Love Actually*). I suggest that *Notting Hill* can be read in the light of what *Love Actually* is getting at, and in the light of the motif of the demands and depths of love which, despite all their apparent superficiality, each of these three films in practice presents.

'Seems to me that love is everywhere. Often it's not particularly dignified, or newsworthy – but it's always there – fathers and sons, mothers and daughters, husbands and wives, boyfriends, girlfriends, old friends.' These words are part of the opening voiceover by the Prime Minister (Hugh Grant) at the start of *Love Actually*. The speech signals what is going to be celebrated in the film. Despite the location of his films within the genre of comedy or romantic comedy, however, the celebrations of love offered go beyond the formulaic requirements of such films. The love celebrated, as Grant's speech indicates, is not only romantic or sexual love. It is the love found in families and in friendships. And where love is sexual it is not only heterosexual. Nor is the love 'easy' despite many fantasy and 'happy ending' elements across the films. In *Four Weddings and a Funeral*, the funeral is of Gareth (Simon Callow), a gay man, whose homosexuality had been hidden even from his closest friends. There is thus the pain of the death for his partner, Matthew (John Hannah), and his family and friends, but also of the knowledge that the couple had felt the need to hide their sexuality.

In *Notting Hill*, a marriage is celebrated: not the impending one of the two main characters William (Hugh Grant) and Anna (Julia Roberts), but that between Bella (Gina McKee) and Max (Tim McInnerny). They are clearly well off – both are lawyers – and their practical struggle is only alluded to, through Max's carrying Bella upstairs. But the fact of Bella's physical incapacity and her newly discovered childlessness are contained within their loving relationship, and borne by it. In *Love Actually*, the pain present in two of the ten relationships stands out: that caused for Karen (Emma Thompson) by Harry's (Alan Rickman) infidelity, and that borne within Sarah's (Laura Linney) relationship to her mentally ill brother Michael (Michael Fitzgerald).

Beyond the fantasy elements in each of these films (financial worries are not prominent in the films, film-stars don't usually walk into small bookshops, travel abroad doesn't automatically lead to a range of satisfying trouble-free sexual relationships with beautiful people), there is a conservatism of both form and content. However, whether the conservatism of content (e.g. marriage is still worth striving for, real happiness is heterosexual) is ultimately determinative of their impact and value as films depends on their reception. For alongside the fantastic and the simple the plot and character elements just mentioned point to a level of satisfying complexity in the films. The films are to be enjoyed and make us feel good. But they also leave the viewer, as we shall see below, with more than the feelgood factor.

Viewing experiences

These films offer four distinctly different types of viewing experience. *Koyaanisqatsi* depends for its effect upon colour, striking imagery, the interplay of mostly non-verbal sound (especially music) and image, and the willingness of the viewer to participate in the task of interpreting images and their juxtaposition. Whether viewers are inspired or bored will depend on whether they are willing to stay with the film and work at the task of interpretation. Consideration of this film marks the first point in this study where one of the differences between a 'popular' and an 'art' film becomes evident. For the viewer who stays with it, the challenge of locating oneself as a responsible human being within the world is both ethical and emotional. Viewers *feel* their co-responsibility within the world for resisting any human tendency towards neglect or destruction. The aesthetic experience of viewing thus opens up a cognitive challenge to think of the 'world' in terms of 'creation', that is as a gift.

Unlike *Koyaanisqatsi*, *Eternal Sunshine of the Spotless Mind* is more widely known through its release in multiplexes. It is, however, in its own way a demanding film. It is not an easy film to follow. The viewer has to move behind what is portrayed in screen time to be able to unravel what is mixed up in the times of both plot and story. For a viewer disinclined or unable to do this, the film will simply end up confusing and confused. Whether the film then functions as an enjoyable and challenging stimulus to reflect upon 'the centrality of memory in defining one's personality' (McCarthy) will depend upon how much the viewer has been prepared for the film, that is, made ready to handle the film's reversing of the story, or is prepared to reflect on it afterwards.[2]

The experience of viewing *Eternal Sunshine of the Spotless Mind* can, however, prove disturbing as well as disorientating. Whatever is to be made of Joel's regression scene (described by McCarthy as 'downright odd'), the clever range of camera and sound techniques – especially the blurring and slurring as memories are being erased – seek to accentuate the level of damage to one's self-awareness which memory loss would cause. Viewers are thus exposed through such technical skill to more than a mere cognitive reflection on the question 'what would it mean to lose my memory?'

Do the Right Thing is demanding in a different way again from *Koyaanisqatsi* and *Eternal Sunshine of the Spotless Mind*. Unlike the former but like the latter, the focus is again upon the inter-human. The film deals less with the intra-human, however, than on the ethnic and cultural groups into which people are born, find their identity and out of which they experience the world and encounter the 'other'. It leaves no viewer emotionally unaffected. *Eternal Sunshine of the Spotless Mind* had not ignored the importance of memory for linking people together. Memory is seen to be always in part memory of having been related to others, and thus one's identity in part depends on the memory of others as well as oneself. But the film largely focused on individuals. *Do the Right Thing* presents plausible, interesting, ambiguous individual characters but it is keenly interested too in the groups and traditions within which each is located and in and through which they discover and shape their identities.

The power of the experience of watching *Do the Right Thing* depends on the nature and degree of identification on the viewer's part. Many middle-class white viewers might conclude that they cannot 'get into' the film much, except through the character of Clifton (John Savage), the well-meaning new local resident who, in response to the query why he lives in a black neighbourhood, indicates he is 'under the assumption that this is a free country and one can live where he pleases'. Wealthy white liberal cinema-goers may indeed find this as an emotional point of access to the film. Yet they may overlook, on grounds of class and on the level of (lack of) immersion in urban culture, potential identification with Sal and his sons, and with the police who patrol the area and are then involved in the killing which sparks off the riot which brings the film to its climax. Diverse groups within the black community – based on age, gender, and ideological outlook – are opened up by Lee. They offer a range of opportunities for black viewers to locate themselves specifically within the film's plot and action. In a way which viewers of other ethnic backgrounds might not be able fully to appreciate, Lee invites black viewers to explore their backgrounds, identities, commitments and prejudices in the context of exploration of the intensity of experience presented in the film, and the reality of tensions between groups, between black and black, black and white, black and Asian. No potential tension is left unexplored, and thus there is no emotional hiding place for any viewer prepared to open up to the impact of their own ethnicity, gender, class and age upon their identity. Film critic Roger Ebert declared: 'I have only been given a few filmgoing experiences in my life to equal the first time I saw *Do the Right Thing*. Most movies remain up there on the screen. Only a few penetrate your soul.'[3] Ebert is surely not alone in feeling the deep emotional impact of the film. And as with any great film, its work is only fully done when people respond and work with their reactions to it, so that the viewing experience does not remain only an evening's entertainment.

The Curtis films take us in a different direction again. They may seem light and superficial compared to the other films considered so far. They are slick packages designed for a good night out and the cultivation of a warm glow for the twenty- and thirty-something cinema-going public for whom they are clearly intended. My use of them here derives largely from evidence adduced from teaching experience. What 'lingers in the mind' of many viewers, beyond the feelgood factor, is an element in their respective plots of the disruption of the romance and the comedy of each. Hence, the funeral in *Four Weddings and a Funeral* stands out, and collections of poems by W. H. Auden sold millions of copies as a result of his 'Stop the Clocks' being used in that scene. In *Notting Hill*, the quality of relationship between Max and Bella overshadows the fantasy romance of Anna and William, because enough is glimpsed (and felt) by the viewer of what they have to struggle with together within their relationship, despite their material wealth. In *Love Actually*, the two plots with loose ends, already referred to above, are the ones that are remembered, not the ones that are tied up neatly or seem far from real life.

In other words, across all three films there is a motif of stark real life, always containing an element of sadness, yet not always consumed by negativity, which disrupts the genre in and through which the films are packaged and marketed. These disruptions become important in the films' reception as they are what viewers commonly remember and therefore 'work with' beyond first or ensuing viewings ('O, I feel so sorry for the Emma Thompson character').

Connecting questions and issues

A wide range of questions arises from these films about what it means to be a human being. These include:

- What is the place of humanity within the whole of the created order? Are humans somehow special?
- What does it mean to speak of 'the created order' as opposed to 'the world' or 'the universe'? (For does not talk of 'created order' already imply a purpose, thoughtfulness or design which may not actually be there?)
- How does human identity emerge? Is it 'discovered' or 'constructed'?
- What place do life-experience and memory play in the discovery or construction of human identity? Is memory solely individual? If it is both individual and communal, then how is memory 'carried'?
- What part is played in the formation of identity by the different groups to which we belong and the diverse commitments that we have? How do we deal with the fact that some of these may be chosen (e.g. ethical, political, religious) and others not (age, gender, ethnicity)?
- What does 'love' mean? What types of love might there be, given that there is something of love which seems identifiably the same across human cultures, and yet even within single cultures there are different expressions of love (e.g. within families, in friendships, in sexual rela-tionships)?
- How are the frailties and limitations of human experience (including illness, accidents, evil, death) to be handled?

These form the framework within which the explorations will be conducted.

Explorations: gift and gratitude; individual and social sin; memory and identity; love and Trinity

Human beings do not come out very well in *Koyaanisqatsi*. It looks as though we are being identified by its director as the villain of the piece. Creation, it seems, would be fine if we had not messed it up. The viewing experience means that reception of the film is, however, more complex than this. The film is beautifully photographed, and the music is haunting. Whether or not we feel good at the end, or have 'got' the message that Reggio seems to want us to hear, if we have stayed with the film we have enjoyed a rich aesthetic experience. The experience of watching, then, itself encapsulates the ambiguity of humanity's place within the world/creation. We are puny when compared to nature's awesome power, but that only puts us appropriately in our limited place within the universe. We (humanity) are part of the problem, and yet have the capacity to resist at least some of our tendencies to damage our environment. Human creativity and technological know-how could be put to better use. And the film itself, in presenting itself to us, is evidence of that. It confronts us, by beautiful means, with the world's beauty.

In Christian theology, ac counts of the limited but important place of humanity within the created order, and of the ambiguity of human experience are ready to hand (Genesis 1–4, Psalm 8, Romans 7). In its focus on salvation Christianity has, however, sometimes not been good at attending to the salvation of the earth as a whole, or on being positive about human capacity to contribute to God's continued saving of creation. This film both presents the ambiguity and embodies evidence of how the ambiguity can be, if not overcome, then at least lived with. The creative skills of human beings are to be turned towards respect for the earth; human communities are to be mended so that people do not need to be isolated.

The film is not, of course, overtly theist. The conclusions drawn by a humanist might be identical to those just summarized. The difference in reception lies in the way in which the world and human beings are understood in the light of the 'givenness' of creation and human nature. Whatever and whoever God is understood to be, the existential conviction that God creates means that human life and its environment are received as gifts. These gifts are received in sometimes complex and fraught circumstances. The freedom of a created order that includes earthquakes and volcanic eruptions, droughts and floods, and produces human bodies that are all imperfect in some way, leaves many questions to be asked of God. But Christian theology suggests a disposition of gratitude as a starting point for the acceptance of who one is and what the world is like. On that basis it becomes possible to assess and develop what one is capable of. It is on the same basis that one's environment may be regarded not in a hostile manner. The surroundings are not to be subdued but treasured and cared for. To treasure and care for who one is and the surroundings within which one lives would, in Christian understanding, be undertaken with a deep sense of the ambiguity to which *Koyaanisqatsi* refers.

Without the final sentence of the previous paragraph, it could be argued that a Christian approach to human living was all too comfortable: written out of comfort for a world in which few problems are identified. Notions of 'gift' and 'gratitude' may be all very well for those who find immediate cause to be thankful (for material wealth, good health, safe surroundings, no environmental threats, political stability). The intensity of human experience portrayed in *Do the Right Thing* stands in sharp contrast to such ease and comfort.

There is gracefulness, tenderness, care and concern between people, and love and respect within and across generations in *Do The Right Thing*. But above all, alongside such positive aspects of human relations, there is profound ambiguity (people can be all those positive things *and* something more negative besides). And beneath all, because of such persistent, present negativity, a simmering rage lurks within many human interactions. It is this simmering rage, related to complex ethnic and ideological loyalties, which explodes violently at the end of the film and which stuns, and lingers with, the viewer. But it stuns and lingers in part because the viewer has been drawn into the emotional, social and political complexity of human living which Lee examines in this film. What theological explorations does a viewer's response evoke?

First, the essential ambiguity of a human being evident from the film invites being put alongside Christian exposition of human beings as always sinful, even whilst still being identifiably made in God's image. In Christian understanding, every human being possesses a tendency to turn damagingly inwards, away from others, away from God, and yet by virtue of being human continues to bear the hallmarks of being created by God. Being 'created' means not being in full control of one's origins or destiny. There are constraints on one's personality and identity (of time, place, gender and ethnicity). But being created in love by *God* means being created by One who desires freedom for those who populate the created world. Human beings are specific; 'humanity' does not exist in the abstract, only in particular forms, as real people, in a particular time and place, and with all the limitations of contingency which go with that specificity. But the degree of freedom which human beings possess, within the constraints of particularity, seems inevitably to carry with it dire consequences. Human exercise of freedom reveals the ever-present tendency to 'sin' (i.e. to neglect God).[4]

Lee's exposition of human relations in *Do The Right Thing* accentuates particularity to the full. The ambiguity and complexity of all the leading characters is real. People are only people in the context of particular locations (here, literally, in the context of one block within a New York neighbourhood). This block does not stand for 'humanity in general', however. The film shows that humanity is only human because it is particular. There is no 'humanity in the abstract'. Christian reflection on humanity is thus challenged both by the starkness of Lee's attention to particularity, and by the reminder that despite the clear presence of lurking rage (evil beneath the surface, evidence of 'original sin', even) goodness can still emerge in human interactions. And yet Christian theology also knows, despite what it has often implied throughout its history, that there is no 'humanity in the abstract'. The doctrine of incarnation (God enfleshed, supremely in the person of Jesus Christ) commits Christianity to close attention to concreteness and particularity. Because of this, Christian theology can work with such cultural-artistic expositions of human experience as *Do The Right Thing* to explore what it means in real situations to be both made in God's image *and* sinful (at one and the same time). 'Image of God' and 'sin' can too easily become abstract terms when not explored through the particularity of human experience within which they take form.

What has Christian theology made of 'sin'? Typically, sin has been understood as self-interest or pride.[5] Human beings turn themselves into gods by worshipping their own selves. This expresses itself in many forms of self-interested behaviour such as the acquisition of wealth and the pursuit of pleasure for its own sake. Common to all such activities is the lack of thought for consequences on others. So-called 'sins' are, however, to be understood as the symptom of the sin of self-interest and neglect of God. This very typical view of sin has been rightly challenged, especially by women theologians, who have pointed out that it assumes a way of operating as a human being in which one has the *choice* to behave in this way.[6] The experience of many women, past and present, across the world has been a *lack* of choice. Sin may thus be better defined as a lack of appropriate self-assertion. On this understanding, neglect of God takes the form of disregard for the God-given goodness of the human self. If human beings are made in God's image, the presence of that image in the human person is to be celebrated by acknowledgement of the human potential for creativity, for relationship, for goodness, for care of others and the earth's resources.

Both of these understandings of sin – as pride/exaggerated self-interest or lack of appropriate self-assertion – are, however, individualistic. They focus upon human sin as an individual disposition. *Do The Right Thing* presses viewers to think about corporate aspects of human identity and self-discovery, and thus of the way that the negative aspects of ambiguous humanity are inextricably woven within social forms of human life. The individual aspect of sin need not be overlooked here. Human beings continue, as individuals, to participate in structures of wickedness. But Lee's film, without letting the protagonists off the hook, shows how complex race, class and gender – and their interweaving – actually are. Furthermore, viewers, like the lead characters, are brought into the complexity. We are left confronting our own ambiguity as we think about the personal, social background which has made us, and makes us, who we are.

The film therefore offers a challenge to Christian thought not only to keep particularity rather than abstractness at the forefront of its exploration of human being. It also reminds theology to address the *social* complexity of human formation. As we shall see in Chapter 9 in due course, Christian theology has a social sense of what it means to be human at its heart. But Christianity sometimes moves too quickly towards a notion of 'church' as a form of human community which seeks to anticipate 'the Kingdom of God' (a kind of ultimate vision of what is possible for human beings to become).[7] In its undue haste, Christianity is prone to overlook the 'kingdoms of sin' within which all human beings live. In other words, notions of 'original sin' have often been too individualistically conceived. The inevitability of human wickedness has thus not been adequately explored in Christian thought in relation to the social and political complexity of human life.[8] *Do The Right Thing* is therefore theologically provocative because it relates the inevitability of human ambiguity to unavoidable social aspects of what it means to be human (ethnicity, above all). In so doing it poses a question about how creative, positive human potential (celebration of God's image) and human wickedness (as the expression of the universality of sin) are to be both understood, and the former encouraged, the latter resisted, given the scale and intensity of social pressures.

There is hope and humour in *Do The Right Thing*. Characters are immersed in the particularity of their neighbourhood. But some also step back from it at times. Mister Senor Love Daddy (Samuel Jackson) offers a commentary – a sort of soundtrack – on all that goes on. Black debates with black as to what kind of black-consciousness and action is appropriate. And, strikingly, at a point when it looks as though the Korean shop-owners may have their store wrecked, they are protected by black residents who can identify with them because of their own past experience. The role of black memory is thus important in the film not only for black people themselves but also as a way of enabling group-interest (in this case ethnicity) to be transcended. Whether as viewers we can 'survive our inevitable multicul-turalism' is Lee's challenge.[9] It is also a challenge to Christian theology, which must likewise work with and through the powerful loyalties engendered by group experience, and resist overlooking their force through too lazy and hasty an appeal to transcendence. As we shall see further in Chapter 9 below, 'church' as a concept invites people to find a new loyalty, and to participate in a different corporate memory than that delivered to people solely by the circumstances of their birth and ethnic background. But without attending to the significance and complexity of what our origins and ethnicities entail, perhaps no fully theological understanding of human being or church will be possible.

Eternal Sunshine of the Spotless Mind is also concerned with memory. Here we switch back to considering individual human beings. But because this film focuses upon the importance of memory for how human beings relate to each other, the emotions experienced by, and the questions posed for, viewers are instructive for exploration of the social formation of the human self. The potential disorientation experienced by the viewer of this film accentuates memory's importance for understanding who one is (What have I done? Who are my friends? What beliefs have I been living by?). A basic question left after the viewing experience (What would it mean for me to lose my memory?) is, however, supplemented by many others. How dependent am I on others for remembering who I am? (For others carry their memory of me on which I can depend when I continue my relationship with them.) Who are the most significant memory-carriers for me? What am I to do with the fact that some groups I am part of I did not choose (family, neighbourhood in early life), whilst others I did choose (neighbourhood in later life – though not neighbours; type of work – though not necessarily colleagues; religious community – possibly)? I am thus dependent on the collective memories of all of these groups in which I participate for part of my identity. I only exist as an interdependent person.

There is surprisingly little direct reflection on memory and the human self in the history of Christian thought. A well-known passage from the early church theologian St Augustine (345–430 CE) uses memory within a triad of memory, understanding and will as an analogy of the doctrine of the Trinity.[10] Interestingly, as this is one of Augustine's psychological analogies, the memory and God are both being considered together within reflection on God being like a human individual.[11] There are then two further major areas in Christian theology where remembering and forgetting has proved vital: confession, and Holy Communion. In any act of penitence – the asking for God's forgiveness – religious believers are asking God to remove from them the consequences of actions which they believe or know to have been wrong. The recollection of them (not the forgetting) is important. It is, then, God who does the forgetting, in the sense that God releases the person confessing from any lingering guilt for past actions, from any burden of memory, and from any sense that God will punish a person for their deeds.[12] Healing thus comes in the context of making public one's repentance of recalled evil actions. In the resolve to live a renewed life, the memory is not then a burden and need not be repressed. Within a life lived in relation to God, then, an individual's good and bad memories can be borne because an individual's own story (identity) rests within a larger story: that of the life of God.

The second main area of Christian life and thought within which memory has always played a crucial part is in the celebration of Mass/Eucharist/Holy Communion/Lord's Supper/Breaking of Bread.[13] A full exploration of what Christians have deemed to occur (to the bread and wine, and to the participants) in the context of a service of Holy Communion cannot be entered into here.[14] In all versions of the celebration of Communion, however, recollection is crucial. The Last Supper that Jesus shared with his immediate disciples is recalled, and words deemed to have been used by Jesus at that event are used again. Two aspects about this eucharistic recollection should be noted. First, the recollection is celebrated not simply as a past event, but as one which stimulates belief, thought and action in the present. Second, the act of recollection is not dependent on the individual memories of those participating. How could it be, of course, for none of us was there! The point is that the memory is contained within the words (of the liturgy or the free prayer used to recall the Last Supper) which the community of Christians who meet carry with them.

Beyond these three uses of memory in Christian tradition, as a subject of enquiry in its own right, 'memory' is otherwise a relatively modern subject for theological and philosophical reflection, receiving particular attention since the rise of interest in consciousness. *Eternal Sunshine of the Spotless Mind* reflects this modern post-Freud concern. Conscious and unconscious memories are recognized as crucial for the understanding and shaping of human identity. There has also been a huge interest in recent years in the healing of memories, individual and corporate. Indeed, it looks in many ways in the West as though the therapeutic role played in the past by religion (especially Christianity) is now being played throughout society by counsellors and therapists. So what is to be made of these parallel declarations of interest in the role of memory for the human being?

Eternal Sunshine of the Spotless Mind taps into a widespread current concern about the relationship between memory and identity.[15] The film confronts the horrific prospect of memory loss in an imaginative way. It demonstrates that to be human means to live with a combination of good and bad memories about oneself and others. It suggests the sub-humanity of wanting to be rid of bad memories. It provokes the viewer to think about the interdependence of a person with others for how memories are carried, whilst leaving unresolved the question of how one actually lives with bad memories.

The weight of Christian thought, ironically, is concerned less with what a human being remembers than with what God will 'forget'. This is the overarching framework within which Christianity places the acts of remembering and forgetting. The individual has long been known to struggle with bad memories.[16] But because Christianity's concern is fundamentally with the salvation of the human person, it is the release from the impact of bad memories and the desire to enable people to live more constructively and purposefully within the story of God that are paramount.[17] This has proved therapeutic for individuals throughout Christian history.[18] Ultimately, however, Christianity is less concerned with the individual, than with the individual within the scope of the fate of the whole of humankind within the created order. It is for this reason that Christianity, building on a Jewish preoccupation with a collective memory, a story of a people (the people of the Exodus), is more concerned with the corporate memory of the church, as a form of the people of God. Unlike the collective memories within which people live in *Do The Right Thing*, the church's corporate memory is not based on ethnicity but on a memory, held corporately, about who God is. The response for a Christian to the question 'who are you?' could thus rightly be: 'I am one of God's people.' It is the participation in the people of God (via church) which gives a Christian person an identity. All other aspects of what it means to be human which pertain to memory − recollections of one's participation within an ethnic group, a social class, a family, or memories of aspects of one's individual life-story − are to be understood within this framework.

In this way, when a person 'loses one's memory' one is also then 'held', as if within the memory of God's own self, by the church which carries a collective memory of the story of God.[19]

The interplay between *Do The Right Thing*, *Eternal Sunshine of the Spotless Mind* and Christian reflection on the human person thus proves provocative on a number of fronts. Central to the exploration have been the role of memory, the many ways in and through which one discovers, explores and/or constructs a human identity, and the relationship and tension between the individual and the group. But even if human beings find or construct an identity for themselves, and work out a place for themselves within the created order in which the image of God within them may be respected, what is it all for? What are human beings to do?

One of the most famous Christian statements about what human beings are for occurs in the seventeenth-century Westminster Shorter Catechism in response to the question 'what is the chief end of human beings?'[20] Human beings, the Catechism states, are to glorify God and to enjoy God forever. 'Enjoyment' is sometimes not associated with Christianity, so this should be noted! But what does it mean to 'glorify' and 'enjoy' God? A simple answer can be given: human beings are to love. In loving, they are glorifying and enjoying. In Christian understanding, they will be able to do this all the more when loving as a human practice is understood as a reflection of who God is. All Christian theology can thus be understood as an attempt to grasp what it means to worship a God of love.

Christology and soteriology – the exploration of the person and work of Jesus Christ – are to be seen as ways of understanding what kind of god God is, for 'in Christ' God has made Godself known. The doctrine of the Trinity is an attempt to tease out what God must be like, given that God has made Godself known in Christ: God *is* love, *is* loving relationship in God's own self. The doctrine of the Holy Spirit is the main way in which Christian theology wrestles with the generous, overflowing in the whole of creation of the free creativity of God. God's love for creation is not confined to a past moment in time (incarnation in Jesus), or even to where we may say that Jesus Christ continues to be present today (as 'Church' or in the form of manifestations of God's Kingdom in the world). God's presence in the world will always, for Christians, be identifiably Christ-like, but attention to the Holy Spirit enables Christians to see the love of God for creation present in many forms. When human beings attempt, then, to explore what love is, they are, in Christian understanding, inevitably working in theological territory. When love songs are sung, love poems are written and films about love are made, then the love of God, as reflected in and through human love, is being celebrated and explored. It is on this basis that the three films of Richard Curtis being examined in this chapter become resource material for theology.

One of the drawbacks when talking about 'love songs', 'love poems' or 'films about love', of course, is that it is often assumed that romantic, heterosexual love is what is being talked about. This is indeed often the case. In the case of the Curtis films, however, as I have already shown, more is being explored. Yes, the customary features of romantic comedy remain present (man/boy meets woman/girl, there's a rocky relationship, but they get together in the end). But as indicated earlier, other features are mixed in. These allow real life to intrude into the fantasy and give the viewer more to 'work with'.

The features of the three Curtis films which viewer-response highlights, and which are especially interesting for Christian theology, are these. First, love is not always romantic. *Love Actually* includes within its narratives the love between brother and sister, and between parents and children. It can admittedly be argued that the Curtis films do trade off an interest in erotic forms of love, and in so doing also feed a contemporary Western cultural tendency to idolize sexual love. But the presence and exploration of other relationships within the films qualifies the way in which sexual love is presented as a norm. Love understood as loving relationship is present in the films. This is also a central concern for Christian theology.

Second, love includes suffering. Sarah's love for her brother Michael entails suffering for both. Harry's infidelity makes Karen suffer. It does not remove her love. Matthew suffers when his relationship with Gareth is broken by Gareth's death. In one sense these are merely real-life examples of what anyone who loves knows. No relationship of any depth which lasts over time will be devoid of such suffering. Such a profoundly human experience is, in Christian understanding, not merely illuminated when parallels are drawn between contemporary human experience and the story of Jesus. By the Jesus story being understood as a crucial part of 'the story of God' and of God's relating to the world, then such forms of human suffering are seen to be forms of human participation in the divine life.[21] This matches the way in which God has chosen to participate in creation, risking 'in Christ' all that costly loving entails.

Third, love bears all things. Suffering is not to be idolized. It is never 'acceptable' in the sense of being sought and welcomed. But it happens, and sometimes has to be borne, not being able to be eradicated. This aspect of love becomes clear in Max and Bella's relationship in *Notting Hill*. The reason that their relationship, and not that of William and Anna, is a good model for people to copy is not simply that they are married.[22] Theirs is a lasting, loving pain-bearing relationship because they have had to face suffering, and yet still they love. As viewers we have confidence that they will bear together, in love, whatever life will present to them.

Where can true love be found?: in God. For film-viewers not already predisposed to offer this answer, however, the meaning of such a response has to be grasped via a circuitous route. In response to all the films looked at in this chapter we see that the meaning of human beings' 'glorifying God and enjoying God forever' takes shape in the context of human loving. Human love, of creation and of one human being for another, is participation in the love of God for the created order. This can only be celebrated in concrete form, however much it may be reflected upon in the abstract.

Working conclusions

A number of important theological themes have emerged from engagement with the six films looked at in this chapter. Many of these themes overlap directly with the subject-matter of other chapters. Here I simply highlight the themes that have emerged and the way in which this chapter's treatment of them links to other material in the book.

First, we have been reminded that human beings are made in God's image. This means being created for relationship – between human beings and between human beings and creation as a whole. Discovery of what it means to be in relationship both occurs within given patterns of human relationship – families, ethnic groups – and within those relationships that we choose to live within – friendships of all kinds. These relationships reflect who God is in so far as Christian theology makes the claim, via its doctrine of the Trinity, that God is relational in God's own self.

Second, who we are as loving beings is not only discovered, but also constructed. The formation of our identity as persons occurs in relation both to the groups we are given to belong to, and those we choose. These groups carry a memory for us, a tradition of believing and behaving which shape the meanings we adopt, sometimes by clear choice, sometimes without knowing. The fashioning of personal identity is thus always an individual and a social exercise. Christian theology recognizes this, and also the many different communal forms (families, friendships, ethnic groups) through which memory is carried and the self is shaped. 'Church' enters into this mix as a challenge to the social forms in and through which what it means to be made in God's image (to relate, to love, to be a steward of God's earth) is discovered and explored. More will be said on this in Chapter 9 below.

Third, obstructions to what makes it possible for human being to celebrate the divine image in their self-understanding and living also have to be addressed. Whatever mars the recognition and enjoyment of God's presence in the world (sin), whether that takes individual or social form, has to be opposed. This links with many of the chapters below. Chapter 7 explores redemption: how human beings are enabled by God to be human in the face of internal and external factors which prevent loving relationship. Chapter 8 explores key ritual practices (sacraments) through which Christianity enables people to recognize their God-givenness, and the way that God goes on loving and shape them in their everyday living. The sacraments, like the church itself, embody in concrete form the tradition and the memory by which people are carried through life. Keeping a focus on what it means to be made in God's image and resisting all that blocks recognition of that image therefore entails being appropriately dependent on others. It is not an individual's task to maintain the image: human beings *are* made in God's image. They need support of many kinds to respect what having such a gift means in practice.

For further study

Biblical passages worth exploring include:

Genesis 1–3 The opening chapters of both the Hebrew and Christian Bibles, in which there are two accounts of creation (1.1–2.4a and 2.4b–25) and an account of 'the Fall', i.e. a story which seeks to characterize human disobedience, and distance from God.

Psalm 8 A statement about the dignity of human beings before God.

Proverbs 8.22–31 A poetic passage praising Wisdom, and Wisdom's fundamental role in creation.

John 1.1–5 One of the most famous passages in the New Testament, linking Jesus Christ with God the Creator via attention to 'the Word'.

Romans 7.7–25 A passage which finds the Apostle Paul vexed by his experience of being unable to do what, in his mind, he knows he wants to do. It is a classic expression of existential struggle.

Texts from the history of Christian thought worth exploring include:

'Augustine on the Trinity' (= extracts from *De Trinitate* IX.i.1–v.8; in McGrath, pp. 187–90). This famous passage finds Augustine exploring the doctrine of the Trinity using lots of different imagery drawn from human psychology.

John Calvin on knowledge of God and knowledge of the self (= *Institutes of the Christian Religion* [1559] 1.1.1 and 1.2.1; in Madges, pp. 103–5). Here, Calvin notes the close relationship between knowing ourselves and knowing God. At the same time, Calvin observed that there is a stark distinction between who God is and who we are.

John Calvin on human awareness of divinity (= *Institutes of the Christian Religion* III.1, 3 [1559]; in Ahlgren, pp. 40–1). These extracts find Calvin expressing the way in which people maintain an awareness of God no matter how far from God they may seem to be.

Sarah M. Grimké on the image of God (= *Letters on the Equality of the Sexes and the Condition of Woman* [1838], pp. 3–5 and 8–10; in Placher, Vol. 2, pp. 119–20). Written in the context of the fight for the abolition of slavery in the USA, this powerful text interprets 'the image of God' in relation to equality between the sexes.

Reinhold Niebuhr on human nature (= *The Nature and Destiny of Man, vol. 1: Human Nature* [1964], pp. 150, 161, 163–4, 178–9, 270–2; in Ahlgren, pp. 54–7). These extracts from an influential set of 1939 lectures contain Niebuhr's understanding of sin as pride.

Emil Brunner on 'the Image of God' (= *The Christian Doctrine of Creation and Redemption: Dogmatics Vol. 2* [1952], pp. 55–8; in McGrath, pp. 442–5). This passage offers a fine exposition of a relational understanding of the term 'image of God'.

'Richard Swinburne on the Concept of Creation' (= *The Coherence of Theism* [1977], pp. 126–31; in McGrath, pp. 222–5). This text sets out with philosophical clarity what it means to speak of 'creation' within a theistic world-view.

John Mbiti on the cultural influences upon understandings of creation (= 'The Encounter of Christian Faith and African Religion', *The Christian Century* [27.8–3.9. 1980]; in Placher, vol. 2, pp. 197–8). In this extract from a journal article, Kenyan theologian John Mbiti points out how the universality of the claim for God as creator influences the way in which local histories are understood.

Sara Maitland on 'Ways of Relating' (in Loades, pp. 148–57). Novelist Sara Maitland reflects on how what it means to 'relate' connects with fundamental questions about how people talk of God.

Vitor Westhelle on a view of creation from Latin America (in Thistlethwaite and Engel, pp. 146–58). This challenging text brings to the topic of creation the insights of theology done in relation to displaced peoples. The concept of 'image of God' is interpreted relationally against this background.

Chapter 6

SPIRIT

CONSIDERATION OF WHAT IT MEANS TO BE human in the context of creation leaves as yet unexplored how the divine and the human interact in contemporary life. It would be quite possible to follow a (deist) line of thought, according to which God created the world, but then 'let it be' to such an extent that there is no ongoing interaction between God and the created order. This deist view could be held to be closer to atheism than it would care to admit. Theism, by contrast, wrestles with the harder question of how God remains actively involved with the world, even when there appears to be much evidence to the contrary. This branch of Christian theology has often been known as the 'doctrine of providence'. 'Providence' is then an extension of the doctrine of creation in the sense that God is thought to be continuing to be involved in the same way that God let creation be.

In its most extreme form, the doctrine of providence leads to the notion of a God who is so directly involved in the world as to leave little scope for human freedom. The 'fore-seeing' implied in the word providence comes to mean 'fore-ordering' or 'fore-ordaining'. The sovereignty of God (God is God, after all) is stressed so much that the extent to which God, in love, leaves room for creation to discover for itself what love is is downplayed. 'Letting be' is, however, not the same as 'leaving alone'. One of the main ways in which the interplay of divine initiative and human response, divine action and human action is explored is through the doctrine of the Spirit (pneumatology). When God's creativity is spoken of, it is the spirit of God which is highlighted (e.g. Gen. 1.1–2). Exploration of the creative human spirit should therefore be one location where aspects and implications of the interplay between the divine and the human in the created order can be drawn out and examined.

In this chapter we shall consider three films which offer very different examples of human creativity and 'spiritedness'. One (*Amadeus*) presents its subject-matter in a theological framework. Another (*Touching the Void*) reflects a fighting human spirit in a battle against nature, on the assumption that there is no God. A third (*Legally Blonde*) barely raises the question of God, yet suggests directly what sort of faith is required in contemporary life.

Films

Amadeus (Milos Forman, 1984)

Based on Peter Shaffer's 1979 stage play, a fictional account of Salieri's response to and jealousy towards Mozart, *Amadeus* is a rich (and long!) celebration of Mozart's music. It is essentially Salieri's story: the story of how he came to try to commit suicide and ended up (the point at which the film begins) explaining to the priest who comes to the asylum to hear his confession and why he sought to take his own life. The film is thus Salieri's interpretation of Mozart, and an expression of his rage at a God who does not appear to reward moral endeavour with artistic gifts. In the midst of the rage and the incomprehension at the unfairness with which Salieri deems God to have dispensed musical gifts to his creatures, however, he does not doubt Mozart's genius. Nor, however, does he doubt that it really was God who gave these gifts unfairly. He mocks God in anger, it appears, not disbelief.

Touching the Void (Kevin Macdonald, 2004)

Touching the Void proved a surprisingly successful film on its release in 2004. Part documentary, part dramatic reconstruction, it tells the true story of two climbers, Joe Simpson and Simon Yates, who got into difficulties on an expedition in the Peruvian Andes. When Joe fell and broke a leg, Simon had to try and help him to safety. During the descent, however, their problems merely increased and Simon was faced with the decision about whether, in order to save his own life, he should cut the rope on his climbing-partner, whom he could not see and assumed to be dead anyway. Having done so, and being unable later to see where Joe's body had gone, he had to leave him on the mountain and descend alone. Joe, however, survived after a three-day crawl back down the mountain. The film records this astonishing escape from the mountain, mixing interviews with the two climbers and their base-camp companion, Richard, with brilliantly filmed reconstructions of the climb and the struggles of the descent.

Legally Blonde (Robert Luketic, 2001)

Legally Blonde is the story of a young woman Elle Woods (Reese Witherspoon) whose boyfriend Warner (Matthew Davies) heads off to study law at Harvard. Disgruntled at being left behind, and treated disparagingly by her boyfriend on his departure, she decides to teach him a lesson by working hard for good grades and earning a place at Harvard Law School herself. She proves an exceptional student, finds a new boyfriend, is invited back to give a graduation speech, and all ends well for her. It is admittedly unusual to find a feelgood 'teen movie', or 'chick-flick', included in a book about theology. This 'fluffy comedy' is, however, included for two main reasons. First, there is empirical evidence that it can inspire and empower young women. Second, the closing speech of the film contains a succinct summary of contemporary Western individualism.

Viewing experiences

As a celebration of Mozart's music, Amadeus is both a stunning visual and aural experience. There is sufficient music in the film to make it more than a soundtrack. The music inevitably leaps out of the film because it has already been at work culturally in its own right as music for over two centuries. But somehow the film brings the music itself to life even more for the viewer. By locating selected pieces in the context of the film's own plot, so that a commentary is provided, the music is simply enhanced. Salieri's respect for Mozart's Serenade in B flat major is a case in point. His evident jealousy merely accentuates the brilliance of the music. As viewers, then, we are drawn into Salieri's world and can empathize with his feelings.

The viewing experience can, however, provoke a range of reactions. In our enjoyment and sympathy we might leave the cinema thinking that the music is beautiful, but know that very, very few people are capable of such brilliance. It is therefore not 'our' world not only because it is a historical drama about a past age, but also because we do not feel we could ever be so creative. Or, if as viewers we get inside Salieri's basic complaint, we might be made to feel conscious by the film of what we are good at, but also about those who are better than us. We are, in other words, reminded of our own jealousy by the film and not only cognitively. We *feel* it too.

Conversely some viewers are repulsed by Salieri's intent to bring Mozart down. This can in turn lead them to sympathy for Mozart. They may not easily claim to share in Mozart's genius. But they are then enabled by the film to be affirmed in whatever gifts and skills they know they have. In being repulsed by Salieri, viewers are thus better able to appreciate grace over merit.

Emotional responses may be even more powerful in the way viewers receive *Touching the Void*. There is not the historical or cultural distance that we might experience in watching *Amadeus*, and we may never be likely to climb snow-capped peaks, but we are skilfully brought by the film inside the fear and the emotional intensity of Simon's moral dilemma and guilt. And we are confronted with some simple questions. Would we have cut the rope? Would we have had the inner reserves to do what Joe did? These are not, as the viewing experience makes clear, straightforwardly rational ethical questions to which objective arguments and criteria apply. They require that attention be given to ideas, beliefs, feelings, what it means to have 'inner resources', to have/be a body, and how all these factors work together in the specific contexts in which we find ourselves. In a stark form, this film demands that viewers do some serious reflection on themselves.

Legally Blonde is lighter viewing and, unlike *Touching the Void*, is not the kind of film one might expect to be talking about deep into the night. It leaves viewers feeling good, and then asking each other where they might go in order to grab some food. However, in Roger Ebert's words, though it is 'balanced between silliness and charm', it is 'hard to dislike'.[1] It is clearly a young person's movie, pandering to (and marketed towards) a cinema-going public of, say, 13–25. For older viewers it lacks the complexity of the phase of life being portrayed.

Nevertheless, for a great many who see this film, especially younger women viewers, the sheer likeability, grit and determination of its lead character makes it an important film to examine from the perspective of its reception and consumption. For a 24-year-old female bookseller who took part in research about the reception of films in the summer of 2004, the case is clear:

> I think that *some* films can have an effect, but the majority are just a . . . fun way of passing an hour or two. But if they are good, then I suppose they have positively affected you by lifting your spirits . . . I watched *Legally Blonde* twice while doing my finals, and both times immediately went home to study, convinced if some cheesy, dumb blonde could get a law degree, I could pass my degree too!

Here is a film, then, to be watched not just when 'you need a lift'. It not only carries a *message* of empowerment. It functions as a *means* of empowerment. What is not clear is whether the explicit message of how or why its lead character found the resources to do what she did is then automatically shared by its viewers. If we are to believe Elle's closing speech, then it is 'through . . . a strong sense of self' that she was able to be successful. Above all, then, she had to believe 'in herself'. For those for whom the film functions in an empowering way, then, the question arises as to how the cognitive processing of a film's content and the emotional impact of a film interweave (if they do). The inspirational quality of *Legally Blonde* raises questions about how films function, as well as about any 'message' it may carry.

Connecting questions and issues

All three films are about inspiration and may prove inspirational in their own way. To talk of being inspired means using language about being 'breathed into' as if we are taken over by some spirit not our own. And when we speak of being 'inspired' we usually mean this positively. We have to qualify the phrase further if we want to imply that a person seems over-taken by a negative force or spirit (e.g. 'inspired by the devil'). Of course, this may be just language. Notions of being 'breathed into' may be simply a way of speaking of what it feels like. It is 'as if' a spirit takes a person over. Even for Mozart, it was 'as if' he could not control what he wrote down. There may have been no specific gift, divine or otherwise, or source external to him on which he drew in order to write his music. He could simply do it; it is as straightforward as that. Likewise, Joe Simpson was not literally 'in-spired' to enable him to survive. Indeed, in the film he explicitly rejects the possibility that God could have helped him. He felt himself to be totally alone. Similarly, Elle Woods was perhaps just choosing to get down to some serious work. It may even be argued that her drive was born of envy or revenge.

But even if all these reductionist arguments are plausible, in theological perspective they do not do justice to what appears to be going on in human experience, in experiences like those which characters in the films explore, and which viewers explore in response. The range of experiences, contexts and issues presented in these films provide a framework for asking basic questions about what it means to 'have spirit' or 'a spirit', to be spiritual, to share (in) the divine Spirit, to be inspired and to have gifts/be gifted. These now need spelling out in more detail.

- Why do we speak of 'gifts' at all? Is it appropriate to speak of 'gifts' without assuming that there is a giver? Is use of the term 'gifts' simply a lingering habit of a pre-modern, theistic age which most of society has, in fact, 'grown beyond'?

- What would be the point of assuming that all creativity is somehow 'derived' (whether from God or not) or 'dependent' rather than original?

- If 'gift' language is to be used, what are defined as 'gifts', and what's ruled out? How broad should creativity be defined: music and art may be acceptable, but what about sport, or dance, or stand-up comedy? And is all kind of music-making a 'gift'? What is to be made of a person with a disability claiming that s/he is a 'gift' to church and society?

- We may speak of people being 'inspired', and are suggesting that something happens to them 'internally'. But what meaning is to be attached to 'internal processes' when so much is known about chemical reactions in the body? What does it mean 'to have an inner life'? And can an 'inner life' be cultivated in any way, or is the notion of an 'inner life' altogether misleading? How does all this link with discussions about body and spirit, body and mind, body and soul?

- If some sense of divine involvement in humanity via 'the spirit' of the human being is assumed, then how do human and divine relate to each other? 'Spirit-possession' has negative connotations. So what kind of co-operation between divine and human spirits are we talking about here?

- How conscious do human beings have to be, if at all, of their 'possession of' or 'participation in' Spirit/the spirit? Does God's Spirit work without human co-operation? Can/must human beings choose to 'invite the spirit in' in some way? What happens to human freedom in all of this?

This range of questions forms the background to the exploration to follow.

Explorations: gifts and skills; re-creation; God's presence in the world

Salieri is enraged. Why should such a snivelling, foul-mouthed little runt like Mozart be so gifted? If God is the giver, then God is clearly unfair. If musical abilities are indeed gifts, then they have been indiscriminately distributed, without respect either for those to whom the gifts have been entrusted, or for others (such as Salieri himself) who demonstrate profound gratitude for what they have been given and work hard to make the most of these gifts. Certainly, Salieri is latching onto a basic Christian insight. In Christian understanding, people's gifts and skills really do come from God. Anything we are capable of doing we can only do because we have been given life in the first place. Human skills and abilities are a gift because participation in life is itself a response to 'the Lord, the Giver of Life'.[2] The embodied and spiritual (emotional, mental, intellectual) forms in and through which we therefore exercise our gifts and skills are but the expressions of our response to the gift of life.

But how specifically are these gifts given? In the Hebrew Bible/Old Testament, for example, it looks as though God has targeted gifts very specifically indeed. The appointment of the workers to work on the arte-facts of the tabernacle, the people of Israel's place of worship, for example, is clearly spelt out (Exodus 31.1–11). Bezalel and Oholiab are named as men called by God. And those involved in the making of the tent and its fittings receive their ability from God (Exodus 31.6). In the New Testament too, even if no individuals are named, there are specific roles that the Spirit of God appears to favour: apostles, prophets, teachers, miracle-workers and healers (I Cor. 12.28). There are no musicians or craftspeople here. There are, however, 'helpers' and 'administrators', and there are also 'speakers in various kinds of tongues'.[3]

The emphasis in both of these passages, of course, is on worship. But in both cases it is not exclusively religious gifts which are identified: skills in arts and crafts and in administration are mentioned too, and can be employed more widely than in worship. The important point to note is that whatever skills are being talked about, it is God who gives them. It is the working of God's Spirit that is spoken of in each case. Bezalel is 'filled ... with the Spirit of God, with ability and intelligence, with knowledge and all craftsmanship ... ' (Exodus 31.2). All of the roles spoken about by Paul pertain to 'spiritual gifts' (I Cor. 12.1); all such gifts, despite their diversity, are given by the one God, who inspires each individual 'for the common good' (I Cor. 12.6–7). None of this would satisfy Salieri, of course. And the more specific the gift-giving appears to be, the more problematic it has become. If Bezalel and Oholiab can be named, then Salieri should be able to be named too. God appears to have overlooked him.

Except, of course, that God has not. The specificity of God's naming might now seem too over-dramatized. If Bezalel and Oholiab were the men for the job, then we might now say that was because they had craft skills which were recognized, and which could then be interpreted as God-given. But they are still acknowledged as gifts. It is therefore logical (when God is held to be the cause of all) to say that God called them by name.

A further, more basic, point of the passage in question is this: get your best craftspeople to do this job; and as they ply their trade, remind them that they are doing more than 'just a job'. This is to the praise and glory of the God who created them and gave them their gifts in the first place. By extension: any human ability or skill, when seen as a gift from God, can always be more than 'just a job'.

Ability and skills may not, however, always be discovered or find their expression in the world of work. Sometimes work is endured for the sake of releasing resources so that other time is made available in life which becomes 're-creational'.[4] *Touching the Void* reminds the viewer both of the intense, gutsy potential of the human spirit and the fact that what happens outside of work/employment may be even more important than what people may 'do for a living'. Exploration of what went on for Joe and Simon in the Andes thus invites consideration of how life is lived in an integrated way. No part is unconnected from another even if some activities (sport, travel, music, worship or cinema-going) may appear like 'escape'.[5] A person's life is made up of different parts. But in theological understanding God as Spirit is active in all parts, even if seemingly more evident in some kinds of activity rather than others.

As for most mountaineers, it is on the slopes and peaks that Joe and Simon stretch themselves, feel truly free, confront their limitations and 'take on' nature. Their sport, and the extreme situation that forms the plot of the film, could be interpreted as their own version of 'spirit versus matter'. No theological gloss on this is needed. It is simply the battle of their own spirits against the forces of a nature that is at once beautifully awesome, and frightening in its power and unpredictability. And though it is their spirits which confront nature, the sense in which human spirits are always embodied could not be clearer in this film, given the battering Joe's body receives on his crawl down the mountain.

What, then, merits considering this film from the perspective of the doctrine of the Holy Spirit? As already noted, the characters themselves do not invite this link. Joe himself refutes any reference to the help of God in the midst of his traumatic experience. In his own view, his own guts and determination got him out of danger. This remains true, though, even if it can be argued that something more was going on. He still needed his guts and determination. The broader question is how and where such guts, determination, and sheer drive and willpower come from within the human spirit.

In Christian theological terms, an answer to this question comes from two angles: humanity's being made in God's image; and the constant interaction of God with the created order, as evidenced in the continuing, creative work of God's Spirit in the world. To put it another way: human 'spiritedness' of the kind displayed by Joe is itself evidence of the working of God in the world. And this working of the spirit of God in and through the human spirit is a crucial expression of humanity's being made in God's image. Human beings reflect God in that they participate by their spiritedness in the Spirit of God at work in the world. A passage such as this from the Apostle Paul – ' . . . the Spirit helps us in our weakness; for we do not know how to pray as we ought, but the Spirit himself intercedes for us with sighs too deep for words' (Rom. 8.26) – is prone to too narrow an interpretation if related only to formal prayer in the context of Christian worship. It surely means more than this. God helps people not only when they cannot pray. Inner resources that can be discovered within the human spirit admittedly do not kick in automatically. Divine and human spirit may struggle to connect in human experience. But, as the Old Testament/ Hebrew Bible shows so clearly, the constancy of an always-available God who remains loyal to God's people whatever they may get up to is a profound message of hope for humanity and the whole created order. God's Spirit remains available because God is available. The Spirit is a form of God's presence. And the companionship of God with a particular people (be it the people of Israel or the church) is always symbolic of God's willingness to be the companion and helper of all.

Three major caveats must, however, be inserted into this rather rosy picture of the working of the divine Spirit in human life. First, an approach to human skill and creativity that takes a vocational approach to work and employment is clearly open to abuse. The close alliance between emphasis upon vocation and the rise of modern capitalism has long been noted.[6] It is rooted firmly in the Reformation-inspired notion of all work being done for God. Even if pre-modern forms of work should not be romanticized, such an emphasis was more possible in pre-industrial times. The monotony of factory work and its postmodern equivalent, the 'call centre', is a challenge to any easy identification of work as always intrinsically fulfilling.

Second, it is easy to speak of fulfilment in human endeavour when speaking of great achievement in the world of the arts. Most of us would be happy to write music like Salieri. We don't need to pretend we could emulate Mozart. But this is still in the realm of the high (or classical) arts. Does all art count? And what about entertainment? Are all forms of diversion inspired by God? It is clear in Christianity that there is a task of 'discerning the spirits'. Not every spirit is of God (I John 4.4–6). The writer of I John provides a Christological criterion of discernment: 'By this you know the Spirit of God: every spirit which confesses that Jesus Christ has come in the flesh is of God, and every spirit which does not confess Jesus is not of God' (I John 4.2–3a). In a first-century context that criterion might have been easier to apply than it is today. It clearly cannot mean 'only Christians speak for God'. In historical context it was clearly meant to fend off those who denied the incarnation. Ironically, then, those who were too spiritual were not of the Spirit of God. In the present, we can say that whatever is Christ-like is of the Spirit of God. At least that satisfies the Christian requirement that all theological statements be related to Christology. But admittedly, it needs a lot of unpacking. So what does applying a Christological criterion to the task of 'discerning the spirits' amount to? And how does it help us decide which arts, which media and what culture/s are worth bothering with?

At the very least, as the Johannine literature in the New Testament makes clear, being Christ-like or in Christ means seeking truth and promoting loving relationships. Furthermore, as the Synoptic Gospels indicate, it means trying to live out the kingdom of God, in anticipation of the future which God alone can bring about. Being inspired by the Spirit of God, then, in any form of human activity always has to be seen in the light of where it leads and what it promotes. Presence of a Christ-like spirit is not simply about the moral worthiness of any human agent, artist or otherwise. Morals may not be irrelevant, but if God were dependent upon moral worthiness to work with the human spirit, then there would be no divine action in the world.

It is clear, too, that God does not only work through brilliance or beauty. Salieri could not quite believe this. The Bible is filled with evidence of God working through 'the least', those whom society has rejected, or those who seem to have little to offer. This means that the Christ-like presence of God's Spirit in human affairs is likely to evident in unexpected, even ugly, places. This important insight constitutes a major challenge for how, media, entertainment and the arts are consumed and interpreted in theological perspective. It does not immediately establish a theological relevance for *Big Brother* or *Friends*. But it is clear that judgments about where God is, and how the presence of God's Spirit is to be discerned in the world, may not always be easy to make, and cannot be made according to prior assumptions about 'set forms' which the presence of God always takes.

Third, although it may be clear that God does not demand perfection, it remains easier to link the Spirit's work with outstanding achievement in a way that privileges, say, the able-bodied. A viewer with a severe physical impairment watching Joe's crawl down the mountain may easily be reminded of their own daily physical struggle. The question of what constitutes an 'ordinary life' is then posed. Reflection on the dimensions of what it means to be human through watching *Touching the Void*, then transforms the meaning of what it means to struggle, to have spirit, and to participate in the given, life-giving Spirit of God by virtue of being human. Joe's battered, disabled, body is precisely the body in and through which so much about what it means to be human becomes visible. His body could be mended, an experience not possible for all. Rage and acceptance are both gifts of the spirit as human beings come to terms with the bodies that they have and are.[7]

But is possession of this spiritedness the same as 'having faith', and does this matter? This is a question sharply posed by *Legally Blonde*. If having faith is the same as guts, determination, skills or abilities, then all human beings already have some of these. Having faith, by contrast, is usually regarded as having some cognitive substance to it. If you 'believe', you believe in something. This is confirmed at the end of *Legally Blonde*. However, Elle exhorts all those graduating to believe, above all, 'in themselves'. The notion of receiving any ability as a gift is collapsed somewhat. Belief in oneself may theoretically contain the possibility that the self is recognized as a recipient of gifts and skills. But it is more likely that the question of the source of gifts does not arise. The independent, isolated self is the source.

A Christian pneumatology is puzzled by such an approach. Without recognition of the dependence of human beings upon a creator God who remains active in the world through the Spirit of God, the human being becomes dangerously narcissistic. Though it is appropriate to speak of the 'inner resources' which a life of faith provides, these are not something generated by an individual or fully possessed by an individual. Human beings have inner resources in so far as they participate in the Spirit of God through the gifts and skills they have received. Faith is therefore the disposition of the person who recognizes this. The belief-system within which one 'has faith' provides the cognitive framework that makes what it means to live in faith comprehensible. 'Having faith' or 'believing' are thus ultimately related but distinct practices, the latter more cognitive than the former. In Christian understanding, however, in each case 'having faith' and 'believing' signify dependence on God, not on oneself. To have faith is to be empowered by the Spirit of God at work in the world. It is to recognize that what one is able to do is derivative. Being (or feeling) inspired is the exercise of engaging and making full use of the gifts that one has been given.

This aspect of the pneumatological character of human activity is crucial as a corrective to individualism, and to over-assertive forms of humanism. It is also an important corrective to forms of Christian faith and theology which have made 'believing' and 'having faith' too cognitive. Participation in the Spirit of God, and discovery of the work of God's Spirit in the world through human artistic endeavour and achievement, is not a solely cognitive phenomenon. All of the three films studied in this chapter bear witness to the emotional, aesthetic and ethical aspects of determined, spirited human behaviour. It is in such activities, in Christian theological understanding, that God the creative life-giver is seen to be at work.

Working conclusions

Divine and human spirits are in constant interaction in human living. This chapter shows that such interaction is best understood not in terms of individual 'spirit possession'. Individuals admittedly manifest the presence of the Spirit of God in creation through creative actions. But understanding how divine and human spirits work together is better understood as participation in something corporate and purposive. There are, furthermore, Christological and eschatological aspects to Christian understanding of the Spirit of God.[8] A Christological criterion operates in the task of discerning what is and is not of God, namely how does what we know of Jesus the Christ inform whatever human activity is being examined. This Christological criterion is always also eschatological, for Jesus was called Christ because of his commitment to the Kingdom of God. Does what is being examined therefore serve the end of the Kingdom of God? Is human fulfilment as God wants this to be understood being served? If not, then, it is not the Spirit of God with whom we are dealing.

Where the Spirit of God is present, therefore, it will not be the one 'possessed of the spirit' alone whose interests are served. The Spirit of God participated in by individuals serves others (through music, through determined action on others' behalf). This insight provides a lens through which to interpret the films we are examining here. Joe's survival is not for himself alone. Others want to relate to him. Even Elle's success as a lawyer is not (or need not be) for herself alone, though admittedly her self-interested creed is open to challenge.

At root, exploration of the Holy Spirit, as the Spirit of God at work in the world, interwoven with human action, means encounter with the dynamism of a life-giving God. Such a God takes people out of themselves: towards others, and in recognition that no-one excels, or survives, alone.

For further study

Major biblical passages that relate to the doctrine of the Holy Spirit include:

I *Samuel* 19.18–24 This is a disturbing, and sobering, passage which highlights the care that is needed in discussions about the Holy Spirit. Saul and Saul's messengers are overcome and end up 'in a prophetic frenzy'.

Isaiah 61 This prophetic passage presents a vision of what the hoped-for future, when God reigns, will look like. It was seen by early Christians to refer to the time of the Messiah, and is therefore found applied to Jesus in Luke 4.

Luke 4.16–21 The passage in the Gospels where Jesus is portrayed as applying the Isaiah 61 prophecy to himself.

John 14–16 The section of John's Gospel where the coming of the Holy Spirit (here called 'the Paraclete' or 'Advocate') is referred to a number of times. These passages, which link together God the Father, Jesus and the Spirit, were crucial in the development of the doctrine of the Trinity.

Acts 2 This chapter gives an account of the dramatic activity of the Holy Spirit at Pentecost. It provides an indication of the eschatological fervour in which Christianity began.

Romans 8 This passage from the Apostle Paul is a theological reflection on what it means to 'live in the Spirit'.

I *Corinthians* 12.1–11 These are the Apostle Paul's reflections on the gifts which are given (by the Holy Spirit) to churches.

Galatians 5.16–6.5 This is a further reflection from the Apostle Paul on how the Holy Spirit affects human behaviour.

I John 4.1–6 This account, from a letter by 'John', suggests how it is possible to tell whether or not a spirit is of God.

Texts from the history of Christian thought on the topic of the Spirit that are worth attention include:

John Cassian on human and divine agency (in Placher, vol. 1, pp. 133–5). These extracts from a text by a fourth-century monk articulate the way that human and divine agency interact. Human dependence on God is stressed. But value is also seen in what human beings do, with the help of God. The text refers to the 'breath' rather than the spirit of God.

'Basil of Caesarea on the Work of the Holy Spirit' (= De Spiritu Sancto IX.22–23 [late fourth century]; in McGrath, pp. 182–3). This text confirms that the work of the Spirit is the work of God. It also notes how the Spirit's gifts given to individuals always spill over, bringing benefits to others.

'Augustine on the Holy Spirit' (= De Trinitate XV.xvii.27–xviii.32 [400–416 CE]; in McGrath, pp. 193–5). This tough text seeks to establish the Holy Spirit's divinity. The notion of 'gift' is prominent throughout, as is the close relationship between attention to God's Spirit and the capacity to love.

Jonathan Edwards on the Holy Spirit and the human imagination (in Thiessen, pp. 172–4). Edwards here defends a link between the use of imagination and the work of the Holy Spirit, whilst recognizing that careful discernment is necessary. (This text links also with material to be addressed in Chapter 10 below.)

Chapter 7

REDEMPTION

R EDEMPTION LIES AT THE HEART OF CHRISTIANITY'S understanding of human
life. Concern for the manner of redemption and for the plight of the
sinning individual might admittedly be claimed to be an especially post-
Reformation preoccupation. But interest in what God intends for the
created order, and how humanity and the whole of creation are to be 'made
right', have been consistently important throughout Christian history.

A number of key theological ideas are implicit within the concept.
Redemption addresses a basic assumption about human being: there is
some aspect of humanity, and of every individual, that needs 'redeeming'
(sorting out, adjusting, dealing with). Without this happening, then
humans are trapped. Redemption also contains within it the notion that
such rescue (salvation, liberation, atonement) is possible. This implies
something about God (God can redeem, save, liberate), and about the way
that God does this redeeming. In Christian understanding, Jesus Christ is
the redeemer figure. The way that God 'saves' must therefore have something to do with the figure of Jesus Christ.

There is, of course, a problem about redemption being so central in a
religion. It could mean that 'God' is made to serve human needs. Whether or
not God exists, the moment that redemption becomes so important, there
is an immediate danger that those who seek or experience redemption

become the focus of religious attention. Rather than God being the centre and focus of a religion, it is the impact of the presence and action of God on religious people which takes precedence. 'God' therefore slips off the scene. A religion of redemption such as Christianity, then, has to take great care to ensure that in paying attention to the work of God as redeemer, it does not allow the 'human interest angle' to dominate.

Redemption is, though, a preoccupation of many Western films. This is probably because of Judaism's and Christianity's influence on Western cultures. It is doubtless also because the 'human interest angle' of film means that films often become great to the extent that they plumb the depths of human experience. Put together a religious concern for redemption and cinema's interest in portraying stretching human stories and a powerful combination results.

American theologian David Kelsey has drawn attention to the ubiquity of explorations of redemption in contemporary culture:

> The language of redemption is used in a variety of ways in this larger social and cultural context [i.e. the social and linguistic space constituted by practices that make up the common life within which Christian communities are located]. For example, as an assiduous reader of reviews of fiction, plays and movies, I have been impressed by the frequency with which reviewers comment on the presence or absence of a 'redemptive' note or theme in the work under review or debate whether there might be such a note. Sometimes the presence of a redemptive note seems to count in favor of the work and its absence to count against it. Although I am often unable to tell just what the reviewer means by 'redemption' or 'redemptive,' it is clear that the words are used in the context of certain practices that help make up Western cultural life.[1]

Kelsey is right, and I have made the same observation myself about reviews in the UK. 'Redemption' is clearly widely recognized as something which needs exploring in the process of examining what it means to be human, and how one becomes human. This feature of Western cultural life has implications for the role of theology in public. 'Redemption' can be talked about in many different ways. But theological contributions will inevitably be made to discussions about the term's meaning simply because it is a prominent theological term. Furthermore, religious people will end up using the term in a variety of ways because they live simultaneously in multiple communities. As Kelsey notes:

Members of communities of Christian faith and practice ... also participate in the practices that make up the cultural life of the societies that are their immediate social and cultural contexts and routinely use 'redeem,' 'redemption,' and related terms in ways that are not peculiarly Christian as well as in ways that are. Furthermore, their extra-Christian uses of the terms doubtless shape the way they use them in the context of the common life of Christian faith communities, and vice versa.[2]

This means that in exploring the ways in which redemption surfaces and is treated in mainstream films, we encounter ways in which Christian usage interweaves with a variety of other uses of the term in public life. Exploration of such public, cultural usage will, however, prove crucial to theological understanding of what it means to be human. At the same time as clarifying key features of Christian notions of redemption in this chapter, therefore, we shall also be able to see how those understandings take cultural shape and are tested in relation to examples of real human stories.

Many films could have been chosen for this chapter. I have selected four. The first two explore evil in two forms in a context where redemption is either unclear or difficult. The third and fourth films explore redeemer figures in unusual ways. One is a (fictional) exploration of Jesus, the other a 'Christ figure', that is a figure who functions like Jesus.

Films

Crimes and Misdemeanors (Woody Allen, 1989)

Crimes and Misdemeanors interweaves two stories. The more comic story finds Woody Allen playing Clifford Stern, a film-maker in an unhappy marriage who is trying to make a documentary about a philosopher. Stifled in his attempt to do this, he must in the meantime make money by directing a documentary about his brother-in-law Lester (Alan Alda), a smarmy, successful TV producer. Stern is envious and tempted to adultery because of his attraction to a documentary film-maker working with Lester, Halley Reed (Mia Farrow). Adultery is present in the second plot, the one which will occupy us most here. Martin Landau plays an unfaithful ophthalmologist, Judah Rosenthal, who arranges to have his lover Dolores (Anjelica Huston) murdered when she threatens to inform his wife both about their affair and about Judah's illegal financial dealings. The film is rich in its portrayal of how complex moral questions are part of everyday life, of the extent to which human beings go to refuse to face the implications of their actions and of the way in which unresolved guilt can lead to evil conduct. As director, Allen manages to produce a rewarding, enjoyable and challenging film, without providing a happy ending. He maps out clearly why, in exploring what it means to be human, human beings also need to examine what it might mean to be redeemed.

21 Grams *(Alejandro Gonzalez Inarritu, 2003)*

21 Grams is an especially interesting film because it came out at roughly the same time as The Passion of the Christ. It was, however, Inarritu's film rather than Gibson's which the film critic of the Observer, Philip French, suggested might offer a better presentation of a Christian understanding of redemption. Certainly, 21 Grams is offering us a true-to-life story. Benicio Del Toro plays Jack Jordan, a former prison inmate who has 'got religion' as part of his attempt to reconstruct his personal and family life. His story is interwoven with the stories of two others: Paul Rivers (Sean Penn), a mathematics professor awaiting a heart transplant, and Cristina Peck (Naomi Watts), whose life is shattered by the deaths of her husband and children in a car crash. The film links the three stories, presenting their interrelationship in non-linear fashion, thus offering a demanding viewing experience. The film is demanding in other respects too because of the intensity of the experiences endured by the lead characters. The action occurs in urban and suburban contexts, though as one viewer rightly said: 'Even the seemingly comfortable suburban family neighbourhoods are given an unhealthy pallor, while other location choices favor the seedy, shabby side of Memphis, which goes unidentified in the film.'[3] Similar to the shabbiness of the context, if this is indeed a film about redemption, then it is clear that redemption is not easy. Any hope present in the film is certainly underplayed.

The Last Temptation of Christ *(Martin Scorsese, 1988)*

If the first two films map out clearly the complexity and seriousness of the contexts within which talk of redemption must prove its credibility and worth, then Scorsese's The Last Temptation of Christ takes us to where Christians have traditionally explored how redemption comes about. The Last Temptation of Christ is a 'Jesus film' with a difference, in that it is based not directly on the Gospels but on a fictional version of the Jesus story, Nikos Kazantzakis's 1955 novel of the same name.[4] Of course, even those films which purport to be direct interpretations of the Gospels (e.g. *The Gospel According to St. Matthew, Jesus of Nazareth, Jesus*) are precisely that: interpretations. In choosing one Gospel over others, or in allowing one Gospel, or key scenes from one or more Gospels, to dominate a presentation of the figure of Jesus, then an interpretative lens in selected which shapes the kind of Jesus offered to the viewer.[5]

With *The Last Temptation of Christ*, the cinema-goer is confronted with arguably the most human Jesus portrayed in film to date. Here is a Jesus who is tender, gets cross, comes over as deluded at times, and, when faced with the opportunity of not going through with what appears to be his divinely appointed task, seriously considers opting out. The possibility of domestic bliss constitutes the 'last temptation' of the title. The fact that he did not take the easier route made Christianity possible, even if, in a memorable (though unhistorical) exchange between Jesus and (the later Apostle) Paul, the role played by the latter in the emergence of Christianity is starkly presented. The scene recognizes that Paul had a key role in articulating what it means for Jesus to be the Christ. Christianity therefore receives from Paul (and others) an interpreted Jesus: the one in and through whom God is somehow bringing salvation about.

Cries and Whispers (Ingmar Bergman, 1972)

In turning to Ingmar Bergman, we switch from Jesus the saviour to figures whose actions mirror those of the Christ. *Cries and Whispers* is a film about three sisters in the late nineteenth century, two of whom, Karin (Ingrid Thulin) and Maria (Liv Ullmann), struggle to cope when faced with the death of the third sister, Agnes (Harriet Andersson). The film deals with familiar Bergman themes such as the hypocrisy of bourgeois life, repression and death's inevitability. As well as being a tense and beautiful, if harrowing, film to watch, it is also a powerful portrayal of the profundity of simple, practical caring. The film is clearly to be interpreted in part through the visually striking imitation of the 'pieta' created by Agnes's servant Anna cradling the dying sister at the end of the film. In this visual echo of Mary cradling the dead Jesus, Bergman indicates one way in which the relationship between Anna and Agnes can be interpreted. Agnes has suffered more than she should have. Anna has been a means through which the suffering endured by Christ goes on being borne in human interactions. There is less hope than Christian theology would want to see presented. But Anna's stark refusal to receive any gift from the family, whose sister she had accompanied to her death, suggests at least a dignified confronting of death which Agnes's family cannot begin to understand.

Viewing experiences

Films which contain redemption as a key motif often have a simple purpose: to tell the story of someone who undergoes a massive change from a destructive form of life to one which is more hopeful. Scorsese's films are full of such characters.[6] Teen movies also offer their own similar version of redemption, majoring less on destructiveness and more on the need for potential to be developed.[7] 'Rescue' is, however, often a theme which accompanies the 'discovery of potential' motif. People are thus 'saved', at a crucial point in their development, from whatever may block their potential (damaging family life, guilt, poverty, lack of opportunity, educational disadvantages, unfortunate circumstances). Happy endings abound in a way which is understandable: the films are meant to please, to inspire, to create dreams in those who may have none. Questions of realism may not be appropriate, even if the far-fetchedness of some plots could be accused of feeding the wrong kind of escapism. With the exception of romantic comedies, which often have their own form of redemption motif, explorations of the theme in post-teen films are less straightforward in their characterization of what salvation, liberation or rescue amount to. Film-makers still have to wrestle with the fact that audiences want to be entertained, not subjected to an ordeal. But there is a fine line between sentimentality of a sugary kind and an exploration of the possibility of redemption that is both plausible and uplifting.[8]

Crimes and Misdemeanors and 21 Grams both show that films which explore human propensity for evil and human concern for redemption can do so without glorifying violence, and without short-changing the viewer as to the complexity and intensity of human experience. And as both films show, 21 Grams especially, the relatively simple purpose behind a film about evil and redemption need not lead to a film with a simple structure. Not only do these films not deliver simple, happy endings, their narrative complexity reminds the viewer both of how entangled life can be, and how redemption will inevitably be caught up within the moral choices, chance occurrences, failings and emotional fall-outs which make up daily life.

But what more is to be said about the viewing experiences of all four films being considered here? First, some further comments on *Crimes and Misdemeanors* and *21 Grams. Crimes and Misdemeanors* is certainly one of Allen's best films. It retains his humour, but builds in a thoughtfulness which in turn makes the viewer think. The scene when Judah is visited by Ben (Sam Waterston), a rabbi, when his surgery becomes a kind of confessional, is a case in point. But Judah is not, even so, distracted from his purpose. Evil seems to triumph. As viewers, we suspect that Judah's life is not going to be a happy one, but he does not get found out within our hearing. He gets away with his crime, and we are left disturbed even whilst having been entertained. The plotline about Clifford Stern has kept us amused and reassured. At least, despite all his envy and bitterness, Clifford has not succumbed to temptation. We can leave the auditorium feeling OK. But the nagging worry about the 'success' of Judah's actions lingers.

It seems strange to call *21 Grams* a more hopeful film by comparison. For it is harrowing viewing. Jack's rather brutal form of religiosity does not allow him to be, or feel, released from the multiple guilt by which he is tormented. And in the meantime, the other two life-stories in which his own life becomes meshed, do not develop positively in any unqualified sense. Paul Rivers (Sean Penn) remains alive, but only just. Crinstina Peck (Naomi Watts) has lost her husband and children and struggles to come to terms with her new situation. But as viewers we are sympathetic to all these three leading characters, and, whilst having shared their rage, have also been encouraged to hope that they will each let the others be and develop, scarred as they are. If the film has taken viewers to a somewhat extreme place in the way in which it has used the interconnectedness of the leading characters' lives, the plausibility of it all merely leaves viewers wrestling with the emotional complexity of their own lives. The recognition follows that it is within whatever complexities viewers themselves experience that redemption is to be sought and found.

Jesus features much in *21 Grams*, though largely on Jack's lips as he seeks to interpret his life with respect to his readings of words from the Bible.[9] The Jesus presented, and thus the God in relation to whom Jack is seeking to live his life, is, however, a God who demands and controls. Jack assumes that Jesus made him crash the car which killed Cristina's husband and children. The extent to which he has to earn his release from the consequences of past actions is so great, that he cannot but assume he needs to be punished for what he has done. His guilt only increases as a result of the crash. There is yet more which he must be punished for.

Viewers are left in no doubt about the extent of self-loathing with which Jack struggles. They may find the image of God with which he works abhorrent. But at the same time, we are caught up in our viewing with the sense that there can be life-situations where any hint of grace, mercy, forgiveness or release is hard to see. We are made sympathetic to what Jack needs, and the difficult road he will have to travel to experience any sense of release from his guilt. It is clear that some kind of redemption will be necessary for him to recover his sense of what it means to be human. The inadequacy, however, of the theological framework within which he is seeking to live will be apparent not only to Christian viewers. In theological perspective, Jack may need redeeming from his perception of who God is.

'Jesus' and 'God' may have been interchangeable names in Jack's vocabulary. When someone tries to live a Christian life, Jesus-talk is the way that God-talk is done. Jesus-talk is used to shape a person's life. The questions 'how' and 'why' this should be so demand more direct consideration about the person of Jesus. But what is a 'viewer's perspective' on a Jesus film meant to look like? Are we to be stunned by the evident divinity, or at least the holiness, of the figure? Are we to conclude instantly that this is someone clearly special who we could never be like? The danger of having such reactions – a problem common to many Jesus films – is that Jesus ends up less human than Christianity has declared him to be.

The Last Temptation of Christ is an especially striking Jesus film in that it leaves us in no doubt about Jesus' humanity. Despite being a novelistic account of his life, it still handles the Gospel material in a relatively straightforward way. The stories used from the canonical Gospels are identifiable, even if embellished. But the Jesus presented, if rather manic at times, is clearly human. Whether the struggles this Jesus endures are quite the same as any human being may experience is a moot point, to the significance of which we shall need to return.[10] But as viewers we are not reacting here to a figure who is inhuman, or supernaturally detached from daily life. Like Kazantzakis before him, Scorsese has portrayed a human being wracked with indecision and unclear about his identity and his purpose in life. The extent of his inner torment might make us glad that this is not akin to anything we are likely to experience. And we may have similar questions to our response to Jack in *21 Grams* about the God implied by this torment, especially in the impact upon Jesus himself, who, in Dafoe's portrayal, become a nearly neurotic figure.[11] Interestingly, then, it is the kind of humanity being portrayed here, and the image of God assumed within it, which might make us balk at feeling any strong affinity with this Jesus, despite Scorsese's intent.

A Christological objection may be that this is precisely the point: none can be like Jesus. Scorsese was thus misguided from the start. But the juxtaposition of Jack's and Jesus' stories leave us with a clear viewer's response: even Jesus, as here portrayed, seemed to struggle to live 'the Jesus story'. If he resisted the final temptation (and we are to conclude that we are glad that he did), then it was at great cost to him. And it is clear that it will be no small cost to those who try and follow the same way. Jack Jordan would agree. But whether we have quite got to the bottom of what it means to live a redeemed life remains to be seen.

Cries and Whispers continues the note of struggle. Redemption does not come easily. Viewing most Bergman films is a tense experience. For viewers who let a Bergman film do its work upon them, the eyes and the mind are captivated by what is presented visually and the emotions caught up in the complexity of the relationships between characters portrayed. Often, as here in Cries and Whispers, it is what is hidden and unsaid by the character on screen which leads to the viewer's body becoming taught and tense. By the end of the film, viewers can expect to be enraged by the treatment of the servant Anna. Bergman even places us, through his camera-work, alongside Anna, as if she is next to us, when family members come to thank her for all that she has done for the deceased Agnes. We stand alongside her in disdain for their lack of respect for Agnes and of Anna's care, and their unwillingness to face their own mortality. The Christ-likeness of the actions in which we, like Anna, are invited to participate enables viewers to critique such a way of life. We are invited to take greater pleasure in simple acts of caring. In this way we live life and face death constructively and with dignity. We do not seek to avoid it by seeking to attach greater significance to our social customs and habits than they merit. This is what our identification with Anna means.

It may not signify a joyous life – and here, Bergman's pessimism will prove open to challenge. But the praise of simplicity in Christ-like following is worth noting. Sin and evil are to be countered in the context of a life lived simply, with full clarity and openness to human propensity to avoid facing our past failings. The viewer is invited to consider that living this way is to live a redeemed life. In companionship with those who suffer death can more easily be faced, and the living are able to receive life as a gracious gift.

Connecting questions and issues

So much for the films: where do they take us theologically? For some readers, admittedly, my comments may already appear to have gone far beyond the viewing experiences themselves. For others, responding to the films has merely got us to the edge of the important questions which arise for Christian theology in the realms of evil and redemption. So what theological questions arise?

- The most basic question of all will linger beyond this chapter, but it still needs posing: what is redemption? Is there any difference between redemption, salvation, and liberation? How do these words relate to concepts like atonement, reconciliation, rehabilitation, release, forgiveness and freedom?
- Is redemption something which happened, or happens, without much human involvement? Is it simply to be received? Or if it is 'participated in' in some way, what does this mean?
- How does the historical figure of Jesus, or the 'Jesus story', link with redemption? Did something happen back in the past – at the crucifixion – which had some cosmic, or metaphysical, significance? Whether it did or not, how do human beings now relate to the story of the birth, life, death and resurrection of Jesus?
- What is the story for? How does it work? What kind of God is being portrayed in this story, and is it an understanding of God which is welcome and/or tenable in the twenty-first century?
- When we speak of 'story' is that it? Is it just a story? Is what people do with the figure of Jesus therefore no different from how people might use any important, helpful narrative work (a good novel for example)?
- Is redemption a matter for the individual? Or even if it is for individuals, how, if at all, does the notion of an individual's being redeemed/saved/liberated link that person with other people?
- Does the language of redemption simply describe something which all human beings experience, whether they are religious or not? Or if it does more than describe, what does it add to human experience?
- And what about the fact that there is a lot of doom and gloom around in the films selected in this chapter. Presumably Christianity wants redemption to be seen as a good thing. But where's the joy? Should not talk of release, freedom, forgiveness and reconciliation be a liberating, life-enhancing thing?

Many of these questions shape what is now to follow.

Explorations: evil; guilt; joy; participation in Christ

Redemption is a concept which signals joy and fulfilment. The way in which redemption often appears in film, when so many awful things have to be dealt with, may conceal this fact. Redemption may indeed be about happy endings. But, as many films about redemption show, it is about struggle too. Theological conversation about filmic presentations of stories of redemption has to explore why happy endings which come too easily are not redemptive, without implying that redemption is something that can be achieved by human effort.

Evil prospers in the world. *Crimes and Misdemeanors* makes this clear. If redemption is to happen, then the context for its experience is a world in which evil does sometimes triumph. Judah is not redeemed. He simply got away with his evil action and has to live with its consequences. Whether he will go on feeling guilt we do not know. As viewers we bring to the film our own experience and sense of morality. Most of us will assume that he will (must!) feel guilt and feel ashamed if we experience any sense of plea-sure that he has been successful. Judah is thus a character who one hopes will see a need for redemption, but as the film ends we suspect he might not. It is difficult to know how genuine any remorse he expressed at any point might have been.

Judah is not an everyman figure. Woody Allen is not suggesting that Judah stands for us all in any direct way. Relatively few viewers would end up in quite the dilemma Judah finds himself in. This is no abstract portrayal of the human condition, despite Allen's persistent interest in the theme throughout his directing career. Evil choices, culpability, guilt and moral complexity occur in concrete situations. If there is such a thing as 'the human condition', then it can only ever take shape in the midst of actual, concrete moral decision-making and acting. Judah's situation is thus his alone. But even if viewers' own moral dilemmas are not directly comparable, they are comparable enough to be able to disturb the viewer. If Allen therefore does not expound the human condition in an abstract way in *Crimes and Misdemeanors*, he asks the poignant question of the viewer as to whether it matters that people feel responsibility for their actions. He leaves us perturbed at the notion of a world without guilt. We know that guilt can debilitate. But we are reminded, too, that guilt is an essential component of human living. Guilt can be good. In order that it does not debilitate, however, it has to be dealt with in some way. Allen has therefore created a film that affirms the need for guilt, and raises the question of redemption. How are people who *do* feel guilt, and thus behave more humanly than Judah, to live with and beyond their guilt in a morally and metaphysically responsible way?

Juxtaposing Judah's lack of guilt with Jack Jordan's crushing guilt, however, presents an unattractive prospect. There may be no human condition in abstract form. But the ease with which viewers can identify with some version of Judah's dilemma suggests that most human beings are going to experience their own form of concrete guilt. If this is necessary in human living, then does this mean that Jack's form of handling guilt is what will result? And given the particular theistic world-view within which he seems to operate, does this mean that dealing with guilt will prove oppressive and even tragic? When placed together, the two films invite reflection on what redemption actually means.

Redemption is joyful and fulfilling because being rescued from evil and its consequences is life-enhancing. It is the rediscovery of the joy of living. In Christian theological perspective this rediscovery of life and life's purpose – to love and to live in peace with God and all people – is not something that it is possible to do unaided. All need help.

In Christian understanding, God's help – God's redemptive activity – takes the form of the work of Christ. The New Testament declares in various ways that Jesus Christ 'rescues' or 'redeems' (Mark 10.45; Romans 3.24–25; I Corinthians 6.20, 7.23; Galatians 3.13, 4.4; Titus 2.14; I Peter 1.18–19). This means that the battle with evil in which all participate by virtue of living has been fought and won. There is no need for people to be consumed by the evil in which we all know we will take part. To seek redemption means to accept that despite the ambiguity, and sometimes downright awfulness, of our actions, we shall neither pretend that we have no guilt, nor expect that our actions have no negative consequences on ourselves or others. We shall accept that we shall constantly need the help of God to be rid of that which we regret, and that which we know will have bad effects.

To say that God has in Christ redeemed the world is to make a metaphysical statement. Something has occurred which has potential consequences for all people. Redemption is found, in Christian understanding, with respect to this cosmic act of God. For viewers and readers not immersed in the Christian tradition, however, positive appreciation of the link between a (cosmically significant) past event, the narrative form in which it is communicated in the present and everyday living may be difficult to grasp.

Jack Jordan has recognized the cosmic significance of God's redemptive activity. This is why he keeps referring to Jesus. He has chosen to connect his life to the story of God as embodied in the narratives about Jesus. His link with the figure of Jesus shapes his life. He has not, however, grasped the fact that his participation in God's redemptive act in Christ does not depend on any particular course of conduct. He will indeed want to amend his life. But it is not his choice to amend his life which is the condition of Jack's receipt of redemption. Redemption is a gift. The redemptive work of God is effective because of what has happened in Christ. Living in the light of that divine action is the means of reception of the gift.

Anna and Agnes (*Cries and Whispers*) participate in the story of Jesus too. But they and Jack Jordan offer two quite different ways of participating in God's redeeming activity. Each represents a way of 'living the Jesus story'. In Jack's case, the living out of the story is explicit and cognitive. He makes explicit how he thinks Jesus (and thus God) is directly affecting his life. In the case of Anna and Agnes, they inhabit roles of carer and sufferer, and experience in their own lives the death of Jesus. This form of participation is not redemption in the fullest Christian sense. There is no resurrection here. The film offers no clear future for Agnes, beyond death, or for Anna, with the sale of the house where she has been working. Both Bergman's bleakness and the subject-matter of the film ('how do we face death?') hold sway here. Nevertheless, the telling of their story indicates how the story of Jesus functions: it is a narrative which is to be inhabited, so that it can in turn help us make sense of who we are, and interpret and face whatever life presents, even (perhaps especially) death.

Working conclusions

There has not been as much joy in this chapter as befits the subject-matter of redemption. I think this is fair to how the medium of film deals and struggles with the subject-matter. Redemption in visual form needs graphic portrayal. Inner turmoil cannot be seen and needs to be externalized for the sake of the cinema. Outer struggle is painful, both to endure and to watch. New life (resurrection) too easily becomes a happy ending in the cinema. Resurrection portrayals in Jesus films are notoriously tacky. This means that film portrayals of redemption focus more readily on what people need to be, or are being, rescued from: guilt (Judah and Jack) or suffering (Agnes), for example.

Christian theology is no different. There are many examples from Christian history of preoccupation with sin, the catch-all term for what humanity needs releasing from. Sin has too often been identified only as an individual matter, relating to an inner state. It has been held to be universal (Romans 3.23), and even 'original' in the sense that no-one can escape it, and is born into it (Augustine). Despite that sense of sin's universality, however, the development in understanding sin as a social phenomenon, or in terms of humanity's longing for redemption as the struggle against being 'sinned against', is a relatively modern affair.[12] But in whatever sense sin is understood, it is identifying what one is being released from, and the cataloguing of the world's evils that often follows, which too easily shapes interpretations of redemption.

What people are redeemed for or into is less readily expressed (or filmed). The Shawshank Redemption is a prime example of the difficulty the medium of film experiences in this respect. The film ends happily. But that's just it: it ends! It is as if all will inevitably be well for Red and Andy after their respective releases. Redemption understood as new, amended life, freedom, social living in the place of isolation, or ultimate peace, beginning in this life and potentially continuing beyond it, is harder to film, and harder to conceptualize theologically. But the resources are there. In Christian theological understanding, 'life in Christ' is a way of speaking about such redemption. For this is the life that one is saved/redeemed into. Jack Jordan and Anna and Agnes's experience are two, if rather harrowing, forms of such life. But they are only examples of multiple ways in which the Jesus story can be inhabited.

In more concrete terms, of course, Christians talk of 'church' as a way of speaking of the social form in which the presence of Christ can most easily be participated in and celebrated. The church is, after all, called 'the Body of Christ' (following the Apostle Paul's statement in I Corinthians 12.27).[13] This is too limiting. 'Life in Christ' takes many forms.[14] It is, however, a helpful lens through which Christian theology can express its grasp of what redemption is, and how it is participated in. Christianity understands redemption as a past and present work of God. God *has* acted in Christ: the effects of that act of redemption are there to be received. God *is* working in Christ: the story of Jesus is not just a story. It is a living tradition within which redemption can be experienced.

This being so, the Jesus story is never just a story about Jesus alone. It is always also a story about God, and about God's relationship with humanity. Kazantzakis saw that very clearly and in his imaginative interpretation of the Jesus story, as faithfully filmed by Scorsese, the divine and human dimensions of the Jesus story are starkly portrayed. But The Last Temptation of Christ, ironically, focuses too much on Jesus. In the exposition, in both novel and film, of the tortuous inner turmoil of Jesus himself we lose the sense of the Gospels' desire that people follow (inhabit) this story too. And yet that is the story of Jesus when told as a redemptive story. It is inhabited in the act of following, by those who are so impressed that they want to imitate the actions of Jesus.

'Life in Christ' thus becomes shorthand for a Christian understanding of the redeemed life. And because Jesus is interpreted as an ultimate figure (= the Christ is 'the Messiah', the one who comes at the end of all time), then the decisiveness of the link between an experience of redemption and inhabiting the story of Jesus cannot be overplayed. Redemption is vital for the human spirit. Life in Christ is a Christian way of speaking about this. Redemption thus has ultimate significance. We can say, then, that redemption always has an eschatological character. And we shall need to say more about this in Chapter 10 below.

For further study

Biblical passages that relate to the understanding of redemption explored throughout this chapter include:

Isaiah 53 A prophetic passage later used by Christians to interpret Jesus' suffering in salvific terms.

Mark 14.1–15.47 One of the four New Testament accounts of 'the Passion' (the trial, crucifixion, suffering and death) of Jesus.

Romans 3.21–6 One of the Apostle Paul's interpretations of the meaning of the death of Jesus.

Romans 5 Further exposition from the Apostle Paul on the significance of Jesus' death.

II Corinthians 5.16–21 This passage from Paul spells out the cosmic dimensions of Jesus' death.

Hebrews 9 A passage from a New Testament book which interprets Jesus' death in the light of Jewish ritual practices.

Texts from post-biblical Christian history that are worth following up include:

'Origen on the Suffering of God' (= *Homilia in Ezechiel* VI.6; in McGrath, pp. 180–1). This text from the first half of the third century is unusual in that it considers the prospect of God suffering.

'Athanasius on the Death of Christ' (= *On the Incarnation of the Word* VIII.4–IX.1 [c.318 CE]; in McGrath, pp. 331–2). Here, the fourth-century Bishop of Alexandria explores the close relationship between Christology and soteriology. It is an early Christian Christological parallel to what has been investigated in this chapter: redemption happens in the thick of real, concrete life. That applied to God's work in Christ too.

'Athanasius on the Two Natures of Christ' (= *Epistulae ad Serapionem*, IV.14 [c.350 CE]; in McGrath, pp. 256–7). Athanasius here offers his own version of the interplay between divine and human natures in the person of Christ.

'Augustine on Fallen Human Nature' (= *De Natura et Gratia* iii.3–iv.4 [415 CE]; in McGrath, pp. 398–9). This passage from Augustine offers a version of his exposition of original sin.

'The Second Council of Orange on Grace and Freedom' [529 CE] (extracts in McGrath, pp. 408–9; the full text can be found, e.g. in J. H. Leith (ed.), *Creeds of the Churches*, John Knox Press 1973, pp. 38–43). This text, usually regarded as a victory for the Augustinian viewpoint, sought to put an end to Pelagianism, the view that human beings somehow contribute to their own salvation.

Immanuel Kant on the necessity of theism for true morality (= *Religion Within the Limits of Reason Alone* [1793]; in Placher. Vol. 2, pp. 103–6). This influential Lutheran theologian-philosopher here defends the view that people need theological traditions in order to be able to live an ethical life.

'Daphne Hampson on Feminist Approaches to Sin' (= *Theology and Feminism* [1990], pp. 121–4; in McGrath, pp. 452–5). Now a post-Christian theist, Hampson here spells out the deficiencies of understandings of sin offered by some male theologians.

Chapter 8

SACRAMENTS

T HE QUESTION OF HOW REDEMPTION IS PARTICIPATED in communally requires, in Christian understanding, some reference to the concept 'church'. 'Church' is the subject of the next chapter. Rather unusually I am opting to consider two of the central rituals of church practice – baptism and Holy Communion – before that. This is for two reasons. First, these two practices go beyond what the church can adequately describe, contain or prescribe. This is so despite the important responsibility the church carries to 'police' the practices of baptism and communion through necessary authority structures in the life of church and society (lest their range of meanings and varied form of practice be obscured or distorted). Second, the practices of baptism and Holy Communion touch on aspects of human conduct which cut across a wide variety of practices, religious and not. In investigating meanings of symbolic washing and communal eating, explorations of baptism and communion both get to the heart of church practice and show how such practice in turn enables people to interpret daily life.

Films

The Piano (Jane Campion, 1993)

The Piano is a story of liberation. In this respect it is an appropriate link with the previous chapter and becomes part of the response to the question posed there: where is the joy? But the journey to the liberation for the lead character in *The Piano*, Ada McGrath (Holly Hunter), is far from smooth.[1] Ada arrives in New Zealand from Scotland, and meets Stewart, her husband via an arranged marriage. She has not spoken since she was six, has a daughter, Flora (Anna Paquin), from a previous relationship. Her piano, which she has brought with her, is the main medium through which she communicates her feelings. It takes some time, however, for the piano to be brought from the beach to a place where she can play it. Stewart has no interest in it. In the end, a neighbour, Baines, with whom Ada will later fall in love, rescues the instrument, brings it to his house, and receives piano lessons from Ada in return.

In the absence of a real relationship with her husband, a more mutual, supportive and passionate relationship begins between Ada and Baines. Jealous of what Baines achieves, consumed by his own rage, yet seeking to keep hold of what he claims to possess, Stewart is physically violent towards Ada, chopping off a finger, and threatening to do more if Baines does not end his relationship with Ada.[2] Neither Baines nor Ada, however, has been without fault prior to this. Both have been behaving in manipulative ways. If Stewart's action can scarcely be condoned, it becomes comprehensible within the intensity and complexity of the plot and characterization.

In the end, Stewart permits Ada to leave the island with Baines and Flora, and the piano travels with them, though only a short way. Soon after setting sail Ada asks for the piano to be thrown overboard. As the piano descends to the depths, Ada deliberately places her foot in the rope attached to the piano so that she too is dragged down into the water. At the point at which she may easily have drowned, she chooses life, releases her foot from the rope and comes back to the surface. In an action which graphically illustrates the way that water can symbolize both death and (re-)birth, she expresses in a ritual-like act her liberation both in terms of what she has left behind (the piano is no more) and what she looks forward to (her new life with Baines).

Babette's Feast (Gabriel Axel, 1987)

Babette's Feast is already well covered in theology and film discussion.[3] But this does not make it any less suitable as a film through which to examine aspects of Holy Communion. For it remains a fine filmic celebration of the interplay between art, simplicity, faith, community and the enjoyment of the material world.

The 'feast' referred to in the title is a meal laid on by Babette, a former Parisian chef who ends up living with two sisters, Martine and Philippa, who run a small Pietist Lutheran community on the Jutland coast. It is the late nineteenth century and Babette has escaped besieged Paris, though losing her family in the process. Until the meal – laid on for the whole religious community and funded by the winnings from a Paris lottery ticket the subscription for which has been kept up by a friend – no-one is aware of her culinary past. The community is stunned by the lavish display (10,000 francs on a single meal!) and the members make an unsuccessful attempt to go through with it without the slightest thought for, or mention of, the food itself. In the event, the food and drink get the better of them, tongues are untied, old wounds exposed and healed, and the community rediscovers itself and its joyous purpose.

For the meaning of the meal to be perceived and interpreted much depends on the role of an outsider, General Loewenhielm, who had been a visitor to the community earlier in his life and happens to be staying nearby with his aunt at the time of the meal. He recognizes what the food is, and who has prepared it, and is rather baffled at the relative lack of appreciation shown by the community members for the quality of the food and drink being placed before them. On the other hand, the community members simply enjoy the meal and its effects, in a way that the General himself can only admire.

Don't Look Now (Nicholas Roeg, 1973)

Don't Look Now may appear to sit oddly in this chapter with two films which have more immediate links with the sacraments of baptism and communion. The film may have Venice as its main location and contain many references to churches (for one of its leads is in Venice undertaking restoration work on a church). But this example of gothic horror, based on a short story by Daphne Du Maurier, does not explore the sacraments in any direct or indirect way. The film features here for two main reasons. First, it is a haunting evocation of the sheer mystery of human life. It shows, within the limits and using the formulae of its genre, that it is unwise to take life at face value and ask no questions about what may lie behind, beyond or beneath what we see and experience. Second, it contains one of the most celebrated sex scenes in Western cinema. The fact that this scene occurs in the context of a joyful act of communion between two happily married characters, functioning as a means of their consolidating their relationship and as a symbol of its depth, links with the meaning of 'sacramentality' in human life which this chapter will explore.

The plot of Don't Look Now is relatively simple. It is, at one level, a study in bereavement. John and Laura Baxter (Donald Sutherland and Julie Christie) are visiting Venice to try and help them deal with the tragic death of their daughter. Despite their hope that they may be given some respite from constantly thinking about her, they keep thinking that they see their daughter in various places around the city. They also encounter two sisters who claim that they are in contact with their daughter. Though sceptical, the father's being haunted by the image of his daughter leads to tragic consequences.

Viewing experiences

Two of these films, The Piano and Don't Look Now, are tough viewing, being exhausting and tense in turn. Two, The Piano and Babette's Feast, end happily, joyfully in fact. Each explores a variety of Don't Look Now's ways in which physical matter can function symbolically and not only mean more but do more than satisfy immediate human need. In The Piano, and much more so in Babette's Feast, human creativity also plays an important role.[4] We are led through a range of emotional and physical responses to the trio of films. We move from the fear and gut-wrenching awfulness of Stewart's violence, through to euphoria at Ada's watery escape and the triumph of her liberated life in The Piano. We salivate in response to Babette's lavish meal. We may be aroused by 'the least exploitative erotic scene in cinema' and yet recoil in horror at Don't Look Now's ending.[5] In each film, however, there are other specific viewer responses worthy of note.

Two points should be stressed about The Piano. First, it is unsurprising in a film focusing on a musical instrument that the film score itself should attract attention and play an even greater role than normal in viewer responses.[6] I have, admittedly, spoken to viewers who have been irritated by the repetitiveness of Michael Nyman's score. But more often, viewers report how well they respond to it. Nyman's attempt to allow the piano music to be the substitute for Ada's voice appears to have been successful. Viewers who are enabled via the music to get inside Ada's character may thus share all the more in her experience of redemption at the end of the film.

A second noteworthy feature of *The Piano*, which Rhoads and Roberts note, is 'the complexity and the contradictions of the characters'.[7] Viewing clips from the film in isolation could suggest rather two-dimensional characterization (George Baines and Ada McGrath as obviously good characters, whilst Alisdair Stewart is clearly bad). In fact, all three lead characters are complex. Baines can be 'crassly manipulative and intensely disturbing'; Ada's behaviour can be 'shocking and self-absorbed'.[8] A usual means by which an enjoyable film 'works', then – through identification between a viewer and a lead character – is not occurring in an unambiguous way. It is true that this film appears to work best for women viewers. (It is after all, about Ada's liberation.) But it is satisfying precisely because this is no easy liberation, and Ada is no simple character.

In comparison, *Babette's Feast* is an easy, warm, gentle, humorous film to watch. It celebrates the religious community for whom the meal is laid on, accepting the relative naivety of many of its members, but without losing a basic respect for the community. A viewer is taken on a gentle journey through the community's life, wincing at their frugality, perturbed by the members' growing restlessness with each other, yet joyous at the impact that Babette's meal has upon them. The frugality is starkly portrayed by the lesson the sisters give to Babette, unaware of her past employment, as to how to prepare the basic food distributed by the community to those in need. The community's tetchiness is reflected in the increasingly worried faces of the sisters, whose pain we share as viewers, as the members begin to quarrel. After our viewing of the meal – a 20-minute scene in film time – we are as warm and celebratory as the community members who dance in the open air. What we think, as well as feel, will depend on many factors: whether we pick up on any allusion to Holy Communion; whether we think Karen Blixen, author of the short story on which the film is based, or Gabriel Axel, the film's director, intend us to make such a link; whether we were intending to have a meal after watching the film, in which case we may appreciate our food and those with whom we share it all the more. Whatever additional factors influence our reception of the film, we will have experienced an unusual kind of happy ending. The film certainly ties its plot neatly together. But it is not this in itself which leaves us satisfied. We are left pleased, filled, smiling, appreciative, pensive and pondering how and why such a meal could achieve so much. To conclude that it was 'just a good meal' would not do justice to what the film itself has offered, or the way in which, as a film, it has worked on the viewer.

As a horror film, *Don't Look Now* is a different kind of film from most being studied in this book. It is meant to shock, surprise and scare, and does this in a more subtle and semi-realistic way than any 'slasher movie'. Despite its horror elements, most of the film is played realistically. What the Baxters experience is spooky because it appears to deviate only slightly from supposed 'normality'. Whatever viewers make of 'other worlds' – whether supernaturalism is to be mocked, whether contact with the dead is possible, how psychic phenomena are to be understood or evaluated – this is not the 'point' of the film. We are to be spooked, yes. But we are also to celebrate what was brought to an end by John Baxter's violent death: the beauty of a relationship both companionable and erotic between two people who faced death by celebrating the life they each had, and had together. We might still be stunned by the plot's denouement. But we are also to be affected by the closing scenes – of John's funeral – at which the serenity of Laura Baxter is apparent. In Nicholas Roeg's words, 'Laura has survived triumphant – death shall have no more dominion over her – their happiness may be in the past, but it was real and will always remain so.'[9]

Whether, as viewers, we are intended to conclude that John's ultra-rationalism was misguided and that he should have had more respect for 'otherness' and mystery is not clear. Perhaps the extent of his resistance to the two sisters who claim to be in contact with their dead daughter indicates he is more affected by (or hopeful of) what they say than he cares to admit. His own psychic disturbance (believing that he keeps seeing his daughter) suggests this. He himself is aware that, 'Nothing is what it seems', but is a persistent sceptic throughout the film, scornful of Laura's desire to pray and light a candle in memory of their daughter. Be that as it may, we are clearly to value what has been: the profound value of human relationship in the multiple dimensions in which it is expressed – friendship, companionship, commitment and physical intimacy. What may be intended does not, in any case, matter as much as what actually happens to us as viewers. At that point we are, as always, again subject to the interplay between how what we bring makes us interact with what we feel and think in response to what we see and hear.

Connecting questions and issues

All of these films require viewers to pose questions about how nature may disclose dimensions that seem to lie deep within or beyond it. In theological perspective they invite the viewer to reflect on what reality is, and whether there is a divine dimension to the created order. When theologically reflected upon, then, these are all examples of films that complement study of how the sacraments are understood and used in Christian practice. For the sacraments are key examples not just of symbols which refer beyond themselves, but mediate that to which they refer. Similarly, these films all contain examples of sacrament-like activities that do more than merely symbolize a deeper meaning.

What specifically theological questions arise, in this light, when reflecting on these films? Here are some of the main ones.

- How much does matter matter? What value is to be attached to water, to food, to the body in themselves? What value is to be attached to them as symbols? What do they symbolize?
- Which symbols have proved especially important in Christianity, and why? What is the difference between a sign and a symbol? How does a sacrament differ from both?
- What are the sacraments? Why do some Christian traditions have two (baptism and Holy Communion), some seven (baptism, confirmation or chrismation, Holy Communion, ordination, penance, anointing, marriage) and some none at all?
- What happens at baptism? When should baptism occur (at birth, or when a person is old enough to know what is happening to them)? What link is there, if any, between baptism and amendment or renewal of life?
- What happens when Holy Communion is celebrated? Why does Holy Communion have so many other names in Christianity (Mass, Eucharist, Lord's Supper, breaking of bread)? What happens specifically, if anything, to the bread and wine during a service of Holy Communion? Why has that question caused so much strife throughout Christian history?
- What is the relationship between sacraments and the rest of life?

As has been the case in each chapter so far, it will not be possible to address all these questions. But these are the questions that would be needed to explore the sacraments fully. And they are the kinds of questions that any exploration of what can be the 'principle of sacramentality' would need to address.

Explorations: sacramentality; baptism; Holy Communion

Neither *The Piano* nor *Babette's Feast* deliver straightforward Christian interpretations of the practice or theology of baptism and Holy Communion respectively. The latter was almost certainly in Karen Blixen's mind as a background against which Babette's meal should be interpreted.[10] Within the context of the film itself, the meal is best understood with respect to the ritual, symbolic meal common to nearly all Christian traditions.[11] Both story-writer and film-director are playfully exploring diverse tendencies in Protestant and Catholic traditions in their respective appreciation of the material pleasures of human life. The meal invites viewers to explore not merely how the food and drink influence the community-members, but also the many levels on which the celebration of Holy Communion works, and the multiple interpretations which are required to do it justice.

The Piano uses water imagery in a way that may be regarded as universal. Even if religious usage of water as a symbol always occurs in specific ways, no single religion can claim a monopoly upon the symbolic uses of water, with all its associations with danger, death, birth and cleansing. That said, the ending of The Piano is a clear invitation to viewers to re-think the content of the film they have just watched in the light of what is a life-changing, symbolic action by Ada. In theological perspective it is in turn a prompt to re-think the meaning of baptism.

Water appears as a symbol of danger in Don't Look Now. The film as a whole, however, is an exploration of life's inherent mysteriousness. For my purposes in this chapter I am less concerned to explore the full richness and potential of what is a very dense and at times baffling film, or to claim any direct intended allusion to the two sacraments I shall examine. My concern is rather to interpret the beautiful, central love scene in the film in relation to the sacraments being explored. In this way, a 'principle of sacramentality' can be seen to be at work in the way that Christian theology enables life to be understood and lived. Life can accordingly be lived in a way that is deeply respectful of the value of the created order, and recognizes that in and through the material realm God is present and disclosed. But what questions and issues link explorations of the three films to Christian theology's concerns in this respect?

I begin by exploring the principle of sacramentality itself. Many definitions of sacrament exist. Here are two influential definitions from the twelfth century.

> a sacrament is a physical or material element set before the external senses, representing by likeness, signifying by its institution, and containing by sanctification, some invisible and spiritual grace.
>
> (Hugh of St Victor)[12]

A sacrament bears a likeness to the thing of which it is a sign . . . Something can properly be called a sacrament if it is a sign of the grace of God and a form of invisible grace, so that it bears its image and exists as its cause.

(Peter Lombard)[13]

Hugh of St Victor's definition calls for three components of a sacrament: likeness to what is signified, the fact that it was set up for a sacramental purpose and the capacity to convey spiritual presence. Hence, the water of baptism symbolizes cleansing, the practice of baptism was instituted to signify new birth, and it brings new birth about. Peter Lombard's definition is similar, though without the emphasis upon 'a physical or material element', even though the two main sacraments, baptism and Holy Communion, do have a clear material element (water, bread and wine).

A sacrament, then, is a material means or human practice in and through which God's grace becomes present. These definitions were clearly worked out in the context of existing church practice. (Practices were recognized as sacramental, and the definition of sacrament was then worked out in relation to what such practices achieved.) But the theology of sacraments that resulted both clarifies what the two sacraments (or seven in Roman Catholic and Orthodox traditions) are and do, and provides a way of understanding the way in which God works outside of the sacraments themselves. Other practices or occurrences may be called 'sacramental' or 'sacrament-like' in so far as they function symbolically of the grace of God, and actually mediate the grace to which they refer, even if they are not expected to be such, through not being instituted for such a specific purpose. On this basis, sacraments become 'guaranteed signs': contexts in which one can expect the presence and grace of God to be mediated. 'Sacramentality', by contrast, is a way of viewing life which is informed by the sacraments, but expects the grace to become evident in all sorts of places and times, communicated through the world's materiality at any point that God chooses to be revealed.

All three of the films looked at in this chapter invite interpretation through the lens of sacramentality. Water and food are symbolically used in The Piano and Babette's Feast and are suggestive of baptism and Holy Communion respectively. They are not direct expositions of these two sacraments. But interpretation of what Ada's 'baptism' and Babette's meal signify and convey invites theological exploration. The physicality of the love-making scene in the context of Don't Look Now as a whole also invites a sacramental interpretation. It is grace embodied in that it both signifies and conveys the love which the couple share, and through which the lovers oppose the death which brought them to Venice in their state of bereavement. How, though, do these three films help us explore baptism, Holy Communion and sacramentality more fully?

Taking baptism and The Piano first, it must first be stressed that Ada's descent into the water at the end of the film is not an act of Christian baptism. It is a sacrament-like event in her life that functions similarly to a baptism given the symbolism which the event contains and the effect upon her life. It is therefore this sacrament-likeness which we are exploring here. Here are some of the reasons why the event is not a Christian baptism. It is not an act undertaken with the intention of being a form of Christian initiation. It is not a symbolic act administered in the name of the Trinity. It is not seen as entry into a community of Christian people.

Nevertheless the sacrament-likeness of the event enables it to be explored creatively within the context of the film's own narrative, and also facilitates understanding of what baptism is on the part of those not immersed in Christian tradition. A number of features are worth exploring. First, there is some human choice involved. Ada decides to put her foot into the rope so that she will get dragged under water. She has (literally) taken the step to be submerged. She then needs to make the choice to release herself from the rope when underwater. But what makes her do this? In her own words: 'What a death! What a chance! What a surprise! My will has chosen life. Still. It has had me spooked and many others besides.' The human choice is not, therefore, the full story of what occurs. Her action was not unambiguous. It was, she believes, her will, and yet it was a surprising choice to make even for her. The symbolic act is therefore a mixture of human choice and something else, which in the context of the film is left undefined.

The theology of baptism wrestles with the same ambiguity. It is a human choice, for the parents or guardians of a child, or for a believer in later life. But participation in baptism is an act of choosing to accept the prior gracious action of God. It is a human 'yes' to a prior divine 'yes' to life. Paedo-baptists believe that the practice expresses the gracious initiative taken by God all the more. This is the complement to Ada's 'surprise'. Baptism is thus always to be understood as a human response to a divine initiative.

Second, this event in Ada's life is clearly an effective as well as a symbolic act. It really changes her. In a film when it might have seemed there could be no happy ending, it is this event which signals the major change in her life. This, too, complements baptismal theology. Debates continue between different Christian tradition as to how effective baptism itself is (Does it simply signal publicly what has already happened in the individual? Is belief in 'effectiveness' the same as superstition? Is the act of pouring water complemented by activity, at that point, of the Spirit of God?). But some form of effectiveness of the working of God in the life of the believer in relation to baptism is rarely denied.

Third, a death happens ('What a death!'). It is the death of Ada's captive, old self. As a consequence of her near-death experience, and the surprising exercise of her will to live, she (literally) finds her voice and is able to relate to others in a new way. The death is symbolized by the fact of her nearly drowning. This complements the symbolism of baptism directly.

> Do you not know that all of us who have been baptized into Christ Jesus were baptized into his death? We were buried therefore with him by baptism into death, so that as Christ was raised from the dead by the glory of the Father, we too might walk in newness of life.
>
> (The Apostle Paul, Romans 6.3–4)

A death therefore happens for the one baptized ('We know that our old self was crucified with him . . . ' Romans 6.6). The fresh start which baptism signifies is as stark as that. Baptism by full immersion therefore captures symbolically the descent into the grave, and emergence from it into renewed life. This is, in Christian understanding, only possible, however, because of the link being made between the believer's experience and that of Christ. Indeed, the new life of the believer is dependent on the new life that the resurrection of Jesus Christ not only symbolized but brought about. Baptism is, then, a striking, physical, symbolic act of identifying with and participating in the story of Jesus Christ.

Finally, Ada's experience propels her into a new, more joyful form of living. Her relationship with Baines blossoms. She begins to play the piano again, using a metal finger that Baines makes for her. Not only, then, has she found her voice. She can make music more freely, not merely depending on it to be her voice. And she can relate fully to someone she had begun to love. Baptism also propels a person into a new set of relationships. By becoming a member of the church, a person is linked, in Christ, to others who are called to care for and support all baptized people. Baptism is reduced in significance when seen only as a public declaration of entry into a/the church. It is this and much more. It is a signal of acceptance that a person is understood to be held by the Spirit of God, in Christ, in the company of others. It signals where a fundamental communal focus of a person's life is going to be. Baptism takes a person beyond their immediate family into a new community, a community in and through which a baptized person's family is also supported. In this sense baptism discloses Ada's experience to be somewhat limited. In Christian understanding, what it means to be a 'person' is signalled by baptism to be a matter of being 'in Christ', a communal reality which always includes but cuts across family ties and friendships.[14]

And what of Holy Communion? How does *Babette's Feast* inform, and how is the film itself interpreted by, understanding of this sacrament? Again, it is important to stress that the meal is not presented directly as a celebration of Holy Communion. What is being celebrated here is as much the work of the artist as the symbolism and effectiveness of the meal upon the community. The allusions to Holy Communion are, however, unmistakable, even if it is the quality and quantity of food and drink provided which enable the meal to function in a sacrament-like way.

In my earlier theological study of this film I noted four features of the meal which invited comparison with Holy Communion. First, the meal includes elements of confession and absolution. Reflecting a key element in services of Holy Communion (in the preparing of people to receive bread and wine), the forgiveness offered and received in the meal itself is a crucial trigger for the healing of wounds in the community. Second, word and sacrament belong together. In other words, it is not simply the fact of eating which proves effective. The event is interpreted (by the outsider, General Loewenhielm, who can see what is going on) in a way that draws out the meaning of the meal. Third, the community restates its identity by recalling the memory of its founder. In retelling its own narrative, then, it re-finds itself. This reflects the way in which every celebration of Holy Communion is also in part recollection: of the Last Supper. The memory of Jesus is intrinsic to the Eucharistic act, though Holy Communion is not merely a memorial. It is also an event in which the presence of Christ is celebrated. Fourth, Babette's laying on of the feast is itself a sacrificial act. She expends all that she has (her entire lottery winnings) on the meal. In a clear if limited sense then, Babette is a Christ-figure here.[15] The meal, and all that it achieves, is thus only possible because of this act of self-giving.

To those four points I would now add a fifth: the sheer lavishness of the meal. Yes, this insight is contained to some extent within the self-offering of Babette. But I think emphasis on the scale of the meal is merited. This is a banquet, an anticipation of the 'heavenly banquet prepared for all people', which is a feature of any celebration of Holy Communion.[16] It is not sacrament-like because of its lavishness. It is sacrament-like because of what is mediated by the celebratory meal. Joy results from Babette's generosity, and comes about through the pain and release of forgiveness, the willingness to receive grace and the preparedness to celebrate.

What do such insights tell us about Holy Communion itself? First, it really is meant to be a joyful occasion. The memory is painful – of what happened to Jesus, and what participants must face in their own lives (when confessing) in preparing to receive. But there is joy in forgiveness. Second, Holy Communion is as much (if not more) about what happens to a community of people as what happens to the individual. The potential impact of sharing the Eucharistic feast upon the community of people who receive is not to be underestimated. Third, the link between Holy Communion and ultimate meaning cannot be stressed enough. Holy Communion is an eschatological act: it looks forward to 'the end', when all will be well, and all will be fed. It seeks to anticipate that end now, and in so doing the meal serves as a prompt to those who participate to play their part in making that 'kingdom' come. In the film's own terms, the function of the meal is to rejuvenate the community in its own work of caring for the poor in its locality, which its members can now do more joyfully than before.

And what about sacramentality as a concept? How do all these three films help us understand the concept better? One reading of Don't Look Now could be: 'Don't delve too much. It will only bring danger. Religion or supernaturalism are no solace. The way to face death is to live life more fully, treasuring what you have.' The irony is that there are elements in such a reaction which relate precisely to what it means to live sacramentally. Certainly, the physical world is to be valued in and for itself. It is not simply to be 'looked beyond', as if all that matters is some spiritual meaning beyond it. Sacramentality denotes a valuing of the material. It is an emphasis which has been very prominent throughout catholic traditions in Christianity and which Protestants have had to re-learn. In Christian understanding, valuing the material is possible because of recognition of what the material is: a gift from God the creator. The physical world can disclose God at many points. Sacraments are points where the presence of God can be expected, but many other fully embodied human activities can function sacramentally too. Such an approach to life is not, however, materialism in a simple sense. Christianity is 'the most materialist of all religions' (William Temple) because of its commitment to incarnation: the belief that God was found in human form, and is thus recognized as the kind of God who is committed to the created order. But God is present in, and mediated through, the physical world. God is not to be identified with it. A sacramental world-view accepts that God is 'other', and is encountered in and through the physical world: in the symbolic use of water, in the sharing of bread and wine, and, for example, in the physical aspects of loving human relationships.

Working conclusions

Consideration of the sacraments seems at first glance to be the study of some of the most internal aspects of the Christian tradition. On closer inspection, we have seen that sacraments open up a way of viewing life as a whole. The created order in all its physicality is recognized as the site of the disclosure of God. God is, however, not identical to the whole of creation (that would be pantheism). To refer easily to the whole world as a sacrament, as some Christians do, is to mislead. Anything in the world admittedly has the potential to be sacramental: God can be revealed where God chooses. God does, though, need to be recognized. Sacraments are effective symbols, guaranteed channels through which the presence of God can be discerned. Through reflection on them, it then becomes possible to see more about who God is, and therefore the forms in which God's presence is likely to take shape elsewhere in the world.

For further study

Biblical passages that inform an understanding of sacraments include:

Matthew 3.13–17 (= Luke 3.21–2) Two accounts of the baptism of Jesus.
Mark 14.17–21 Mark's version of the Last Supper.
John 6.22–40 The Gospel of John does not offer an account of the Last Supper, but does offer this interpretation of 'the bread of life', linked to his version of the feeding of 5000 people (John 6.1–14).
Romans 6.1–14 The Apostle Paul's reflections on the meaning of baptism in relation to the death and resurrection of Christ.
I Corinthians 11.17–33 The Apostle Paul's account and interpretation of the Last Supper, offered in the context of reacting to early Christian practice in Corinth.

Important post-biblical texts on various aspects of the sacraments include:

Tertullian's defence of the full humanity of Christ [early third century] (in Placher, Vol. 1, pp. 46–7). This is Tertullian's opposition to Marcion, who had contended that Jesus

Christ did not really have a human body. The defence is important because it shows how insistent early Christianity was on the reality of God's incarnation.

From the Second Council of Nicaea [787 CE] (in Thiessen, pp. 64–5; in Leith, pp. 55–6). This influential text is actually a defence of the spiritual value of artistic images, produced to defend the production of icons. It is important in this context in so far as it expounds the religious value of something from the created order in and through which the revelation of God is deemed possible.

Radbertus v Ratramnus [ninth century] (in Placher, Vol.1, pp. 139–43; in McGrath, pp. 525–8). This exchange of views lays out some of the issues involved in debates during the medieval period about what happens to the bread and wine during a service of Holy Communion.

From the Council of Florence [1438–45] (= Leith, pp. 60–1). This text, based on the theology of Thomas Aquinas, spells out why there are seven sacraments.

Martin Luther, from 'That These Words of Christ, "This is My Body," etc., Still Stand Firm Against the Fanatics' [1526] (in Placher, Vol. 2, pp. 23–6). This text shows Luther at his most combative ('Listen now, you pig, dog, or fanatic, whatever kind of unreasonable ass you are . . . '). He offers an understanding of Christ's 'real presence' in the bread and wine of Holy Communion, whilst distinguishing his view from the Catholic view of transubstantiation.

Chapter 9

CHURCH

R EADERS MAY HAVE EXPECTED THE TOPIC of 'church' to have been considered well before now in a book about Christian theology. After all, the church is the most public face of Christianity. It is the church which makes the headlines for its failures, and when Christian statements are sought by the media. And in theology, it is recognized that the church 'carries' Christian theology as a tradition, and is the context within which the ritual practices of Christianity are performed. So why wait till now to examine it as a concept?

I certainly do not want to play down the church, either as theological concept or socio-political reality. It is naturally vital for an understanding of Christianity. But I have delayed addressing the theme for two reasons. First, to place it too early in an exposition of Christian theology may imply that it has an importance over and above the one to whom it bears witness (God as known in and through Christ). The church only exists because it is a social reality that tries to live in relation to God. By its very existence, the church acknowledges that unless a theology is embodied socially, human beings will not be able to 'live' that theology. But if theology starts with the fact of church, then the danger is that it is the ones who believe, or the institution to which they belong, that become the object of scrutiny. God may then move down too low on the agenda.[1]

Second, by considering a number of other theological topics first, we end up adopting a much more creative approach to the topic of 'church'. By identifying first what theological questions and insights emerge from exploring doctrines of God, creation, spirit, redemption and sacramentality, we are in a better position then to see how church as a social form relates to all of these.

The three films to be studied are quite different from each other. Two – *Eat Drink Man Woman* and *Brassed Off* – approach the topic of church from an oblique angle. Neither is specifically *about* church. But each addresses aspects of human social living which a doctrine of church (an ecclesiology) needs to consider. The third – *The Magdalene Sisters* – is directly critical of the church. Looking at that film reminds us that Christian theology cannot make do with abstract reflections on the theological concept of church. It must also take into account the church as an actual social reality, and of the history of the church's practice. Failing to do so would raise into question the truthfulness and viability of church as both a social reality and a theological concept.

Films

Eat Drink Man Woman (*Ang Lee*, 1994)

Eat Drink Man Woman is a gentle, thoughtful comedy (in Taiwanese) directed by Ang Lee.[2] It is a study of family life, in particular the relationship between a father (Chu, played by Sihung Lung) and his three daughters Chen (Kuei-Mei Yang), Chien (Chien-Lien Wu) and Ning (Yu-Wen Wang). All three daughters still live at home and one, Ning, is still at school. All are in the process of finding their own way in life. Each relates to her father, a chef, in a different way, displaying diverse ways of reacting to or rebelling against him. Nevertheless they hang together as a family and eat together, even though the father has lost his sense of taste. Their meal-times are the focal point of the way in which the family's history is carried and of their inter-relationship. The preparation of food and its consumption is a large part of the way they do, and do not, communicate with each other. Two of the daughters, Chen and Ning, eventually leave home. It is a surprise that Chien, a high-flying businesswoman, does not. When Chu decides to sell the family home, Chien buys it rather than going to work in her company's Amsterdam office. It is she who is the most affected by the thought of losing the tradition of family meals. In the film's closing scene, roles are reversed. Chien cooks for Chu and Chu realizes that he has rediscovered his sense of taste. His daughter's cooking has been the means for this happening.

Brassed Off (Mark Herman, 1996)

Brassed Off is the fictional account of a Northern mining community, Grimley. The study of the closure of the coal-mine in the village is, however, based on the experience of many communities in the North of England in 1992, against the background of earlier political conflicts in the 1980s between the miners and the Conservative government. The particular aspect of the film that is pertinent to this chapter's topic, both in theme and in its emotional impact on the viewer, is the role played by the community's brass band. The pit is threatened by closure and the miners are themselves divided about whether to accept the redundancy money offered to them. Phil (Stephen Tompkinson) is especially under pressure, having not recovered financially from the 1984 strike-action, which had a huge impact upon the quality of life of his family. A young researcher, Gloria (Tara Fitzgerald), originally from Grimley, returns with the task of assessing the long-term future viability of the pit. A descendant of a famous band-member, and a flugelhorn-player herself, she is allowed to join the band. Her professional work, always suspect in the eyes of some of the miners, is eventually disregarded as the closure of the pit goes ahead. Throughout all of this, the band plays on, its future uncertain, yet as both site and symbol of communal life.

The Magdalene Sisters (Peter Mullan, 2002)

Peter Mullan's study of one of the Magdalene Convents is set in 1964. Set up to house 'fallen women' sent by families or parishes from the Roman Catholic Church in Ireland, the institutions were working laundries at which residents were held to atone for their sins through hard labour. The last laundry finally closed in 1996. They functioned more like prisons, as the residents lived and worked in isolation from the wider world. Furthermore, the reasons for women being there in the first place often invited sympathy, and commended support and help, rather than punishment. Mullan's film explores the experiences of three women, Margaret (Anne-Marie Duff), raped at a family wedding, Bernadette (Nora-Jane Noone), a teenager who enjoyed flirting with boys, and Rose (Dorothy

Duffy), an unmarried mother. It is unremitting in its criticism of the Roman Catholic Church, yet still manages to include elements of humour whilst presenting the tragic personal stories. (The three tales are fictional, yet are all based on accounts of women housed in such convents.) It has rightly been said that the film 'balances a light touch with searing intensity and a sense of moral outrage'.[3]

Viewing experiences

It is important that adequate and equal attention is given to cognitive and emotional responses to all three films in this chapter. If not, then the film in which the church dominates (*The Magdalene Sisters*) too easily becomes the focus of the chapter. On the basis of an imbalance of focus, the moral outrage which Mullan expresses, and the viewer is likely to echo when watching, would prevent viewer and reader having any possibility of reaching a broader and deeper appreciation of what the concept and reality of church *can* be.

There are relatively few positive images of the church in recent Western film. There may be occasional positive (priestly) characters. And the ambiguity of the church's mission can be examined in historical perspective (e.g. *The Mission*). But it is much easier to present the church's failings or problems. This in part explains why it is necessary to try and get at what the church is about via an indirect route. How, then, are viewers likely to respond to the three presented here?

In response to *Eat Drink Man Woman* viewers are likely to be invited to reflect upon their own family experiences, particularly their roles as parent or child. The film is gentle, but offers an accessible way into the emotions and basic dynamics of adult children breaking away from parental influence. In the very different experiences of the three daughters, Lee offers diverse ways in which the loosening of a parental hold on a child takes shape. The shift of focus from family to other relationships – romance and work – and the tensions which result are also presented. For most of the film, however, the family meal table remains the focal point. It is here where reports are given of developments in each of the four family members' lives. If it is true, as Chien declares, that, 'We communicate by eating' (whilst the karaoke-playing neighbours do so by singing), it is also true that it is in the context of family life, as Chu notes, that the worrying happens. *Eat Drink Man Woman* therefore invites the viewer into a family's life, to share in its role as an emotional foundation for its members, at the point where the family-members move into new patterns of relating.

Brassed Off is uneven as a film, depending to some extent on caricature to make its points, even though there is richness in the characterization. The film uses the brass band music well, however, to create intense viewer participation in the emotional struggles of the main characters. If it borders on the manipulatively sentimental at times, this is simply to ensure that viewers *do* get some grip on how much the issues and events presented affect and matter to the kinds of people being portrayed. The film leaves a clearly unhappy ending (the closure of the pit) lurking within the happy ending of the band's success in the brass band competition. Despite the social realism of the second half of the film, therefore, the viewer may be left feeling warm and satisfied by the film.

Two aspects of viewer response do, however, deserve specific attention. The first is the potentially different responses of male and female viewers, brought on by the primary focus of the film (the redundancy-threatened miners), though also the clearly defined respective roles of male and female characters within the film. Men who are fathers take a limited role in childcare. The men of different ages and across generations show limited capacity to identify and reveal their emotions and often lack assertiveness. The women characters appear to be background figures and yet are strong and influential. Those who are mothers do the bulk of child-care and control household finances.

Depending on their own backgrounds (sex, class, economic) viewers will relate differently to the relationships and social context configured by the characters. But the film is unlikely to permit viewers to stand apart from the everyday complexity – of financial concerns, employment insta-bility, of gender roles – which the film presents, whatever their own background. In this respect, the film proves successful.

The one caveat to the film's success in this respect forms the second aspect of viewer response to *Brassed Off* which merits scrutiny: a viewer's political response to the film. In a teaching context I have known students report that they 'don't like the film' in a way which quickly discloses itself to be a response based on political disagreement ('I don't like its politics'). *Brassed Off* is clearly a film that wears its political heart on its sleeve: the Conservative government damaged whole human communities through its policies towards the mining industry during the 1980s and 1990s. Viewers who dispute this believe that the Conservative government had little option, or are not sympathetic to the social or ideological context out of which opposition to the Conservatives' course of action emerged. They may therefore not connect with the film and are certainly unlikely to participate in the film in the way that many of its strategies for viewer involvement suppose.

Most viewers will, however, be invited through their watching of *Brassed Off* to reflect upon the sets of relationships within which they themselves live – work, leisure, family – and the interplay between them. Furthermore, through its presentation of the financial constraints operating for most of the lead characters, the film invites viewers to consider the material dimensions of their own existence. It therefore sets up a clear platform for a viewer's critical reflection upon the multiple, interlocking, communities within which human beings discover and construct their identity, and the practical pressures and constraints that affect people's lives. *Brassed Off* is not, of course, a film about the church. But reflection on what viewers are drawn into through the way the film works begins to open up the subject-matter with which ecclesiology must deal.

Viewers are clearly intended to have a different, and explicitly ecclesiological, reaction to *The Magdalene Sisters*. In response to this film, it is clear that director's intention and viewer response are meant to coincide. The 'searing intensity' and 'sense of moral outrage' which the film embodies are meant to be felt and shared by the viewer. As one respondent on the Internet Movie Database (IMDb) states: 'Religion's role in the sheer brutalization of its adherents has been evidenced throughout history – no mass religion has brought anything other than terror, subjugation and self-hatred to women – this film proves it beyond doubt!'[4] Including such a film in a chapter designed to stimulate reflection upon understandings of the church may thus not be deemed a positive move. Certainly, no space is given in the film for a hearing of what the church may have intended positively by the creation of the laundries. Admittedly it is hard to see how they could be defensible. But it can be argued that seeking to understand the Roman Catholic Church's actions in a broader social and historical context may have at least enabled viewers to understand more about why the laundries existed in the first place.[5]

As it stands, only viewers who might have other reasons for defending the church as an institution would come away from this film thinking and believing that the church was something worth supporting. Those predisposed to think of the church negatively have their assumptions confirmed. Those unsure about the church, or with little experience of it, leave questioning its conduct and reason for being, wondering whether 'such things still go on'. The experience of watching this film, in short, leaves viewers with much work to do if they are to move towards a positive appraisal of the church as theological concept and social reality. From a viewing of *The Magdalene Sisters*, the church is to be criticized. Even if there is a distinction to be drawn between the church's potential and the work of the laundries (as Mullan himself acknowledges[6]), the difficulty of articulating that potential in the face of the actual failure of the church as an institution is clear from this film.

If watching these three films creates in any way a typical viewing experience for a regular cinema-goer, then it is not to the church that a viewer might turn in thinking about social institutions that shape a person's identity positively. Family life may be a struggle too, but can be positive. Work and leisure may not be easy. But *Brassed Off* has more hope and warmth in it than the church, as often portrayed in the cinema. What questions, then, does this create for a theology student seeking to grapple with the church as concept and reality?

Connecting questions and issues

The church as a social reality may be very distant from the experiences of many readers. It is for this reason that the topic has been approached indirectly. Putting Mullan's critical film alongside two films which are not directly about the church at all does, however, enable a wide range of appropriate questions about what the church is, and is for, to be posed in real rather than ideal terms.

- What is the church? What is its primary purpose: worship, mission, spiritual development of its members, proclamation, pastoral care, social and political influence?
- How is it to be best described: as a human organization, as a divine reality, as visible or invisible? Can the phrase 'the true church' have any meaning?
- What is to be made of the fact that there are so many different churches? Does it make any sense to talk about 'the church'?
- What does belonging to a church entail? How does participation in the life of the church relate to belonging to other communities and groups? Is the church, by definition, expected to be the main community to which a person belongs, so that a Christian is defined by their church-involvement?
- Does church therefore inevitably replace the family as the primary community to which a Christian belongs? Is this why churches are

often likened to families? But in what ways is the church like and unlike a family? What may be the limits of seeing the relationships between church-members in terms of family bonds (brother–sister, parent–child)?

- How is the church best organized? How are its priests/ministers/ pastors (and bishops, deacons or elders) to behave? What are their roles in both church and society? How do its leaders relate to the rest of the church membership? (In most traditions, this means: how do the ordained relate to the laity?[7]) What kind of people should be its leaders?

Once again, as with all chapters in this part of the book, this list of questions cannot possibly be addressed in its entirety. But discussing the themes and issues that arise for viewers in response to the three films selected will get us inside some of the main questions listed above.

Explorations: unity; holiness; catholicity; apostolicity; church as 'base group'

In the Apostles' Creed, the church is called 'one, holy, catholic and apostolic'. This is the church that Christians are expected to declare their belief in. The church is *one*: united worldwide, despite whatever differences may appear between different Christian traditions. Its unity is based on the fact that all members are united in Christ, worshipping through the Holy Spirit the one God as known in and through Jesus Christ. The church is *holy*: it is a worldwide community which seeks to manifest itself in many local forms as bodies of people seeking to reflect in their lives the holiness of God. Such churches make no claim to succeed in their hopes. Any sense of holiness is a derived holiness, for God alone is holy. Nor should holiness be identified too quickly with moral rectitude. Holiness is not earned in any sense. But it is true that churches believe that the holiness of God reflected in human life will issue in the desire to be good.

The church is *catholic*: extending across the whole of the world, and seeking to share the same faith. Even allowing for variations, unity in Christ is expected to issue in forms of belief that stand in continuity with each other. A Pentecostal Christian from Birmingham, England, should therefore be able to identify that she stands in the same religion as a member of the Russian Orthodox Church in St Petersburg, a Roman Catholic from Sydney, Australia, and a Mennonite from Bolivia. The church is *apostolic*: the continuity of belief should stand in identifiable continuity with what the church has always believed. There should be ways of showing how a basic tradition of belief has been maintained (in content and through church structures) across nearly two millennia. Doctrinal ideas do develop. Circumstances do change. The philosophical and cultural partners with and in relation to which Christians articulate their beliefs in different contexts have a marked influence on how the apostolic tradition is formulated. But continuity remains.

That, at least, is the theory. It is, of course, a theological ideal. But it is important to acknowledge this ideal nevertheless. Not to do so would fail to respect why any local church exists, what worship is for, and how participation in the church in its local form is deemed to connect with humanity as whole. There are undoubted problems when any group makes claims of a universal nature and has an organizational reach which is global (and this applies to most religions). Theologies and philosophies are usually engaged in the business of seeking to clarify understandings of humanity which they think are true of human beings everywhere. The implication is therefore that if only everyone believed the same (especially as what is proposed is 'obviously' true) then all would be well, for every-body. Without such universal visions, human groups remain in isolation from each other, so the beliefs and visions need to be articulated.

And yet dangers lurk. For no-one can actually step fully outside of their own community and tradition to take a God's eye view. At this point, the necessity and difficulty of inter-faith and inter-ideological dialogue become apparent. In the meantime, what is celebrated week by week in the social groups known as churches shapes those who participate in them, and offers a vision of what humanity might be. But the ideal and the real remain far apart. For whatever the church seeks to be in the light of its understanding of God and what it deems to be God's vision for humanity, it remains a collection of fallible human organizations.

The Magdalene Sisters is not a direct attack on the Roman Catholic Church as a whole. Mullan's film does, however, pose poignant questions about this gap between the ideal and the real, between the church as a theological concept and the church as a collection of fallible human organizations. How any church could both set up the Magdalene laundries and then leave them running for so long is a legitimate question and one which Mullan's film presses home with some ruthlessness. The film at least implies that there is something about the church that prevents it being able to see how immoral some of its own practices have been. The church's fallibility is plain to see.

Taken in isolation, this film might encourage viewers and readers who have little time for the church (as ideal or organization) to skip the chapter and move on. It is here, however, where the interplay between a film that is critical of church practice, and two which are not directly about the church at all proves important. My contention is that critical attention both to what *Eat Drink Man Woman* and *Brassed Off* are 'about' and what they can do to and for viewers can enable an understanding of what the church as both theological ideal and social organization is for, and how it works.

The simple idea I suggest we work with is that of a 'base group'. The term draws on insights from psychology and sociology and is used in youth and community work. It provides a way of understanding how churches work in practice, and thus how we may move from churches as real examples of human social practice function in relation to the theological ideal to which they aspire.

A 'base group' is a primary community. It is the main community to which one relates as a human being. All people relate to many communities and groups: families, friendships, work teams, leisure groups, political parties, sports clubs, religious groups. It is sometimes not easy to determine which of these groups prove most influential upon us. In the case of a political activist who has devoted their life to a party cause, or a professional sportsperson for whom work, vocation and the need to maintain physical well-being coincide, the primary group may be relatively easy to pinpoint. But this will not always be so. Furthermore, some groups we belong to (e.g. work or family) we may wish we did not. We know they influence us deeply, but we seek to choose to define ourselves and be defined by other groups to which we belong. In addition, it may be very difficult to pinpoint *one group only* as a 'base group' if, say, a group of friends and a particular religious or political group both seem equally to shape us. Yet the concept of 'base group' remains significant and helpful to understand what 'church' is. Reflection on the concept forces us to ask about the social groups to which people are committed, through which they recognize, and often choose, to develop as people (emotionally, intellectually, inter-personally and spiritually) and thus through which their identities and aspirations take shape.

Eat Drink Man Woman and *Brassed Off* can both be interpreted in this light. On the basis of exploration of these two films in this way, it will then be possible to return to the questions of what the church is, and is for, and to get inside the church's practical, theological significance in a fresh way.

Eat Drink Man Woman is a film about the family. In its handling of the evolution of Chu's relationship with his three very different daughters, it shows us how the family functions as a base group for all four people involved. In so doing, it addresses many other aspects of human living which impinge upon, or are brought into, family life. First, a family operates across generations. A feature of Chu's struggle with his daughters is the new ways they operate in personal and working relationships. Second, we see an example of patriarchy under challenge. Chu is clearly the family's head. But things are changing. Third, we are invited into the way in which the family ritually handles the crucial points of meeting between its members. The film revolves around the 'Sunday dinners', when all four members meet (at a round table) to exchange news. These become places of conflict too. But even though there are examples of avoidance, this is also where all four are clearly supported by the others in what they do in the rest of their lives. Fourth, because of the bonds existing between the family members, the support offered by each of them extends beyond their times of meeting to what happens in between. The clearest example of this is when the busiest daughter, Chien (the one who buys the family house off her father), offers support to her father through the illness and eventual death of Old Wen, her father's work colleague.

All of these four aspects of family life can easily be correlated to life in the church. The church is one of the most striking cross-generational bodies that exists. Churches note that they can grow more easily if they attract similar ages or types of people. But in following such a path they overlook an important (positive, challenging) aspect of church life: churches throw people together who would not have chosen each other, and who are located in different stages of life. Churches remain, by and large, heavily patriarchal. Even in the many traditions that now ordain women, patriarchy is alive and well. Things are changing, but very, very slowly. There is no point in pretending otherwise. Third, the church has its regular times of ritual (worship) when people meet. These may not always be times of intense, personal meeting in the way that Chu's family meet at meal-times. Some churches ensure that this kind of meeting happens at other times (e.g. in small groups meeting for prayer, Bible study, fellowship or social reasons). Other churches do not see this as important because worship is what the church is for, and people participate in worship, and access its benefits in whatever way they deem appropriate. Food is important in church life too, in two senses. Food is, of course, shared symbolically in Holy Communion.[8] The sharing of food occurs, however, in other ways too. I recall being present at a Greek Orthodox service in a city in the UK, during which family members brought food to be shared at the lunch following the service. When the service 'began' I was one of three people present. The congregation grew as the morning went on, with the priest chanting the liturgy throughout. The sharing of the meal was dovetailed with the congregation's gathering and was to be part of their celebrating what it meant to be a Christian community. Similarly, empirical studies have often disclosed that it is often the kitchen, rather than the sanctuary, which functions as the place where people meet each other. It is as if people meet God in church, and each other in the kitchen (or round the dinner table). But in the life of the church one type of meeting is simply the flip-side of the other. Finally, with regard to pastoral care, it is clear that churches often prove to be social groups whose members look after each other. Admittedly, one of the greatest challenges for churches is to resist only looking after 'their own' and to be aware of those in need around them. Here, pastoral care and mission interweave. But churches are very rarely so inward looking that there is no concern for others.

In these four respects, then, churches are clearly like families. Whether this is a helpful image for what the church is, however, is a legitimate question.[9] In making the comparison we can see ways in which churches function in practice as a base group for people. In two significant ways, however, the parallel between the church and the family should be resisted. First, the church can be a chosen base group. You can opt into the church from the outside. Second, the church has a more clear, explicit focus on an end beyond itself. If a family's 'purpose' may be defined as the provision of a stable environment in which children may grow up into mature adults, all of whom can then continue to develop and relate to each other creatively for the rest of their lives, then the parallel holds. But the church exists not just for its members. It also carries an understanding of God and a corresponding vision of humankind which is connected with 'the Kingdom of God' – a vision of what the world could be.[10]

Brassed Off raises many of the same issues about how a base group functions in practice. Here, however, the focus shifts from family to a work-related leisure group that plays a crucial role in the life of a local community. Arguably, the Grimley Colliery Band is already more church-like than a family because of the way it connects other groups to which people are attached, through a mixture of necessity and choice. The miners must work, and job opportunities are limited (yet somehow, this is what the men are 'meant' and 'want' to do, as it has always been so). They also choose to belong to the band, and it fulfils needs which are expansive and deep. It offers welcome respite from work, and is recreational through being a pastime and enabling them to be fed through the making of music. Furthermore, the friendships they form through the band sustain them emotionally, being contexts within which they can express and explore all that matters to them.

There are, however, respects in which the church is unlike the Grimley Colliery Band, even when only the social and psychological aspects of belonging are considered. First, there are clear border controls on membership. Until the arrival of Gloria, the band is for men only. And naturally, given its purpose, it is only for the musically able. The church, whatever its own historical and present struggles about membership, has no such bars to membership. Those who want to count themselves amongst God's people can do so freely. Different traditions then interpret in diverse ways how commitment to God in and through church should then take shape. But churches do not usually demand prior requirements as conditions of entry. Second, *Brassed Off* wrestles with the question of cultural specificity in a stark, even caricatured, way. The working-class band from the North of England takes on the capital (and all that 'the South' symbolizes in terms of wealth and high culture) in making it to the finals of the band competition. Churches are caught up in similar dynamics too (in terms of wealth, class, ethnicity or geography). But at its best, the church recognizes that no culturally specific group can speak normatively about and for God. Encounter with God can happen in and through any cultural context. Who and what God is, is discovered, reflected upon and explored in the constant interplay between different groups' encounter with and celebration of the presence of God in their lives. Christian theology is thus always 'theology of the church' in the sense that it has to relate to real encounters with God occurring in the concrete contexts in which people meet as Christians. But Christian theology errs when it makes ecclesiology (the doctrine of the church *per se*) the focal point of theological exploration. In order to maintain its focus on God, theology has to wrestle with the very diverse understandings of God which may emerge from different cultures, despite the evident continuity of tradition evident throughout the one, holy, catholic and apostolic church.

On the basis of this enquiry we are now in a better position to grasp what the church is for, and to offer a response to Peter Mullan's powerful implied critique of the church in *The Magdalene Sisters*. First, the church exists to be an agent of what it deems God wants for creation. In its own eyes, then, it is serving a vision that it believes it has received from God about what creation is for (the Kingdom of God). It does not have the exclusive responsibility to bring this about. Indeed, as we shall see in the next chapter, because the Kingdom of God is God's alone to bring, there is a clear sense in which the church cannot *work* for the Kingdom at all. Its job is to seek to embody its coming in a small way. But that is its job. That is why the church sees it role as important, its task as enormous, its responsibility as immense, and why it can only be expressed in theological terms.

Second, if the church functions in any sense as a 'base group' for its members, then it will do so in co-operation with and sometimes in competition with other base groups which shape people. But the church inevitably invites its members to think of the church as their primary group, their most basic base group. For if they really do seek to serve the Kingdom of God then there will be something about the church which will inevitably shape people whatever their base group actually is.

Here, though, the distinction between the church as theological concept and social organization becomes very apparent. For the church may function as an important theological ideal, whilst in practical terms other social forms function as people's base groups. People may, in other words, serve the Kingdom of God, whilst their primary groups are (and have to be) work or family.

The church is therefore, inevitably, third, the carrier of a tradition. The church shapes people through the belief system and ritual practices which people can inhabit, whether or not it can function as a base group. A delightful scene from *Eat Drink Man Woman* indicates how this works. It is the occasion when the daughter Chen, when she has begun to fall in love with the volleyball coach, sees the coach on his scooter one day as she is leaving the school where she teaches. We already know that she is Christian, and a regular church-goer. We also know that her devotion extends to supplementing her participation in worship by regular listening to hymns on her Walkman on her way to and from work. As viewers we see the coach speaking, but cannot hear what he is saying, for we adopt Chen's point of view. All we can hear are the hymns she is listening to. It is a striking scene which both illustrates how the task of inhabiting a tradition works, and raises the question about how inhabiting a tradition relates to membership of multiple communities. Chen is a Christian, so therefore her head literally contains Christian beliefs (carried here in musical form) which shape her life. However, the ways she inhabits these beliefs does, at times, block her capacity to interact with others. She is an active church-member. Church may indeed be functioning as a base group for her (she certainly wants the volleyball coach to become Christian too). But as viewers we gain greater insight into her family life. In addition, we see the beginning of a new form of life through her friendship and then romance with the coach. She also relates to school as her working environment. Whether or not it is church or family which actually functions as Chen's base group is less important than the point that she lives in multiple communities, and does live within Christian tradition, which the church carries for her. She also lives within the Christian tradition even when she is not at church.

Fourth, although the church serves the Kingdom of God, functions as a base group, and carries a tradition, it knows that it will fail on all three counts. It is always likely to fail in strictly human, organizational terms, because it will simply not be able to fulfil its mission statement (God alone can fulfil that). Living with such awareness of failure is not a comfortable position to be in. It creates a human organization often unwilling or unable to speak of 'success' or 'achievement'. Awareness of likely failure and unwillingness to speak of achievement together conspire against the church critically evaluating its own work, in human organizational, let alone theological, terms. Development of this point would take us well beyond the remit of this book. But it does relate to where this section began: the church lives within the context of seeking to reflect a huge theological ideal and yet, as Peter Mullan reminds us, all too publicly fails to reveal its own critique of its own workings.

Working conclusions

The church is, then, both a theological concept and a socio-political reality. It is a collection of vastly differing communities of many sizes and cultures. It functions as a base group for Christians. However, it also exercises a cultural-theological function for many who may or may not call themselves Christian, and for whom it does not function as a base group, and yet have some link to it as one of the multiple communities to which they feel they belong. It does this by being a carrier of a theological tradition that articulates the meaning and purpose of creation as leading towards the coming of the Kingdom of God. As Western societies become less and less supportive of organized Christianity in formal terms, and the patterns of consumption become more individualized, this way of relating to the church as the carrier of tradition may be more widely practised. Whether such tradition-carrying is sustainable in the long term without continued, extensive participation in churches as base groups is a moot point. Examination of this aspect of Christian practice, as both a theological and sociological matter, is sure to be ongoing.

For further study

Biblical passages which are important to aid understanding of what the church is, and how it works, include:

Isaiah 43 This is an example of a passage from a prophetic book in the Hebrew Bible/Old Testament in which God is portrayed as addressing the people of Israel. It is such passages as this that the early Christians then interpreted as relating to themselves too. Hence, they become descriptions of who the church is.

Matthew 16.13–20 This is a crucial New Testament passage as it portrays Jesus making Simon Peter especially significant in the church's origins.

Acts 2.37–42 and 4.32–5 These two passages from the Acts of the Apostles provide examples of what the early church sought to be like in terms of the quality of its communal life and its ethical practice.

Romans 12.3–8 and I Corinthians 12.12–31 These two extracts from the writings of the Apostle Paul speak of the way in which the church is to see itself as a body with its members playing different but equally significant roles.

I Corinthians 1.10–27 This passage finds the Apostle Paul reflecting on the unity of the church, opposing the way in which the Corinthian church too easily split into different factions.

Ephesians This whole New Testament book could be read in one sitting. It may or may not derive from Paul (it is likely to be from a pupil of his) but it spells out in six chapters a number of different aspects of the church.

I Timothy 3 This chapter provides an example of guidance about what church leaders (in this case bishops and deacons) should be like.

I Peter 2.9–12 This text offers a succinct description of how the churches are to view themselves, drawing on rich Jewish imagery.

Texts from later periods in the church's history which offer insight into understanding the church include:

'Irenaeus on the Function of the Church' [second century CE] (in McGrath, pp. 461–2). This short text places emphasis on the church as the carrier of tradition, which needs to ensure careful transmission of that tradition through time.

'Leo the Great on Ministry within the Church' [fifth century CE] (in McGrath, p. 469). Linked directly with the biblical passage I Peter 2 (see above), this text from Pope Leo I emphasizes the way that all members participate in the church's ministry. It is a striking text given that it appears 1000 years before the Reformation.

Extracts from Thomas Aquinas, 'Exposition on the Apostles' Creed' [1273 CE] (in Ahlgren, pp. 107–9; shorter extract in McGrath, p. 471). This text finds Thomas Aquinas offering his interpretation of what it means for the church to be 'one, holy, catholic and apostolic'.

Martin Luther's understanding of the role of the Holy Spirit in the Church [1528 CE] (from 'Sermons on the Catechism'; in Ahlgren, pp. 112–14). Luther's exposition in this sermon concentrates on the church as a living community, inspired by the Holy Spirit.

George Fox on the church as a group of inspired people [seventeenth century CE] (from *The Journal of George Fox*; in Placher, Vol. 2, pp. 79–81). This extract from the journal of the founder of the Quakers places emphasis on the inner life of the church's members.

Friedrich Schleiermacher on the Church as a Fellowship of Believers [1834] (= *The Christian Faith* [E.T. 1928], pp. 525–8; in McGrath, pp. 490–2). Schleiermacher's exposition of the church emphasizes the quality of the spiritual life of individual members and of the church's communal life, because of the dependence of the church upon Christ the Redeemer.

Texts from the Second Vatican Council [1962–65] (in McGrath, pp. 500–3 and Ahlgren, pp. 131–3). These two extracts from documents deriving from Vatican II (*Lumen Gentium* and *Gaudium et Spes*) offer insights into the Roman Catholic Church's understanding of the nature of the church and on how the church relates to the world.

John Macquarrie on the four marks of the church (= *Principles of Christian Theology* [1977]; in Ahlgren, pp. 152–60). British theologian John Macquarrie here offers a recent interpretation of the church as one, holy, catholic and apostolic.

Chapter 10

THE END

T HE FINAL SUBSTANTIVE CHAPTER OF THIS PART of the book is fittingly devoted to eschatology – the study of all things to do with 'the end': the end of life, the end of all things, and of whatever may lie beyond 'the end' (e.g. resurrection, immortality, heaven, hell). As a medium, film has proved a fertile ground for the development of stories and visions about the end and 'what lies beyond'. If the horror genre explores both the dangerous mystery of what lies beneath or beyond this present life, then apocalyptic visions of all kinds in the cinema offer speculations and reflections on what may or may not lie beyond it. Theology cannot but be interested in such speculations. This chapter considers three films offering quite different approaches to aspects of the future.

Films

Truly Madly Deeply (*Anthony Minghella*, 1989)

Truly Madly Deeply is a study of bereavement. Nina (Juliet Stevenson) is distraught after the death of her lover Jamie (Alan Rickman), a cellist. However, Jamie returns to her. When she is at the piano, playing a favourite piece, she finds herself again accompanying his cello-playing. His embodied reappearance is played straight, with humorous effect, for he returns from death with many other new (dead) friends, so that viewers begin to forget wondering whether they are 'really there'. Gradually, Nina comes to accept that Jamie has gone, or at least cannot remain with her in the form he now is. A new friendship begun with Mark (Michael Maloney), an art therapist, can then develop more freely.

Jesus of Montreal (*Denys Arcand, 1990*)

Jesus of Montreal is one of the cleverest Jesus films ever made. It is rightly identified as belonging both to the 'Jesus film' and 'Christ-figure film' genres because of its interweaving of a Passion Play within a contemporary narrative.[1] The film is highly effective in exploring both the meaning of the story of Jesus of Nazareth and the way that the Jesus story influences and is influenced by contemporary experience. Daniel Coulombe (Lothaire Bluteau) brings together a group of struggling actors to form a group to revitalize a Passion Play performed at a shrine of which Father Leclerc (Gilles Pelletier) is the warden. Their re-writing and re-staging of the play is a huge success, though is not popular with the Roman Catholic Church. Father Leclerc himself voices his disquiet at some of the changes made. An accident occurs during one of the performances, however, and Coulombe dies, but not before he has had chance to wander ghost-like through the Montreal underground. His life as an actor thus mirrored Jesus' own. Even in death he gives life to others, as his heart and eyes are used in transplant operations.

Field of Dreams (*Phil Alden Robinson, 1989*)

Field of Dreams, a film which has spawned a tourist attraction, many websites and provided the name of many small businesses, is a haunting piece of work. Running the risk of coming over as treacly in its homeliness,[2] it explores fundamental themes in an accessible, and seemingly realistic, way, and yet introduces elements of fantasy that make it more a work of magical realism. Ray Kinsella (Kevin Costner) is a farmer in Iowa. In response to what he believes to be a divine voice, he puts his entire farming business at risk by creating a baseball field in his valuable corn-field. Sticking, Noah-like, to his task in the face of much opposition ('If you build it, they will come'), Kinsella's vision consumes him. He is not entirely sure why he must create the baseball diamond. And his task also requires him to set off in search of others who might be able to share his vision, above all baseball-player Archibald Graham (played at two different life-stages by Frank Whaley and Burt Lancaster) and author Terence Mann (James Earl Jones). In the end, great baseball-players from the past come to practise in Kinsella's field, though only he and members of his closest family see them playing. Both Kinsella and others with whom he comes into contact are reconciled to their pasts through the baseball field. In Kinsella's case, he undergoes a healing of memory with respect to his late father.

Viewing experiences

When I first showed *Truly Madly Deeply* in the context of teaching a class in theology and film, I was experimenting with difference methods of acknowledging and recording responses to films. After a group had watched the film together, I asked them to write down their emotions immediately after the film before they had an opportunity to discuss its contents with anyone else in the group. The plan had been to get responses down on paper prior to a coffee-break, after which we would then explore the film both in relation to the immediate responses recorded and more considered reflections. In the event, some of the students rebelled. How could I possibly expect people to write anything down immediately? It was an unreasonable demand! Not everyone, therefore, completed the task. Needless to say, this did not cause a great problem for my pedagogical method. On the contrary, it simply gave the group as a whole even more to reflect on after the coffee-break.

This experience produces a simple observation: *Truly Madly Deeply* is a film which provokes strong responses. Through its subject-matter, the cleverness of its crafting and the intensity it evokes, viewers with any experience of a close bereavement are unlikely to remain untouched. It also means that viewers who have strong emotional reactions in the light of being able to compare their experience with Nina's will feel compelled to confront the question of what they *really* believe about what, if anything, lies beyond physical death.

Jesus of Montreal is not simply about death or the after-life, even though I have chosen to include it in this chapter. It is an imaginative, contemporary interpretation of the Jesus story which is prepared to pose critical questions of orthodoxy, whilst nevertheless highlighting the Jesus story's relevance to current media culture. As far as viewer response is concerned, the viewer is lured into the Jesus story, and invited to consider how it works existentially. In other words, features of the narratives about Jesus' life (the Gospels) appear both as stories about Jesus as a past figure and as examples of challenges and dilemmas in contemporary living. Viewers are thus confronted with Jesus' anger at the money-changers in the Temple in Jerusalem (as told, for example, in the Gospel of Mark 11.15–19[3]) in the form of Daniel's wrath at the way Mireille (Catherine Wilkening) is treated at an advertising audition. The Temptation Narrative – in which Jesus is portrayed as being tempted in the desert by Satan (in the Gospels of Matthew, 4.1–11, and Luke, 4.1–13[4]) – is reflected in the way that Daniel and his actors are taken to the upper storey of an office-block and shown the whole city. It is presented to them as if it could be theirs.

Admittedly, such existential participation in the film depends on familiarity with narratives about Jesus as they appear in the Gospels of the New Testament. But the dovetailing of Passion Play and contemporary story is so well done in the film, that even a most basic familiarity encourages viewers to reflect on how the two narratives may interweave at many points.

At the end of the film, viewers of a nervous disposition may wince as Daniel Coulombe's body is cut open to enable his heart to be used in a transplant operation. His eyes are also used. This is a further example of how the Jesus story is existentially interpreted in the film, and perhaps the most striking. As 'the only postmodernist resurrection available',[5] this scene continues the film's invitation to the viewer to inhabit the Jesus story. At the same time, it suggests the limitations of the Christian story to carry meaning in the same way as has happened for most of Christian history. The viewing experience itself marks out an aesthetic limit for the communication of Christian meaning. The experience of watching *Jesus of Montreal* is ethically empowering. But it is implied that the Jesus story can be no more than this in the present. The viewer is to be involved in the film in order to consider living differently. But no afterlife is possible, and whether the church is needed remains a moot point.

Field of Dreams is ultimately a warm, nostalgic film, which can function for viewers at a deep psychological level. Though it, too, seems to deal with a form of life beyond death, through the baseball players who return from beyond death to play in Kinsella's field, concern for 'life beyond' is not the film's main concern. Viewers are invited to consider their own past hurts that may need resolving. The primary way in which the film works is through its invitation to viewers to consider the way they handle their capacity to imagine. The film is an exploration of the function of the imagination in human well-being. Without facilitating a philosophical exploration of what constitutes 'reality', the film nevertheless provokes viewers to tackle the question of what Kinsella really thinks is happening, and what they themselves do with the seemingly irrational aspects of their lives. Does Kinsella hear voices? What does he simply imagine in his head? It cannot be doubted that Kinsella's life is affected by what he dreams, and what he deems to be an instruction from beyond himself ('If you build it, he will come'). But the film's cosy warmth admittedly runs the risk of obscuring the significance of the material it is handling.

Film critic Roger Ebert comments: 'It's a religious picture, all right, but the religion is baseball.'[6] I am not myself sure it matters whether this is any kind of 'religious picture'. It certainly leaves the viewer wondering what the borderlines are between reality, fantasy and madness. That the film can be called religious at all therefore reminds viewers and interpreters of the film alike that religion is concerned to probe those borderlines. To those who do not understand religion, all religion seems like madness. When its use of fantasy and imagination are respected, however, through its attention to the role of vision in human life, then religion's role can be more positively appreciated. *Field of Dreams* offers an exposition of how bizarre religious faith can seem, because any such form of living out of 'another world' can provoke the same kind of responses as Kinsella receives when he seeks to articulate his vision.

The film may therefore be readily comprehensible to a religious person who knows what it is like to live with a seemingly irrational, yet life-shaping vision as a passion. The film may seem strange, though evoke wholesome nostalgia, in a viewer who sees no obvious parallel between Kinsella's way of living and a religious approach to life. Yet by the way the film works, for any viewer touched in their own experience by the impact of Kinsella's vision upon his life, then the interplay of imagination, life-experience, healing of memories and future orientation is striking.

Connecting questions and issues

None of the three films studied necessitates any clear, single conviction about life beyond physical death. In this respect they reflect contemporary caution about believing anything concerning what lies beyond death. Nevertheless, death, its impact on this life, the possibility of existence beyond this life and the meaning of resurrection are directly addressed in these films. They therefore evoke a range of questions with which Christian theology has long dealt. The contemporary, and distinctly this-worldly, forms in which the films relate to such questions both shapes, and is challenged by, the way in which Christian theology formulates them. Furthermore, to pick up a key theme left hanging from the previous chapter, it will be important to explore how all considerations about 'the end' relate to the concept of the Kingdom, or Reign, of God. What form, then, do contemporary eschatological questions take?

- How is death to be understood? Is physical death the end of a person? If not, what happens to a person, given that it is clear that the body comes to an end? Does Christianity support resurrection or immortality, or try to combine both? What can resurrection possibly mean? Why has Christianity emphasized resurrection *of the body*?
- What is the link, if any, between belief in the resurrection of Jesus Christ and the resurrection of others? Are only believers resurrected, or all people?
- And what about the concept of judgment, which is often linked in religious thinking about the end-times? Is it an idea which is no longer tenable? Has judgment been redefined as something which occurs already in this life? If so, in what way is this still divine judgment?
- Can the concept of heaven and hell carry any real meaning today, other than as symbols of wonderful and awful contemporary human experiences?
- How is the Kingdom of God to be understood, and how useful is it as a concept today? In the New Testament Gospels it is used to denote something about the future which also shapes the present. Is the Kingdom of God therefore tenable as anything other than a concept denoting an imagined future?
- Where do all these questions leave the question of God itself? What does it means to speak of 'God' in relation to death, judgment, resurrection, immortality, heaven, hell and visions of the future?

As with all chapters in this second part of the book, these questions again set out a much larger agenda than our discussion of the films requires or than can be entered into here. They do, however, indicate how broad Christian thinking about 'the end' has been throughout the history of the church.

Explorations: after-life; judgment; Kingdom of God; vision

The question 'what's going to happen to us when we die?' may not crop up very often in daily life in any explicit way. But the question lurks behind most of what we do as human beings. For how we answer the question affects how we live. If we think that when we die, that's it, then the entire focus of living is on this present life. There is, in addition, unlikely to be much sense of being held to account in any way for actions undertaken, except in terms of their immediate or long-term conse-quences upon people around us. If we introduce some notion of continued, or resurrected, existence beyond physical death – be that immediately on death, or at some future point – then questions arise not only about the form of that existence, but also the nature of the continuity with our present lives. We are likely to consider the possibility of a causal link between our conduct in this life and any future form of existence ('if we behave like this, then . . . '). This way of thinking is certainly present across most of the world's religions, and Christianity is no exception. Eschatology is thus the branch of theology which asks the ultimate questions about life (where is it all going?) in a way which links faith with ethics and with basic questions about who God is, what God is able to do, and what God will do (in the end).

For much of Christian history it seems unlikely that there was much concern about individual survival. It was assumed on the basis of many Old and New Testament texts that all people would continue to exist beyond their physical deaths. There are passages in the Hebrew Bible/Old Testament that imply that death really is the end.[7] The overall picture for those who receive Old and New Testaments together as Christian scripture, however, is that there is life beyond physical death. In the same way that Jesus was raised from the dead, so will all people be resurrected. A passage from the Apostle Paul's writings has functioned normatively in Christian tradition:

> Now if Christ is preached as raised from the dead, how can some of you say that there is no resurrection of the dead? But if there is no resurrection of the dead, then Christ has not been raised; if Christ has not been raised, then our preaching is in vain and your faith is in vain.
> (I Corinthians 15.12–14)

Such passages are unlikely to have been as individualistically interpreted for most of the church's history as they are in the modern period. It was arguably only with the rise of attention paid to the individual that emerged in various stages throughout Western cultural history – with the Renaissance, the Reformation and the Enlightenment – that concerns about resurrection would be preoccupied with the survival of the individual.[8] In the modern and postmodern worlds, in the context of rising incredulity that any form of existence beyond physical death is tenable, this focus on the sheer possibility of the individual's survival is understandable.

It is this background which creates the context for the three films we have considered. None of them provides a convincing, clear-cut case for considering that any belief in existence beyond physical death should be maintained. Each addresses the question in a different way. By the way it treats the 'return' of Jamie to Nina's life, *Truly Madly Deeply* suggests that embodiment is such a constitutive part of human identity, that no understanding of the existence or presence of a person is possible without a body. This could be taken one of two ways. Either it confirms the widely held Western cultural assumption that when a person has died, their life has indeed been totally extinguished. Jamie's return therefore really is wholly in Nina's head. Or it indicates a recognition that if there is any continued, or resurrected, existence then it clearly must be in some sort of embodied form, because we can only conceive of people who have identities being embodied. This second interpretation therefore finds the film sharing the Apostle Paul's wrestling with what form a resurrected body could possibly take:

> But some one will ask, 'How are the dead raised? With what kind of body do they come?' . . . God gives it a body as he has chosen . . . What is sown is perishable, what is raised is imperishable . . . It is sown a physical body, it is raised a spiritual body. If there is a physical body, there is also a spiritual body . . . flesh and blood cannot inherit the kingdom of God, nor does the perishable inherit the imperishable.
>
> (I Corinthians 15.35, 38, 42, 44, 50)

Paul comes close here to speaking of the immortality of the soul or spirit, even whilst arguing for resurrection. But in speaking of resurrection he knows that death really does occur. The human spirit or soul does not float off from the body and continue unaffected. Any new existence is totally God's doing. It is God who does the raising. And because existence needs a body, then there must be a resurrection body. But as to what form that body will take, Paul naturally flounders too. Nevertheless Paul and *Truly Madly Deeply* are in agreement. If we are to talk of continued, or resurrected, existence at all, then it is understandable that we must speak of bodies. Otherwise we would not be able to speak of human identity at all.

Truly Madly Deeply leaves open, however, what it really 'means' as a film. In its handling of bereavement it knows it cannot offer a conclusive answer to the question of what happens after death. We can only deal in practice with what happens to those who continue to live. In the meantime, differences in belief and thought persist. Nina's conversation with her Greek Orthodox friend Maura (Stella Maris), where options in belief about the afterlife are considered, are a case in point.

The dominance of attention to the impact on this life of beliefs about the future and what lies beyond death continues in both of the other two films considered in this chapter. In the case of *Jesus of Montreal* we see both how resurrection is interpreted in relation to this present life (others can go on living through organ donation) and how the Jesus narratives can prove useful for contemporary living (through experiential echoes of stories about Jesus). The Jesus story therefore has an ethical use. We can act to enable others, beyond our death, to go on living. And people can choose to have their life shaped by seeing how the story of Jesus as narrated in the Gospels informs the way they view their lives now. *Jesus of Montreal* thus presents the theologian with the prospect of all eschatological concerns being collapsed into ethics. If there is nothing beyond physical death, then we really must be wholly concerned about the present, knowing that there is no appeal to future judgment, or to heaven and hell, to enable us to shape contemporary decision-making. Recourse to such concept would at best be imaginative, and at worst manipulative. Jesus remains helpful. But he remains helpful as the figure within a richly evocative story the re-telling of which is best thought of in terms of the ethical life.

This challenge of *Jesus of Montreal* to Christian theological thinking about 'the end' should not be treated lightly. Few Christians would want to dispute that the eschatological dimensions of the Jesus story have ethical import, whatever beliefs are held about death, resurrection, judgment or heaven and hell. The Kingdom of God – the main emphasis of Jesus' preaching and activity – is presented in the New Testament Gospels as Good News for the poor, the meek, the persecuted, those who are hungry and thirsty, who mourn, and those who seek peace (Matthew 5.1–11, Luke 6.20–23). Jesus was seen as being the embodiment of this Kingdom, through his own teaching and healing activity. In and through Jesus' words and actions the Kingdom that was promised *had* arrived (Matthew 12.28, Luke 11.20). Jesus' actions were recognized as the beginning of the end, for, as Isaiah had prophesied, people would be set free and the blind would be able to see. This was happening as a result of what Jesus said and did (Luke 4.16–20, quoting Isaiah 61.1–2). It is therefore scarcely surprising that early followers of Jesus brought together contemporary events and their sense of the end of all things.

In the context of first century eschatological expectation, furthermore, the urgency and ultimacy of acting on the basis of the insights that resulted from Jesus' action and the interpretation of his immediate followers would have been clear. The Gospel of Matthew injects an element of threat into its narration of the Jesus story that may or may not have been in the earliest tellings, but the importance of recognizing both the truth of early Christian proclamation and of its ethical consequences is very apparent:

> the King will say to those at his right hand, 'Come, O blessed of my Father, inherit the kingdom prepared for you from the foundation of the world; for I was hungry and you gave me food, I was thirsty and you gave me drink, I was a stranger and you welcomed me, I was naked and you clothed me, I was sick and you visited me, I was in prison and you came to me.' . . . 'Truly, I say to you, as you did it to the least of these who are members of my family, you did it to me.' Then he will say to those at his left hand, 'Depart from me, you cursed, into the eternal fire prepared for the devil and his angels; for I was hungry and you gave me no food, I was thirsty and you gave me no drink, I was a stranger and you did not welcome me, naked and you did not clothe me, sick and in prison and you did not visit me.' . . . 'Truly, I say to you, as you did it not to one of the least of these, you did it not to me.' And they will go away into eternal punishment, but the righteous into eternal life.
>
> (Matthew 25.34–6, 40–3, 45–6)

The ethical challenge of Christian eschatology has thus been there from the start. Yet questions remain. What image of God is communicated by such apparent threats? What if images of God in Christian belief have undergone shifts at other points that question God's desire to inflict such punishment? What if judgment of this kind has no real place in Christian thinking and notions of hell or total annihilation are misplaced? On the other hand, what happens to human conduct if there is no sense of judgment? Is this text not just one way of recognizing that some sort of sense of cosmic justice must be true? (Or was Sartre indeed right? If there is no God, everything is permitted.) In response to all of this, how can Christian theology possibly proceed?

It seems to me that Christian theology has a responsibility to interpret such difficult, but ethically challenging, texts in the context clearly mapped out by such films as *Jesus of Montreal*. The film recognizes clearly the continued capacity of the Jesus narratives to function creatively and ethically in the present. But it also discloses that the ethical function cannot work in the same way as it may have done in much of the Christian past. Judgment may or may not happen. Heaven and hell may be tenable as no more than imaginative pictures. We do not know, and cannot know, for sure. But we have to decide how to live. One aspect of *Jesus of Montreal's* challenge which perhaps underplays how Christianity has worked (and will continue to work), however, is in the extent of the film's reductionism. The mutation of resurrection as a theological concept and as a hoped-for reality into an exhortation to organ donation is symptomatic of the film's downplaying of the nature and function of religious language. The collapse of eschatology into ethics that the film brings about fails fully to respect the way in which the Jesus narratives can and do function religiously. In other words, Christianity may well be quite wrong in the present to echo the Matthean threat of eternal fire in any form as a means of ensuring that the hungry are fed and the naked clothed. But the fact remains: the hungry still need feeding. How is a moral imperative to be sounded in a postmodern age? On what basis should anyone care for their neighbour? This is a central question for any form of living, religious or not. Christianity has to play its part in clarifying how its resources can help that question to be addressed and answered, so that people *are* actually fed. The imperative contained in its own narratives may need some re-thinking. But the urgency of its ethical impulse is striking and challenging.

Turning attention to *Field of Dreams* invites us to explore further how religious language functions, even though the film is not directly about religion at all. There need be no suggestion from this film that the baseball players really do return from death to play in Kinsella's Iowa cornfield. The film is a work of imaginative fiction.[9] As with the other two films considered in this chapter, this film wrestles with death and death's meaning. But in keeping with contemporary culture, its handling of death is with respect to its impact upon this life. It is, however, of interest to theology because of the way it presents the persuasive power of a visionary way of thinking. Furthermore, in its trading off nostalgia it asks the uncomfortable question of whether religions may not merely be longstanding, proven traditions of wisdom, but trading off nostalgia too.

Two features of the film are especially worthy of exploration. First, there is the almost primordial aspect of Kinsella's purpose in creating the baseball diamond. He is initially unable to detect the reason for his receiving the call to create it. But as time elapses it is clear that responding to the vision he has been given as a gift, both he and others are given also the opportunity to be granted forgiveness and reconciliation in respect of events which remain unresolved from early in their lives. The film thus offers a version of religion as therapy.[10] Rather than assume the reduction of all religion to therapy, however, a Christian theological reading of the film can acknowledge that religion can be therapeutic, and then go on to examine how and why this is the case.

Christian faith can be therapeutic precisely because it gives shape and form to a person's life, and offers a hope for the future. This is not simply a hope that enables a person to live for the following day – though it is that too. Christian hope is a dramatic, cosmic, eschatological hope. Living with respect to the Kingdom of God becomes a practical possibility. Death is not feared as final. Judgment is not considered a negative thing but becomes a prompt to live for others. Resurrection (whatever it means in detail) is up to God. All of these contribute to a practice of living in hope in a positive manner.

This entails living within a vision. The Kingdom of God thus provides a narrative framework within which people can live. The narrative about Jesus the Christ, who embodied in his own life the concept of the Kingdom of God, fills out its meaning. It is then possible for those who seek to follow Jesus to use this narrative, and relate constantly to it, in order to live according to the vision which the Kingdom of God presents. Field of Dreams brings to the screen an imaginative presentation of what it means to live according to a vision.

The dream of the Field of Dreams is not necessarily to be read, of course, as the Kingdom of God. The elements of forgiveness and reconciliation that lie at the heart of the film are compatible with thinking about what participation in the Kingdom of God entails. But it is not the whole picture. The Kingdom of God is insufficiently respected as a concept when interpreted individualistically, and solely in terms of inner well-being. As the history of the reception and use of the term in Christian thought and practice shows, the Kingdom of God is to be interpreted individually and socially, in relation to present and future, and has both spiritual and political dimensions to it.[11]

Nevertheless, Field of Dreams is instructive in that it enables viewers to gain a sense of what it means to inhabit a vision. For those who have little personal experience of how an all-consuming religious way of life might work, therefore, the film provides an experiential point of entry. The all-

consuming character of the vision by which Kinsella lives is both primordial and eschatological. It is fundamental to enabling him to take account
of his past and to reach a settled identity. At the same time it wholly shapes
his life. Similarly, a religious outlook on life really can take over all things
in a person's life. In some respects it is important that it should, otherwise
faith will not prove life-shaping. This element of 'ultimacy' is crucial, as a
religious faith provides a total framework within which a person lives their
life, including the future. But it is the all-consuming character of a religious vision that can also prove its danger. Religious ways of looking at life
can be so dominant that no room is left in a person's outlook for any
encounter with another's view, or for critical appraisal of one's outlook. It
is understandable to some degree. For all is not reducible to reason. Vision
includes that which goes beyond reason, without being simply irrational.
But the danger of how religions work does have to be acknowledged.

The second feature of the film worth exploring connects directly with
this. That is the fact that only Kinsella and his family can see the baseball
players who come to play in the cornfield. This mixture of nostalgia and
vision that Kinsella's action produces, therefore, is for a chosen few. It is
difficult not to interpret this in terms of the ever-present danger of
Gnosticism in religious thought: the view that some people are born with
a divine spark and others without.[12] How is a visionary approach to life to
be sustained with succumbing to Gnosticism? Those who live with
purpose, within an explicit framework of meaning which it is claimed is
God-given, will face the opposition of being 'secretive', or detached. They
will face the incredulity of many, whether or not such opposition is justi-
fied. Living within the context of a powerful, life-shaping vision inevitably
raises questions about that vision's accessibility and comprehensibility.

It is here, I think, where the film's effect and its after-life raise questions
which attention to the film itself cannot support. The website of the movie
invites tourists to come to visit the site where the movie was filmed.[13] The
invitation contains the following statement:

> The best thing about this place is what isn't here – instead of providing
> images and dreams, it is content to be a mere stage. It falls to each
> individual guest to supply whatever drama and whatever cast he or she
> desires.[14]

It is understandable why this statement is made. As a tourist attraction it is
to be claimed by no particular ideological outlook, no single religious
vision and no specific political agenda. This is pluralism at its broadest and

most generous. But it is also pluralism at its most unrealistic. This is not because any claim to have or know 'the truth' can prove itself to be ultimately true. There may indeed be many truths. It is unrealistic and problematic because there *are* conflicting truths and not all can be right. All-embracing tolerance is neither feasible nor necessarily moral.

It matters what the content of dreams is and how accessible that content is to people. Gnostics are misguided. This does not mean that it is easy to make the myths and visions by which one lives accessible or persuasive. If, however, a vision cannot be articulated and shared, so that others may potentially inhabit it, then it is by definition likely to be mistaken. The content of visions must be shared and tested. Religions are not exempt from this, however questioning they may be of much that goes on in the wider societies of which they are inevitably part. Dreaming in itself is not enough. It matters what you dream and what is done with the dream.

In the case of religion, visions of the future function as visions from the future, encompassing and shaping the present. Assumptions about who God is, what God has done, is doing and will do, including beyond death, profoundly affect how believers live their lives. In Christian theology and practice, the Kingdom of God and the resurrection of Jesus Christ are theological motifs that dominate all thinking about the future. In the narrative that Christians inhabit, they become the grounds of all hope and hopeful living.

Working conclusions

No one knows for sure what lies beyond physical death. Whatever religious, or other, convictions people have, this remains true. Everyone therefore lives within interpretative worlds that may or may not be ultimately true. At this juncture we just don't know. But this cannot be a matter of indifference. The interpretative worlds (world-views, outlooks, myths, cognitive frameworks, schemas) we live within actually shape who we are. And they contain assumptions about death, what lies beyond it (if anything) and what this means for now.

The Kingdom of God and the resurrection of Jesus Christ are two key theological motifs that shape the Christian narrative. Both relate directly to the account of the life of Jesus Christ. Both are therefore ways in which Christians undertake their God-talk. (God lifts up the poor, feeds the hungry, and so on; God is source of all life, even beyond death.) Narrating the life of Jesus provides a story for people to live within. The story enables people to live ethically responsibly in the present. Arcand saw this clearly in *Jesus of Montreal*. But it does more than this. It encapsulates the vision of what it is believed God will do ultimately. In this sense, then, the story of Jesus cannot simply be a story. It is a set of theological truth-claims cast in narrative form. This 'ending' of Christian theology is linked to the beginning in two senses. In the first sense, creation, in Christian understanding, is heading towards the Kingdom of God. This conviction is grounded in God and God's vision for the world. The second-century theologian Irenaeus of Lyons placed a heavy emphasis in his writings on the restoration of creation. He saw the work of Christ as the re-working of God's intention for humanity, through correcting what had gone wrong in Adam, and looked forward to the restoration of the whole of creation as a consequence of salvation. This interpretation of biblical themes has reverberated through Christian thought.

This ending of Christian theology is also, second, an ending of this part of the book. Here we return to the subject-matter of Chapter 2 when we looked at the ways in which God is 'imaged'. Here we are dealing with images too: pictures, visions and dreams. No version of 'the end' can simply 'tell it like it is', because we cannot. There is bound to be a gap between ideal and real, between vision and reality. So we are caught up, still, in words, and networks of meaning. But we still have to fashion visions. For without them, though it is a fraught exercise to articulate and use them, people perish.

For further study

Biblical passages that can assist reflection on the themes covered in this chapter include:

Isaiah 24 A stinging passage from the classical prophet concerning God's judgment.
Isaiah 32 A more hopeful message from Isaiah, about the way in which God will deliver Israel.
Ezekiel 37.1–14 A celebrated passage which both speaks both of the restoration of Israel, and is suggestive of bodily resurrection.
Joel 2 A prophecy about the Day of the Lord (the day of judgment). The link between the coming of the Day and the outpouring of the Holy Spirit should be noted.
Matthew 12.22–8 An example of a healing conducted by Jesus, in the context of which healing and the coming of the Kingdom of God are equated.
Mark 4.26–34 Some examples of sayings of Jesus about the Kingdom of God.
Luke 24 One example of narratives reporting the resurrection of Jesus. Jesus' appearance to two followers on the road to Emmaus (24.13–35) has been especially influential in Christian tradition (including the history of art).

I *Corinthians* 15 The most extensive passage concerning resurrection and the after-life from the Apostle Paul's writings.

I *Thessalonians* 4.13–5.11 An example of the graphic way, in a climate of feverish expectation of the end of the world, that the notion of a (second) coming of Jesus was entertained by the early Christians.

Revelation 21.1–8 A passage from the last book of the Christian Bible, expressing the vision of 'John' of a new heaven and a new earth.

From the later history of Christian thought, the following texts are worthy of attention:

'Irenaeus on the Final Restoration of Creation' (= *Against Heresies* V.xxxii.1; in McGrath, pp. 611–12). In this passage Irenaeus, Bishop of Lyons in the late second century, spells out a clear belief that God's purpose is to restore creation to what God intended it to be at the start.

'Gregory of Nyssa on the Resurrection Body' (in McGrath, p. 619). This fourth-century text, based on Paul's reflections in I Corinthians 15, suggests that resurrection entails 'reconstitution of our nature to its pristine state'.

'Francis of Assisi on the Creation' (= *Canticle of the Sun* [early thirteenth century]; in McGrath, pp. 413–14). This hymn to God is mostly about creation. Its concluding stanza, however, highlights that death need not be feared.

Thomas Muentzer on the political significance of Christian faith (= *Sermon Before the Princes* [1524]; in Placher, Vol. 2, pp. 28–30). This powerful, direct sermon by one of the leaders of the radical wing of the Protestant Reformation illustrates both the intensity and dangers of religious faith. Muentzer's call on political leaders to join the overthrow of the oppression of the poor is cast in eschatological terms. It was not well received, Muentzer joined the Peasants' Revolt, and died in the cause a year later.

Walter Rauschenbusch on the concept of the Kingdom of God (= extracts from ch. 13 of *A Theology for the Social Gospel* [1917]; in Hodgson and King, pp. 317–19). Known as the theologian of the 'Social Gospel', a movement in the USA which linked theology with social activism, Rauschenbusch here spells out the importance of the Kingdom of God in the movement's theology.

Jürgen Moltmann on 'The Resurrection as Hope' (in Hodgson and King, pp. 349–50). Moltmann was one of the prime movers in bringing eschatology firmly to the forefront of Christian theology in the final decades of the twentieth century. This short text shows how.

'Richard Bauckham on Jürgen Moltmann's Eschatology' (in McGrath, pp. 638–9). This text offers a succinct exposition of Moltmann's views on eschatology.

Chapter 11

A CHRISTOLOGICAL POSTSCRIPT

IT MAY HAVE COME AS A SURPRISE to readers that there has been no chapter in this part of the book on Christology. For is not Christology the heart of Christian thought and practice?[1] And do Jesus-films not constitute a whole sub-genre of the 'biblical epic'? Christology has not, though, been absent from Part II. On the contrary, it has been present throughout. The way this has occurred constitutes a theological point that needs drawing out at this stage.

Three Jesus films have appeared in Part II: *The Passion of the Christ*, *The Last Temptation of Christ* and *Jesus of Montreal*. None of these sits easily within the genre 'biblical epic' but each has been important at a different stage as we have sought to examine how theological reflection is provoked by film. When discussing God, redemption and eschatology, explicitly Christological reflection surfaced. Christological reflection has surfaced, however, in other chapters. It was not possible to speak of God as love, in Chapter 5, without reference to Christ. In Chapter 6, it became clear that in Christian understanding Christology informs how one can discern what is and what is not 'of the Spirit of God'. The sacraments (Holy Communion especially), examined in Chapter 8, relate to Christ. Furthermore, the church, the subject of Chapter 9, understands itself to be the Body of Christ in the world, a prefiguration in the present of the Kingdom of God which Jesus embodied.

But why not, then, a chapter on Christology? There is no chapter for two reasons. First, dispersing, whilst making explicit, the Christological content of Christian theology throughout this part of the book makes clear how Christocentric Christian theology is. There is, then, a good theological reason for not detaching Christology from other themes in order to highlight Christian theology's utterly Christological nature.[2] Second, a chapter on Christology would not, I think, have had the same effect as tackling Christology in the way I have. A Christology chapter might have led to a need to parade a number of Jesus-films before the reader. And, let's face it, many Jesus-films are simply not very good as films. They are so careful not to offend, and seek to serve Christian orthodoxy, that this affects their impact as films.[3] Because it is Jesus that the films are about, and because orthodoxy is often being served, the Jesus portrayed ends up not being fully human. For how *do* you portray a 'God-Human Being' on the screen? In effect, then, they become docetic: Jesus ends up only seeming to be human, and it is the divinity that inevitably gets the upper hand. Or, at the other extreme, it may be felt that they do not make Jesus divine enough. Some evangelicals, for example, did not like *The Last Temptation* because Jesus was 'too human'. In short, film is a very, very difficult medium through which to do Christology. Therefore the Jesus-film is not conducive to doing good Christian theology.

This is why the three Jesus-films I did choose ended up dispersed throughout different chapters. *The Last Temptation of Christ* got flak because it portrayed such a human Jesus. Whether it works as a film is up to viewers to judge. But at least it is successful in offering a Jesus who, despite the extent of inner torment presented to us, is more believable than many similar filmic portrayals. *Jesus of Montreal* works because it is not only a Jesus-film. The film itself poses the question of what we, the viewers, are going to do with this story, whether we believe the Christian reading of the Jesus story or not. And *The Passion of the Christ*, in not being a Jesus-film – for it narrates but a short, if highly significant, part of Jesus' life – invites us to place it other than only in a Christology chapter anyway. This film is about God, or, at least, it is about how the death of Jesus is to be interpreted theologically, given what Christians have made of Jesus' life, death and resurrection throughout history.

It is, then, appropriate that a chapter on God, and this postscript on Christology, should frame the entire second part of this book. For it is in the oscillation between Christology and 'theology proper' (thinking about the reality and meaning of God) that all Christian theological reflection occurs. And that is what has happened throughout this part of the book, stimulated by the films that people watch, and rooted in the questions which crop up as a result in the context of everyday living.

PART III

CHRISTIAN THEOLOGY IN PRACTICE

Chapter 12

THEOLOGY AND LIFE

But life's not like that!

A TEACHING COLLEAGUE WITH WHOM I WAS in conversation when compiling this book posed a straightforward question when I sought to explain its rationale: 'But why not just get the students to read Augustine, and Calvin, and Barth, and so on? Why go all round the houses by getting them to watch all these films?' It was a fair point. I do, after all, teach in a Department of Theology and Religious Studies. I should not need to get students interested in theology's subject-matter, especially as the module on theology and film that I teach is offered at a fairly advanced level. But the exchange discloses what is at stake here. I have no need to get students interested in theology; they already are. And presumably I have had no need to get readers interested in theology either (otherwise you would not have looked at the book, and certainly would not have read this far). But how the texts from the history of theology can best be 'accessed' is often an issue. They are not just to be grasped in some cognitive or intellectual way, or located within a stream of thought, but 'got inside' existentially. It is too easy to say that 'you have to believe it to live it', for theology can be studied by those who stand outside a religious tradition. But the content of a theology *and* how it works for those who live by it will not be adequately grasped unless ways are found by which people can imaginatively and empathetically enter into the thought- and life-world of a religious believer.

In the case of this book, that means the Christian religion. In Chapter 3 I drew attention to how Christianity carries its theology. In this chapter I explore the significance of the point just made in terms of the way theology relates to living. For one way in which theology can be 'got inside' is from the perspective of informing the everyday life-decisions made by those who inhabit a religious tradition. I begin by addressing the simple point that life does not take the neat, ordered shape that Part II may seem to imply.

Do not the practices of 'being religious' and 'doing theology' simply refuse to accept life the way it is? This may, of course, be so for some individuals. Religion can indeed be escape of a negative kind: avoidance of what life actually comprises and of the challenges which life presents.[1] Furthermore, the association of religion and theology with the 'ordering' of life may disclose that anthropologists have been right all along. Religion is about structuring life in order to fend off the cosmic chaos which lurks behind all human experience.[2] To this I offer a simple response: life does have to be lived, and we need all the help we can get. If any religious tradition is involved in proven, deliberate deception, then it should be vehemently opposed. If, however, it is engaged both in the task of the searching for truth and of helping people to live in ways through which they value themselves, others and the world of which they are a part, then its efforts ought to receive the profoundest respect.

This, it seems to me, is where we have come to in handling religions in the postmodern West. Truth – with a capital 'T' – is hard to come by. No religion can claim to have it any more. But this does not make every world-view equally true, truthful or valuable. It is simply very hard to establish whether one way of looking at, and living within, the world is better (and more true or truthful) than another. But we have to try. Religions are back on the cultural radar screen in postmodern times because total secularization has not come about. They have proved not to be reducible to other forms and explanations of human experience (psychology, anthropology, sociology, or whatever). But religions are confusing, complex things. However, human beings seem to need them in some form. The attempt to 'order' life, then, is not something which explains religion away. It simply identifies something which all human beings do, whether or not they do this in an explicitly religious way.

Life therefore is 'like that'. What occurred in Part II of this book was merely a very focused example of a basic, human process. First, it was acknowledged that thinking about what it means to be a human being entails us in thinking about a whole range of matters: how our identity is formed, how we relate to others, how we relate to nature, what value we attach to the material world, what we think a human being is, how we respond to evil (in ourselves and in the world around us), which groups we attach ourselves to and why, what will happen when we die. These are all straightforward questions, without simple answers, which vex philosophers and yet are the stuff of living. They do not *require* theological answers, but have been given such answers across many religious traditions for a long time.[3] Theological responses are thus part of the range of possible answers from which people may draw as they respond to these questions when they surface in the context of everyday life.

Second, Part II offered a point of entry to looking at how a single religious tradition, Christianity, handles its own range of answers to the questions which arose. This highly structured approach to Christianity's beliefs and ideas is often not adopted even by Christians themselves. For who does believe or think systematically all of the time? But here is where *theology* has a clear role to play. As an analytical, critical discipline it presses a religious tradition to look at coherence between its key beliefs (does this belief square up with that belief?) and the comprehensiveness of its reach (does it actually address sufficiently what life throws up to be helpful?).

As a result of theology's reflective process – on the tradition that a religion carries with it, in the light of constant ongoing experience of human life – a continually evolving 'body of theological knowledge' is created which can then be brought to bear in the process of reflection on living that every human being undertakes. A version of Christian theology in that form was used in Part II. It is, however, a mistake to see that 'body of knowledge' as a rigid, fixed form. Knowledge is not static, but fluid. Religious knowledge is not simply cognitive ('knowledge that') but practical too ('knowledge how'). The content of theology reflects this.

Theology is therefore ideally suited to handle life's messiness. Far from avoiding what life throws up, theology as a discipline is about handling a living tradition, fed by the insights of a living body of people, in the service of understanding and living life to the full.

The systematic character of Christian theology

More, though, should be said about Christian theology's systematic character. All of the existential, philosophical questions identified above (how our identity is formed, how we relate to others, how we relate to nature, what value we attach to the material world, what we think a human being is, how we respond to evil, which groups we attach ourselves to and why, what will happen when we die) have theological forms. In Christian understanding, as we saw in Part II, identity questions relate to discussions about the image of God (Chapter 5). Reflection on the image of God presupposes we know something about God (4). Our relationship to nature invites us to articulate what is meant by creation (5). Asking questions about our relationships with others and the groups we attach ourselves to forces us to ask about God as love, and about church (5 and 9). How we respond to evil challenges us to think about sin and redemption and the action of God in Jesus Christ (7). Where we are heading and what, if anything, happens after death invite eschatological reflection (10).

But the questions do not arise from life or from film-watching in neatly packaged forms. I therefore shaped the responses to film-viewing. As author and theologian, I am the one pulling the strings here. I selected the films. I grouped them in a particular way, to make specific points about how theology 'relates' to what these films can be shown to do to people who view them. I may have gone part way to convincing the reader that the films really do (or can) provoke the kinds of responses I was working with. But in then locating those viewer responses within a theological framework I was perhaps distorting them and (ab)using them for my own ends. Haven't we now really reached the nub of the matter? Theology boxes human experience into pre-determined shapes. It is doing exactly what religion always does: prevents people from handling life as it really is. It is a form of psychological control, telling them how they should think and behave.

Perhaps I cannot fully escape the charge. I do accept that there is an exercise in limitation going on here. I am not claiming for a moment that the theological explorations conducted in Part II exhaust what may be provoked in viewers by the films examined. On the contrary, I am aware that all the films considered are much richer than that. I am, however, claiming that the cognitive shaping which occurred in the reflection process is not different in kind from what would happen in other disciplines (e.g. philosophy, psychology). Indeed, as the findings of cognitive psychology show quite clearly, human beings need a cognitive world – a schema, a thought-world – out of which they can make sense of human life.[4] The theological tradition within which a religious believer lives, therefore, functions in precisely this way. Theological reflection on what films do to and for people is, then, merely a worked example of one way in which human beings cognitively process their life experience.[5] In contrast to the view that a religious tradition stifles a person, Part II illustrates how the content of a theological tradition can illuminate and inform life experience.

Calling the body of theological knowledge drawn upon a 'systematic theology' does, though, undoubtedly have its drawbacks. For one thing, the implication that theology 'packages' human experience in a neat way also implies that the issues and questions which life-experience or film-watching might raise will need to be formulated in such a way that theology can relate to them at all. Theology will not, therefore, be able to do much listening, because its categories are so rigid. Talk of 'creation', for example, already contains within it a clear assumption about what a 'creator' must be like.

There is undoubtedly something in this. In theology's defence it should be said that theological traditions may only be as good as the people who use them. Can Christian theologians, then, do the listening? And are they familiar with, and critical enough of, the traditions with which they work to see whether, and how, they are applicable to the issues and questions raised? Theological convictions are not intended to be so flexible that they simply adapt to fit whatever is required of them (otherwise how would a theological tradition maintain a clear identity?). But they are not so rigid that they do not change. The history of Christian thought is a history of doctrinal change, as well as a history of continuity.

Second, the term 'systematic' may suggest a level of comprehensiveness that is simply unrealistic, implying that every topic is covered. It may be thought that every conceivable emotion, aesthetic response, ethical issue or philosophical question which a film might provoke in a viewer, has already been 'dealt with' in theology somewhere.

Again, there is something in this charge. But this is only because theological traditions in mainstream religions are wide and deep. Christianity has a 2000-year head start on a contemporary film-watcher. It should come as no surprise that a longstanding religious tradition might have something to offer a person wanting to reflect on the meaning of life. Once more, the issue boils down to how traditions are handled. Are 'links' found *too easily* (between film, reflection and theology)? If so, then this may be doing a disservice both to the theological tradition and the film in question. Reflection takes time, patience and needs careful attentiveness. Otherwise the most fruitful results of a dialogue may not have opportunity to surface.

Third, the term 'systematic theology' raises suspicions because of who, for much of Christian history, has actually been doing the systematizing. As women theologians have been stressing for decades, white, middle-class educated men are not the only ones who can do theology. If 'system' therefore comes to mean that theology consults only theological compendia written by white, male Europeans of the past when engaged in theological exploration, then it is not living theology that is being practised.

Part II, I suggest, breaks out of that way of thinking about theology anyway. But if there was any hint that the 'real theology' is primarily found in the 'For further study' sections, then I have failed to get my message over. No, these sections are used in order to facilitate the to and fro between question or issue and theological tradition. (And many of the more recent readings suggested get us, in any case, beyond the pool of white male theologians who have usually constituted 'the history of Christian thought'.) The living theology is then undertaken in the activity of questioning and reflecting which occurs between the resources. To remain theology, something must be said about God at every turn. To be Christian theology, something must be said about God with respect to Christ and the Christian tradition. But no theology is simply the re-statement of someone's words from the past.

Christian theology's systematic character is thus best understood in terms of coherence, rather than rigid (over-)structuredness. It is worth recalling this systematic character in remembering that themes that are explored do affect each other. You cannot, for example, say 'all theology is about spirit, really' and then try and argue for a very strong doctrine of incarnation, or sacraments. The critical points about the term 'systematic' are, though, well made. This is why many Christian theologians have come to talk more of 'constructive' rather than 'systematic' theology. The emphasis can then be placed on the positive, contemporary end that theological reflection seeks to serve.

'Theology through film' as 'theology of/from/through culture'

Constructive theologies do not, though, simply emerge from the re-working of religious traditions in isolation from the societies and cultures of which they are a part. This has been a clear agenda of this book, and is a main lesson from the explorations conducted in Part II. The constant process of interaction between a theological tradition and engagement in life (and watching films) contributes to the way in which theology is constantly evolving. Only when this interaction is respected, and the presence of God in the midst of the world's life is acknowledged, can theology remain a living discipline. But how, then, can the relationship between theology and culture be best characterized? It is now time to return to the theoretical models of the relationship between theology and culture sketched in Chapter 2 above. I shall nuance further the model of 'theology in critical dialogue with culture' on the basis of what was achieved in Part II.

Theology undertaken in conscious, critical dialogue with culture (using film as a case-study) requires us to attend closely to prepositions. By that I mean that we need to clarify where we think the content of theology is actually coming from as theological enquiry takes place: is it 'of', 'from' or 'through' culture? If we think that theological conversation with film is an exercise in a theology 'of' culture, then this implies that theology's content is to be 'read off' from film. It is somehow already 'in' film waiting to be extracted. A theology 'from' culture may carry the same assumption, though also implies that films have to be sifted for their useful material and theology's content is thus picked out. A theology 'through' culture again implies an extraction process. But 'through' implies that films are somehow left behind in the process. It may also imply that the content of the theology was already so wrapped up beforehand that it was always simply a matter of seeing how this content became evident in films. Films thus end up being more illustrative than a truly dialogical approach implies.

All three prepositions, then, have their drawbacks. There is theology 'in' film. But even when there is theology in them, theology may not simply be interested in extracting it from film. Mel Gibson's *The Passion of the Christ*, for example, is interesting not simply because of the theology that is in it. It is intriguing also because of what it does to viewers (Christian or not) and because of what can be disclosed by critical comparison between its apparent theological outlook and a whole range of different traditions about the meaning of the death of Jesus from Christian history. Theology thus happens 'through' film. But it is, strictly speaking, theology 'between film and tradition', that is, theology through critical dialogue between film and Christian tradition. To be done well, an interpreter needs to know a film (something of its background, how it has been received, and how films 'work' generally) and a tradition (its content, and how it 'works' for those who inhabit it) very well indeed. It is a much more demanding task than first meets the eye.

Ultimately, I find the preposition 'through' the most fitting to charac-terize the theological explorations undertaken in this book. It is *theology* that I am interested in. But whatever preposition is chosen, it cannot be stressed enough that the creative approach to theology adopted here has sought to show a high regard for the products of culture, media and the arts that all people are engaged in consuming as they make and discover meaning. It is not assumed that all cultural products are of equal worth. But it is presupposed that it is very dangerous to make prior assumptions about what will or will not prove useful for theology. The theological rationale for this stance is simple: if God is indeed present and active in the world, then none can presume in advance where God is present. 'The Spirit blows where it chooses' (John 3.8).

Theology through film as practical theology

Finally, the theology of/from/through culture which results from critical dialogue with film and with what films do to people needs to be identified as 'practical theology'. What does this mean? Practical, or pastoral, theology has long been the poor relation of the sub-disciplines of theology throughout the West. Biblical studies, philosophical theology, historical theology and church history have dominated. The reasons for this cannot be documented here.[6] Where practical theology has been undertaken explicitly throughout the modern era, it has been understood as training for clergy (e.g. in liturgy or homiletics) or, more recently, in counselling skills. Over the past few decades, however, the significance of practical theology has been more widely acknowledged and its definition and relationship to other theological disciplines clarified. Furthermore, it has been recognized as a sub-discipline that is far from a specialism for the ordained. It is arguably the most basic form of theology, requiring all other theological sub-disciplines to feed into it. It is not too far-fetched to say that the father of the disciplinary structure of theology throughout the Western world, Friedrich Schleiermacher (1768–1834), has seen his aim realized. Practical theology is now the 'crown' of theological study, though not quite in the way that he expected.

Admittedly, it could be argued that practical theology has come so much to the fore in theology because of the steep decline in overt support for Christianity in the West. Perhaps the interest in all things practical is nothing more than an expression of the concern to demonstrate theology's 'relevance'. It is, then, for this reason that theologians are showing such interest in culture, media and film, as well as the social and human sciences. Such a negative view is much too cynical. It could be shown time after time throughout Part II that what films evoke by way of response from viewers invites theological reflection. On this basis, it is legitimate to conclude that as a form of practical theology, 'theology through film' simply illustrates in a contemporary way how theological reflection happens most naturally. Practical theology is recognized to be a process of critical reflection, using all available theological resources at one's disposal, on the issues and questions which life experience and the consumption of the products of culture present to people.

Chapter 13

THEOLOGY AND GOD

Why 'God' matters

Society depends on churches for carrying Christian theology, but depends on many interacting communities for making theology work. The arts and the media remain interested in religion. Academic institutions enable people to reflect critically on religion and theology. Readers of this book are bringing the critical study of theology alongside a critical approach to film. Such observations are descriptive of what happens in society. They also imply that society thinks this is all a good thing. But what of those who say that all theology is mistaken? Society may well accept that Christianity and many other religions carry traditions about God, and narratives for people to live within. But what if these are not just misguided but harmful?[1] If religions do harm, then any attempt to examine theological frameworks within which people are being encouraged to discover or make meaning is therefore merely adding to the harm done. Part II could then be understood as a disturbing example of brainwashing rather than a creative way of exploring aspects of what it means to be human in the light of a proven, longstanding, illuminating tradition of belief and thought. In this final chapter I therefore come back to the most basic question of all: the question of God. For if there is no God, then surely the whole edifice collapses and the only issue is whether God-talk is indeed harmful, or can be left as the private pursuit of mistaken, but relatively harmless, people.

In addressing the question of theology's potential dangers, I shall use insights that derive from recent discussion between realists and non-realists in theology. This debate centres on the question of the impor- tance of the term 'God' within human language and experience regardless of whether one can prove whether God 'exists'. Non-realists, as we shall see, are convinced there is no God 'out there', but, unlike atheists, they argue that 'God' nevertheless remains an essential concept in human thinking. This discussion is of crucial importance for what has been under- taken in this book, for it opens up all readers to potential appreciation of how religious language and theological traditions function, positively and creatively, even whilst questions of belief may be 'on hold'. I shall then conclude the book with a short section assessing the ethical, social and political significance of keeping vibrant God-talk prominent in public life.

Realism and non-realism

It may come as a surprise to many readers to think that the value of much of what has been explored throughout this book is not, in fact, dependent on the question whether God exists. Certainly a great many statements have been made throughout the text which imply God's existence. All such statements would admittedly need a radical re-think if it could be shown that there were no reality, God, existing independent of the human mind. This step has, however, been taken by some Christian theologians in the last three decades. In this part of the book I shall examine their work and its impact, and consider its relevance for understanding the theological task as it has been approached throughout this book.

What is the realism versus non-realism debate about?[2] The first thing to note is that the debate between realism and non-realism is not the same as between theism and atheism. Though it is true that atheism and non- realism are in some respects closer together than realist and non-realist forms of theism, we should not set off from the assumption that we are dealing here with a distinction between belief and unbelief. Rather, we are dealing with different forms of belief, and what the very concept of 'belief in' amounts to.

The issue with which the realism versus non-realism debate deals is not new. It examines the extent to which what the human mind can conceive and imagine relates to any reality beyond itself. Such concerns have been basic questions in theology and philosophy for millennia. But there is a sense in which the form and content of the recent debate is a modern and postmodern phenomenon. The terms of the recent debate were set in the wake of the Enlightenment, and very specifically by the nineteenth-century theologian and philosopher Ludwig Feuerbach (1804–72).[3]

But what do the terms 'realism' and 'non-realism' mean, and why are they so significant? *Realism* in theology assumes that there is a reality, God, independent of the human mind. Human beings therefore relate to God as 'other' and God relates to human beings as other, standing over against human beings as a creator to creatures. Committing oneself to a realist position in theology does not, however, mean that God therefore becomes an object in the same way as a table or a chair is an object. I may want to claim that God is a real 'other', and yet is an invisible, spiritual being rather than a visible, tangible 'other'. This would be possible within the range of views that a realist might hold. But being a realist would not necessarily commit me to such a position. I might, for example, with Paul Tillich, want to speak of God as the Ground of Being in order to ensure that, whilst thinking of God as 'other', I don't simply think of God as just one more object in the world.[4] In order to prevent God being thought of as just one more object in the world, then, and yet nevertheless being really real, theologians have to find ways of speaking of God's otherness that respects God's role as the source of all things. It is, however, primarily in order to defend and maintain a belief in the otherness of the creator God that realists hold to a realist view. If some form of realism – some form of reality independent of the human mind – is not maintained, then in realist perspective, God has become a human creation and, being subject to human control, has become a dangerous ideology.

Non-realism, by contrast, accepts that God really is a human creation. There is, in non-realist perspective, no transcendent reality 'out there', whatever name be given to it (God, Yahweh, Allah, Vishnu or whatever). All of these concepts are imaginative constructs. Taking a lead from Feuerbach, however, non-realists claim that they are not atheists. Or, rather, they are only atheists in the sense that they are against a traditional realist form of theism that claims to have knowledge of God as a transcendent being. In opposition to such a view, non-realists believe they know what is really happening with God-talk, that is they know that God-talk is really talk about human beings and that therefore all God-concepts are projections of the highest values to which human beings aspire. To call God supremely good, then, is to accept that human beings may not be good but aspire to be good. To say that God alone has or is truth is to acknowledge that human beings do not see the full picture of things, but aspire to move towards truth.

Such an approach to God-language assumes that religion is a human work and that God is a figment of the human imagination. Unlike atheism, however, non-realism does not reject God-talk. On the contrary it believes it to be essential for human well-being. For human beings need to aspire to something beyond themselves. They need always to envision better worlds, and they need conceptual forms and narratives within which to express that for which they hope. And once such concepts and narratives exist then others can live their lives within these stories of aspiration. In non-realist perspective, that is how religions work.

Both realists and non-realists are thus equally convinced that God-language is essential for human well-being. They differ over whether there is a reality outside of the human mind being referred to and related to when humans speak of God. But how does this discussion help us understand what has been happening in this book?

It is clear that the explorations in Part II could now be claimed to have happened either within a realist or non-realist theological framework. In other words, all the discussions may have been possible, and have made constructive use of Christian theology as a narrative tradition, whether or not it was believed that God is 'out there' in any sense. Personally I do not believe that all discussions would be equally possible, or many of the theological views expressed sustainable, in a non-realist framework. But to examine this would go well beyond what is possible to explore at this juncture and that is not the point I want to make. The purpose of drawing the reader's attention to the realism versus non-realism debate is to accentuate further the point that theology does its work in relation to traditions, using theological language, and with reference to collections of narratives. It does not stop there, and certainly not for those who believe in God as 'other' and seek to live a Christian life. But even for non-realists, theology does not stop at language. Non-realists see the importance of using the language about God in order to guide ethical practice.

Appreciation of the realism versus non-realism debate within 'theology through film' discussions, then, highlights in a very practical way how God-language functions. And it does this at the borders of traditional belief. It thus shows how the value of theological language is disclosed in a number of ways, yet with a profound, ethical significance. Whether one is inside or outside the church, firmly within, on the edge of, or baffled by traditional belief, the resources of Christian theology are still recognizable as of immense importance.

A spectrum of theism

The realism versus non-realism debate is important for what has been attempted in this book in one other significant respect. It has created a need to clarify that there are different kinds of belief in God and different ways of using God-language. Atheism and theism are easily polarized. But the range of ways in which people practise theism, even in Christianity, deserves more attention. It is for this reason that I have begun to speak of a 'spectrum of theism'. By this I seek to denote a range of types of belief in God from atheism at one end to naïve realism at the other.

Atheism denies the existence of God, and of the value of God-talk. It exists in two forms. Its hostile form (e.g. that of Dawkins) not only denies the existence of God and the value of God-talk. As noted, it also argues for the harm such talk causes. A gentler form of atheism makes similar denials, without concluding also that theism is harmful.

Next along the spectrum comes *non-realism*. This could also exist in two forms, a general and a particular. The *general* form is that of a non-realist 'universal spirituality'. On this understanding God may be identified as a unity that all religions and world-views seek, or as love, or as peace. There is no claim that this unity, love or peace has any reality independent of human thoughts or actions. But it may be accepted that 'God' is a way of speaking of such striving. A *particular* form of non-realism takes shape within specific religious traditions. For example, as in the work of Don Cupitt, the particular language of Christianity is re-interpreted in a non-realist form.

Agnosticism is in the middle of the spectrum. Again this can exist in two forms. A soft form of agnosticism accepts that knowledge is difficult to come by and that we cannot know for sure that God is or is not. This form may not, however, dispute the value of carrying on with God-talk so long as it proves useful in assisting human flourishing. In its hard form, agnosticism claims that it cannot by definition (and will never) be known whether or not there is a reality 'God'. Indeed, no claim can be made about truth because there is no position from which any claim for truth or untruth could be adjudged. In this version, relativism is supported so starkly that it can become a morally irresponsible position to hold. We may indeed not know. But choices have to be made, and our lack of knowledge must not prevent us from making those judgments so that we and others may live.

Critical realism begins from the assumption that God is. It respects the range of types of language that are used about God (e.g. narrative, poetic, epic, prophetic) and acknowledges fully the gap between human language about God and the reality of God which non-realism exploits. However, unlike non-realism it maintains a conviction that God is a reality. In other words, critical realism accepts that there is always human creativity in belief. Both when God is spoken about, and when envisioned or spoken to, human imagination is always at work. We may or may not have direct, unmediated access to God.[5] But critical realism acknowledges that all our attempts to describe or reflect on such experience are always mediated by language or imagery, and thus always reflects the time, place and culture within which such encounter with the reality of God occurs.

Like non-realism, critical realism exists in two forms. Particular forms of realism occur within religious traditions; for example, there are Christian critical realists and Jewish critical realists within their respective traditions. Such supporters of critical realism accept that any form of God-talk needs a specific tradition within which to operate. Critical realism may, however, also exist in a more general form. Believers may want to look beyond the specifics of their tradition in the claims they make about 'the Divine'. John Hick, for example, speaks of 'the Real' in trying to speak outside of his Christian tradition about the God who is, in a way which is comprehensible to those of other traditions.[6]

The final position on the spectrum of theism is held by *naïve realists*.[7] This position assumes that God is, and that what religious statements say about God are literally true. So, when the Apostle Paul, in I Thessalonians 4.16–17, says that at the coming of the Lord 'the dead in Christ will rise first. (17) Then we who are alive . . . will be caught up in the clouds together with them to meet the Lord in the air . . . ', it means literally that. Naïve realism therefore leaves little room for poetry or metaphor in religious language. In its literalness, it seeks to take at face value what religious language states.

'Naïve realism' may be regarded as an unnecessarily negative term to use for those who hold to this viewpoint. In truth, though, it is difficult to know how not to be critical of this position, for it fails to let religious language use the variety of forms that religion and theology need in order to do their work. How, for example, can you speak of the afterlife except in imagery, given that none of us has been there? There is, though, one important aspect of this position that should not be overlooked: its refusal to let language be the focal point of religious belief and practice. Language always refers beyond itself. So if language refers to God, then it really has to be about *God*, there is no room for talk of God somehow being 'in' the words, or as if the words are important in their own right. This position is so insistent on clarifying what the words refer to. That's why it's literalistic. It is ultimately flawed, as all fundamentalisms are. But given that non-realists would have us believe that 'all is language' it is easy to understand why fundamentalism of this kind flourishes in response.

This spectrum of theism is, I suggest, vital to respect at the end of all that has been undertaken in this book. For it reminds us that theological language can be accessed in a number of ways. It is too easily assumed by critics of religion *per se* that naïve realism is the only way in which religious language functions. Naïve realism about God-language is, however, not the only option. Bringing theological language into play in the discussions that films evoke in those who watch them thus needs great care.

I myself am a particular (Christian), critical realist who accepts a strong dose of soft agnosticism within the faith I hold and in the way I use the theological tradition I seek to inhabit. Others who access theological language will do so differently. My basic point through all of this, however, is that whatever approach is adopted, theological discussion is necessary, for those who do it, and for the society of which they are a part. For religions are carrying vital resources for people to work with in their quest to understand how to live.

And finally . . .

And why is it all so important? Simply because without such theological discussion, the kinds of experiences that people have, and questions they end up with, when watching films will be inadequately explored. Theology needs to be part of public discussion. Theological insights represent only one type of framework within which people are invited to do their reflecting. Theologians will (do!) have a hard job just now to make their voices heard in public. But this book, and others like it, are written in the conviction that societies will be all the poorer without theological traditions to inform them. That is why theology is so exciting as a discipline. So if theology is exciting, and cinema-going is fun, it is no surprise that it is highly stimulating when you put them together.

NOTES

Introduction

1 T. Inbody, *The Faith of the Christian Church: An Introduction to Theology*, Grand Rapids and Cambridge: Eerdmans 2005, p. xiv.

2 This observation about ventriloquism is made by Gerard Loughlin in 'Cinéma Divinité: A Theological Introduction' in E. S. Christianson, P. Francis and W. R. Telford (eds), *Cinéma Divinité: Religion, Theology and the Bible in Film*, London: SCM Press 2005, p. 5.

3 It thus builds constructively on the approach to film and theology adopted in my *Cinema and Sentiment: Film's Challenge to Theology*, Milton Keynes: Paternoster Press 2004.

4 I cannot offer in this book a full consideration of the questions whether this is wishful-thinking on the part of those who study religion, whether the primary purpose of cinema (to entertain) is being overlooked, and what empirical evidence exists to support the views being presented. Suffice to say that work is increasingly being undertaken which shows how film-watching plays its part within a whole range of socio-cultural practices (sport, theatre, watching/listening to comedy, music) which enable people to develop/construct their identities and to find/create meaning in life.

1 Theology in a chaotic climate

1 See, for example, the work undertaken over many years by the likes of John Cobb Jr and John Hick, and the more recent work in 'comparative theology' undertaken by Keith Ward.

2   This point will be addressed further in Chapter 2 below.

3   See, e.g., trenchantly – and at times not very rationally – Sam Harris, *The End of Faith: Religion, Terror and the Future of Reason*, London: The Free Press 2005.

4   Without some such experience within religion or theology classes, the existential aspect (and potential personal excitement) of such studies can easily be lost.

5   I have addressed the religious aspects of the contemporary Western context in 'Still Spiritual after All These Years: The Religious Context', ch. 2 of *Christianity in a Post-Atheist Age*, London: SCM Press 2002.

6   Even when viewed only in sociological or psychological perspective, religion can be seen to be more like sport than shopping: people remain committed to teams not for wholly rational reasons, but perhaps through family tradition, birthplace or regional association. The values of such association are, however, immense, in terms of belonging, identity and purpose.

7   The empirical evidence shows that people do not go to the cinema primarily for intellectual stimulus, but to escape. However, what the cinema actually does to and for cinema-goers is broader and deeper than they expect.

8   One striking example of this is the political work of the singer Billy Bragg, who campaigns with a specific anti-racist agenda for multi-racial ownership by English people of the flag of St George, lest its use be hijacked by the British National Party and its sympathizers. Bragg is supported in his work by many trade unions and campaigning groups.

9   See e.g. the evidence for decline through the twentieth century in the UK in C. Brown, *The Death of Christian Britain*, London and New York: Routledge 2001. Steve Bruce has been the most consistent supporter of the 'secularization thesis', according to which the continuing decline of support for organized Christianity is held to extend a long-term trend of secularization throughout the West (see e.g. *Religion in the Modern World*, Oxford: Oxford University Press 1996 and, more recently, *God is Dead: Secularization in the West*, Oxford: Blackwell 2002). Grace Davie offers an opposing view about the situation in the UK (*Religion in Britain since 1945: Believing without Belonging*, Oxford: Blackwell 1945) and argues for Europe as a special case, that does not suggest that continuing secularization is inevitable (*Religion in Modern Europe: A Memory Mutates*, Oxford: Oxford University Press 2000; *Europe: the Exceptional Case. Parameters of Faith in the Modern World*, London: DLT 2002).

2   Doing theology in a media age

1   Stewart M. Hoover, *Religion in the Media Age*, London and New York: Routledge 2006.

2   Hoover, *Religion*, p. 1.

3   Hoover, *Religion*, p. 9.

4   Hoover, *Religion*, p. 20.

5   In the world of theology, more so than in religious studies, it is clear that it is acceptable to have an interest in 'the arts' ('high culture': theatre, classical music, opera), whereas attention to popular culture is rarely considered theologically useful. I have addressed this issue in '"High Theology"/"Popular Theology"?: The Arts, Popular Culture and the Contemporary Theological Task' in *Expository Times* 117 (2005–06), pp. 447–51. See also

G. Lynch, *Understanding Theology and Popular Culture*, Oxford: Blackwell 2005, and K. Cobb, *The Blackwell Guide to Theology and Popular Culture*, Oxford: Blackwell 2005. The latter contains a helpful annotated bibliography of related works (pp. 324–34).

6 Allowing for the fact that the theological study undertaken may, in fact, force the student to clarify and articulate the 'values that they live by' for the first time.

7 In other words, what will happen in Part II of this present book is not different in kind from what happens for anyone watching a film. It is the resources one converses with and the frameworks within which one operates which produce differences.

8 I have considered this aspect of film's challenge to theology more fully in *Cinema and Sentiment*, Milton Keynes: Paternoster Press 2004.

9 Or, more likely, both, in the context of the gradual emergence of a rich and complex plural culture. But Christianity therefore has to adjust to its new place in such a culture.

10 It should be stressed: this does not indicate one way or another anything about the potential truth of Christian theology. Simply because meaning-making may happen less with respect to Christianity does not make Christianity wrong or misguided. But nor is the question of truth necessarily addressed by identification of where meaning-making is happening, or what activities are deemed to be especially worth-while (be they religious or not). I am simply challenging the view that Christian theology's purpose is solely to re-work the Christian dogmatic tradition from within Christianity, without reference to the complex culture within which it must do its work.

11 In 'Film and Theologies of Culture', in C. Marsh and G. Ortiz (eds), *Explorations in Theology and Film*, Oxford and Malden, MA: Blackwell 1997, pp. 21–34, esp. pp. 24–8. The options resulted from critical engagement with the widely used taxonomy of models of the relationship between Christ and culture offered by H. Richard Niebuhr, *Christ and Culture*, New York: Harper and Row 1951. See the discussion of my proposal in R. Arrandale, 'Drama, Film and Postmodernity' in G. Jones (ed.), *The Blackwell Companion to Modern Theology*, London and Malden, MA: Blackwell 2004, pp. 485–98, esp. pp. 485–6.

12 Wade Clark Roof, *Spiritual Marketplace: Baby Boomers and the Remaking of American Religion*, Princeton: Princeton University Press 1999.

13 Hoover, *Religion*, pp. 77–83 (for the summary of types) and pp. 147–204 (for the critical correlation of the insights with the interpretation of gathered empirical data).

14 Hoover, *Religion*, p. 78.

15 Hoover, *Religion*, p. 81.

16 Hoover, *Religion*, p. 193.

17 Hoover, *Religion*, p. 82.

18 Hoover, *Religion*, p. 203.

19 Hoover, *Religion*, p. 276.

20 It should be stressed immediately that hardly any religious tradition is likely to see itself as being, or ever having been, about a passive acceptance of a world-view. Religions are practices which influence people's lives. The point, of course, is that the 'negotiation' aspect of meaning-making which is so apparent in media culture has rarely been prominent in the study of the way religions work.

21 Two essays arising from this research, undertaken by Charlotte Haines Lyon, are due to appear in 2007 in collections of essays edited, respectively, by Robert K. Johnston, and by Stephanie Knauss and Alexander Ornella.

3 Theology and the Christian religion

1 p. 24 above.
2 The term 'community of practice' is explored most fully in E. Wenger, *Communities of Practice: Learning, Meaning and Identity*, Cambridge: Cambridge University Press 1998. I have explored the concept of 'community of practice' and its relevance for theology in *Christ in Practice: A Christology of Everyday Life*, London: DLT 2006.
3 To put this another way: if a person is not in a church, and not doing theology in the academy, yet sees the value of theological reflection, who is going to support them? Who is going to keep them actively engaging with, and reflecting on, theological themes in relation to life experience? Theology could be a solitary undertaking, but it would not be a very human endeavour, as it is best conceived of as a collaborative venture.
4 In this I am building on ch. 1 of *Cinema and Sentiment*, Milton Keynes: Paternoster Press 2004.
5 Two related comments are needed here. On the one hand, regular attendance at a multiplex may not, of course, expose a cinema-goer to much diversity. The frequent complaint that 'the films are all the same' is never quite true. But it is true that many interesting films (e.g. low budget, independent, sub-titled or deriving from outside Europe or North America) never make it to multiplexes. It could also be argued that Hollywood dominance conveys a rather uniform myth or set of myths about human life. On the other hand, religions are diverse within themselves in a way that those who do not inhabit them may not fully understand.
6 Catherine Bell has identified six basic types of ritual: (1) rites of passage, (2) calendrical rites, (3) rites of exchange and communion, (4) rites of affliction, (5) feasting, fasting and festivals and (6) political rites (in C. Bell, *Ritual: Perspectives and Dimensions*, New York: Oxford University Press 1997), cited in J. Lyden, *Film as Religion*, New York University Press 2003, p. 80.
7 This insight supports the objection to spirituality's frequent current detachment from religion/s. Spirituality can become mumbo-jumbo because of the lack of connectedness with traditions of proven worth.

4 God

1 These are studied in detail by Robert L. Webb in 'The Flashbacks in *The Passion*: Story and Discourse as a Means of Explanation' in K. E. Corley and R. L. Webb (eds), *Jesus and Mel Gibson's The Passion of the Christ*, London and New York: Continuum 2004, pp. 46–62.
2 This was shortened for a 2005 release, six minutes of brutality being removed in order to reach a wider (younger) audience.
3 Kimberley Blessing does, however, offer this as one of her discussion questions at the end of her chapter 'Deceit and Doubt: The Search for Truth in *The Truman Show* and Descartes's *Meditations*', in K. A. Blessing and P. J. Tudico (eds), *Movies and the Meaning of Life: Philosophers Take on Hollywood*, Chicago and LaSalle Illinois: Open Court 2005, pp. 3–16.
4 The best survey of Jesus-films is by W. Barnes Tatum, *Jesus at the Movies: A Guide to the First Hundred Years*, Santa Rosa: Polebridge Press 1997 (2nd edn, 2004).

5 This point is brought out tellingly by John Dominic Crossan in 'Hymn to a Savage God', in Corley and Webb, *Jesus and Mel Gibson's The Passion of the Christ*, pp. 8–27.

6 This also means, of course, that religious communities can be averse to critical examination (internally or externally) of the images and concepts of God with which they work.

7 And as is clear from the evidence of responses to the film it is not always clear to many Christian viewers. Admittedly, Christianity itself does not help matters through the way in which it has fostered traditions which have over-emphasized the death of Jesus and/ or have fostered reflection or meditation on the death in isolation from the life and resurrection of Jesus. See on this further Chapter 7 below.

8 The importance of recognizing how religious imagery is carried in societies by religious communities was noted in Chapter 3.

9 Keith Ward's work should be emphasized here. See, e.g., his tetralogy *Religion and Revelation*, Oxford: Clarendon Press 1994; *Religion and Creation*, Oxford: Clarendon Press 1996; *Religion and Human Nature*, Oxford: Clarendon Press 1998; and *Religion and Community*, Oxford: Clarendon Press 2000. See also the volume of essays on his work: T. W. Bartel (ed.), *Comparative Theology: Essays for Keith Ward*, London: SPCK 2003.

10 In the same way that philosophers, economic theorists or sociologists, for example, may choose a particular 'school of thought' within which to undertake research and develop fresh insights. The parallel is not perfect, of course, but it is a helpful one to make if only to counter the view that theology is inevitably somehow 'biased', 'unacademic' or insufficiently rational or objective, whilst other disciplines are more detached, rational and free from prejudice.

5 Human being

1 The former verdict is offered in J. Walker (ed.), *Halliwell's Film and Video Guide 2004*, London: HarperCollins 2003, p. 469. The latter judgment is that of Gareth Higgins, *How Movies Helped Save My Soul: Finding Spiritual Fingerprints in Culturally Significant Films*, Lake Mary, Fl.: Relevant Books 2003, p. 119.

2 The McCarthy quotation is from his *Variety* film review of 12.03.04 (www.variety.com).

3 R. Ebert, *The Great Movies*, New York: Broadway Books 2002, p.138.

4 This point will be explored further in Chapter 7 below.

5 See, e.g., the Niebuhr reading at the end of this chapter, and that by Augustine recommended at the end of Chapter 7.

6 See the Hampson reading suggested in Chapter 7.

7 The 'Kingdom of God' is a concept describing the will of God for the whole of creation. It will be considered further in Chapter 10 below.

8 For brief comments on this point see my *Christ in Focus*, London: SCM Press 2005, pp. 194–9, and the extensive treatment in A. McFadyen, *Bound to Sin: Abuse, Holocaust and the Christian Doctrine of Sin*, Cambridge: Cambridge University Press 2000.

9 Ed Guerrero, *Do The Right Thing*, London: BFI 2001, p. 82.

10 A relevant extract from Augustine's work is listed under 'For further study' below.

11 God is therefore 'like' a human being in so far as a human being has a store of memories, which need to be understood and lovingly shaped. This is a way of understanding

God the Father's going out from Godself in the form of the Son, with the Spirit being the loving will between them.

12 The Psalms contain many references to such notions, e.g. Psalm 25.7: 'Do not remember the sins of my youth or my transgressions; according to your steadfast love remember me, for your goodness' sake, O Lord', and Psalm 51.1–2: 'Have mercy on me, O God, according to your steadfast love; according to your abundant mercy blot out my transgressions. Wash me thoroughly from my iniquity, and cleanse me from my sin.'

13 These are the different names given to the sacrament across different Christian traditions, some of whom resist referring to it as a 'sacrament' due to their seeing the ritual act more as a memorial meal with symbolic significance. This topic will be considered further in Chapter 8 below.

14 The further reading suggested at the end of Chapter 8 provides leads for the reader to follow up.

15 In film see, e.g., *Memento* and *Being John Malkovich* and the chapter ('Personal Identity') devoted to these two films in M. Litch, *Philosophy Through Film*, New York and London: Routledge 2002.

16 With respect to the burden of individual misdeeds, Thomas Cranmer's prayer of confession, included in the *Book of Common Prayer* of 1662, for example, contains the especially expressive line: ' . . . the memory of them is grievous unto us and the burden of them is intolerable . . . '.

17 Salvation will be explored further in Chapter 7 below.

18 When misunderstood or misconstrued it has also proved profoundly damaging. The capacity of Christianity to induce guilt and repress understandably provokes the opposition to Christianity in particular, and to religion in general, from such contemporary writers as Ludovic Kennedy, Sam Harris and Richard Dawkins, not to mention a whole stream of UK journalists, including, e.g., Johann Hari, Joan Smith and Philip Hensher. Whether this feature of Christian practice is specific to Christianity, or is evidence more of what happens when a valuable (and socially necessary) function of religion goes awry, lies beyond the scope of this study. I naturally tend to the latter view.

19 This can prove quite literally true in the case of people who suffer from Alzheimer's disease. There is considerable evidence from pastoral work that though people lose their sense of self, they can also 'come to life' within the context of recalled words of liturgy or hymnody. There is thus a sense of deeper belonging than is evident to the conscious self.

20 Cited in W. C. Placher (ed.), *Essentials of Christian Theology*, Louisville and London: Westminster John Knox Press 2003, p. 7.

21 More will be said on how Christianity uses narratives about Jesus to inform the Christian life in Chapter 7 below.

22 Though as a covenant relationship celebrated before God, marriage institutionalizes (and treats sacramentally) the deep commitment of two people to each other.

6 Spirit

1 Cited in John Walker (ed.), *Halliwell's Film, Video and DVD Guide* 2004, London: HarperCollins 2003, p. 488.

2 The quotation is from the Nicene Creed (which is strictly speaking the Nicene-Constantinopolitan Creed) of 381 CE.

3 The legitimacy and function of the 'speakers in tongues' has created much consternation and division throughout Christian history.

4 The relationship between theology and work, leisure, recreation and anything which can be considered 'entertainment', becomes important here. Exploration of a 'theology of leisure', or of the importance for theology of entertainment or popular culture is not a matter of theologizing about people's spare time. On the contrary, in the contemporary West it is crucial for understanding, at a time of steep decline in the support of organized religion, how meaning-making is happening. On this see, e.g., my '"High Theology"/"Popular Theology"?: The Arts, Popular Culture and the Contemporary Theological Task' in *Expository Times* 117 (2005–06), pp. 447–51, but especially also Stewart M. Hoover, *Religion in the Media Age*, London and New York: Routledge 2006.

5 I began to explore aspects of the 'escape' motif in *Cinema and Sentiment*, Milton Keynes: Paternoster Press 2004.

6 Especially as a result of Max Weber's 1904–05 work on *The Protestant Ethic and the Spirit of Capitalism*.

7 Other films which enable exploration of this issue include *My Left Foot* and *Inside, I'm Dancing!*

8 Aspects of eschatology will be considered further in Chapter 10 below.

7 Redemption

1 D. Kelsey, *Imagining Redemption*, Louisville: Westminster John Knox Press 2005, pp. 5–6.

2 Kelsey, *Imagining Redemption*, p. 5.

3 David Rooney, Review of *21 Grams* on www.variety.com.

4 1955 is the date of the Greek original. The English translation appeared in 1960. For a discussion of the significance of the novel and the film, see Darren J. N. Middleton (ed.), *Scandalizing Jesus?: Kazantzakis's The Last Temptation of Christ Fifty Years On*, London and New York: Continuum 2005. For discussions of the film within theology and religious studies, see, e.g., M. R. Miles, *Seeing and Believing: Religion and Values in the Movies*, Boston: Beacon Press 1996, ch. 2; W. B. Tatum, *Jesus at the Movies: A Guide to the Fist Hundred Years*, Santa Rosa, CA: Polebridge Press 1997, ch. 11; Lloyd Baugh, *Imaging the Divine: Jesus and Christ-Figures in Film*, Kansas City: Sheed and Ward 1997, ch. 4; R. C. Stern, C. N. Jefford and G. Debona, *Savior on the Silver Screen*, Mahwah: Paulist Press 1999, ch. 8; Bryan P. Stone, *Faith and Film: Theological Themes at the Cinema*, St Louis: Chalice Press 2000, ch. 5.

5 On the interplay between film and Jesus study, see my 'Jesus as Moving Image: The Public Responsibility of the Historical Jesus Scholar in the Age of Film' in S. Porter and T. Holmen (eds), *The Handbook of the Study of the Historical Jesus Vol. III*, forthcoming, Leiden: Brill 2007.

6 On redemption as a motif in Scorsese's work, see, e.g., D. Graham, 'Redeeming Violence in the Films of Martin Scorsese' in C. Marsh and G. Ortiz (eds), *Explorations in Theology and Film*, Oxford: Blackwell 1997, pp. 87–95, and C. Deacy, *Screen Christologies: Redemption and the Medium of Film*, Cardiff: University of Wales Press 2001.

7 *Hoop Dreams* (Steve James, 1994) is a good example.

8 I have dealt at some length with the effectiveness of *The Shawshank Redemption* (Frank Darabont 1994) in *Cinema and Sentiment*, Milton Keynes: Paternoster Press 2004, ch. 3. See also Mark Kermode, *The Shawshank Redemption*, London: BFI Publishing 2003, for an exploration of the film which actually takes into account viewer responses.

9 See, for example, Jack's exchange with the prison pastor in Scene 15 (on the DVD version) and the comment in Scene 17 that before he 'didn't believe anything' but that now 'everything has to do with God'.

10 This has been Scorsese's claim about the film. See Stone, *Faith and Film*, p. 75.

11 Both Baugh (*Imaging the Divine*, p. 71) and Stone (*Faith and Film*, p. 75) are concerned about the masochistic elements in Dafoe's portrayal of Jesus.

12 On this, see my *Christ in Focus*, London: SCM Press 2005, pp. 193–7.

13 This will be explored further in Chapter 9 below.

14 I have explored this more fully in *Christ in Practice: A Christology of Everyday Life*, London: Darton Longman and Todd 2006.

8 Sacraments

1 The following description of the plot of the film is adapted from the insightful study of the film by D. Rhoads and S. Roberts, 'From Domination to Mutuality in *The Piano* and in the Gospel of Mark', in C. Marsh and G. Ortiz (eds), *Explorations in Theology and Film*, Oxford: Blackwell 1997, pp. 47–58, here esp. pp. 47–51.

2 Rhoads and Roberts point out the link between possession of people and of land at work in the film ('From Domination', pp. 48–9).

3 See, e.g., L. Baugh, *Imaging the Divine: Jesus and Christ-Figures in Film*, Kansas City: Sheed and Ward 1997, pp. 137–45; B. P. Stone, *Faith and Film: Theological Themes at the Cinema*, St Louis: Chalice Press 2000, pp. 156–66; R. M. Anker, *Catching Light: Looking for God in the Movies*, Grand Rapids and Cambridge: Eerdmans 2004, pp. 191–214.

4 It is also true that there is an artistic motif in *Don't Look Now* in so far as John Baxter is a restorer of old churches, though this is not significant for the interpretation of the film I am offering here. Within the plot of the film itself, it symbolizes the restorative work being undertaken in John and Laura's life as a married couple through their trip to Venice and functions as a counter to the belligerent rationalism which contributes to his death.

5 The comment on *Don't Look Now*'s love-making scene is from S. Benson, 'Don't Look Now' in J. Bernard (ed.), *The X List: The National Society of Film Critics' Guide to the Movies that Turn Us On*, Cambridge, Mass.: The Da Capo Press 2005, pp. 81–3, here p. 83.

6 I am conscious that such a statement may underplay what film scores *always* contribute to films, and comments about the extent to which those of us writing about film in theology and religious studies often overlook film music are sometimes made (see, e.g., Jeremy Begbie, 'Unexplored Eloquencies: Music, Media, Religion and Culture' in J. Mitchell and S. Marriage (eds), *Mediating Religion: Conversations in Media, Religion and Culture*, London and New York: T & T Clark 2003, pp. 93–106). But here the film score not only works well in the film but has had an afterlife in its own right as an aid to reflection and meditation, both as a piece of music and through evoking memories of the film-

watching experience. On the use of music in the film, see Claudia Gorbman, 'Music in *The Piano*' in H. Margolis (ed.), *Jane Campion's* The Piano, Cambridge: Cambridge University Press 2000, pp. 42–58.

7 Rhoads and Roberts, 'From Domination', p. 51.
8 Rhoads and Roberts, 'From Domination', pp. 50 and 51.
9 Roeg cited in Mark Sanderson *Don't Look Now*, London: British Film Institute 1998, p. 80.
10 I have explored this association more fully in 'Did You Say "Grace"?: Eating in Community in *Babette's Feast*' in C. Marsh and G. Ortiz (eds), *Explorations in Theology and Film: Movies and Meaning*, Oxford: Blackwell 1997, pp. 207–18.
11 In mainstream Christianity, only the Society of Friends and the Salvation Army do not celebrate Holy Communion in some form.
12 Cited from Alister McGrath, *The Christian Theology Reader*, 2nd edn, Oxford: Blackwell 2001, p. 531.
13 Cited from McGrath, *Christian Theology Reader*, p. 532.
14 I have explored this point at length in *Christ in Practice: A Christology of Everyday Life*, London: DLT 2006.
15 Limited in the sense that unlike Jesus Christ she does not give her life.
16 The quotation is from *The Methodist Worship Book*, Peterborough: Methodist Publishing House 1999, p. 197. This aspect of the celebration of Holy Communion has been especially prominent since it featured as one of the ways of understanding the sacrament in the very influential World Council of Churches Faith and Order report *Baptism, Eucharist and Ministry*, Geneva: World Council of Church 1982.

9 Church

1 I have considered the danger of placing too great an emphasis on the church in my *Christ in Focus: Radical Christocentrism in Christian Theology*, London: SCM Press 2005. I note there that the church can take centre stage (ecclesiocentrism), when it is actually the person and work of Christ that needs to be central in both Christian thought and practice. See ch. 3, esp. pp. 60–1.
2 Ang Lee is now better known for such films as *The Ice Storm, Sense and Sensibility, Crouching Tiger, Hidden Dragon* and *Brokeback Mountain*.
3 David Rooney, review at www.variety.com (posted 30.08.02).
4 http://www.imdb.com/title/tt0318411/.
5 Accepting the fact that however much one might wish to defend the church, one may have to confront the fact that the most basic reason they existed may be because of Christianity's difficulties in dealing with sexuality.
6 See, e.g., the interview cited by Warren Curry on the cinemaspeak.com web-site.
7 Strictly speaking, this should read 'to the rest of the laity', as the ordained are part of the *laos* (the whole people of God). 'Laity' has, rather misleadingly, come usually to denote the non-ordained membership of the church.
8 On which, see further Chapter 8 above.
9 I have explored this more fully in *Christ in Practice: A Christology of Everyday Life*, London: DLT 2006, pp. 103–13.
10 On this, see further Chapter 10 below.

10 The end

1 Lloyd Baugh, *Imaging the Divine: Jesus and Christ-Figures in Film*, Kansas City: Sheed and Ward 1997, calls *Jesus of Montreal* a 'Film of Transition' (pp. 113–29).

2 *Variety* refers to its script as 'hobbled with cloying aphorisms and shameless sentimentality' (http://www.variety.com/review/VE1117790890?categoryid=31&cs=1&query=%2A). Even the film location's website appeals to 'traditional values' (http://www.fieldof dreamsmoviesite.com/distance.html).

3 The story also appears in the Gospels of Matthew (21.12–17), Luke (19.45–48) and John (2.13–22). The early position of the story in John's Gospel is usually thought to relate to John's theological purpose. Historically, the event is more likely to have taken place late in Jesus' life, and been a major cause of Jesus' provocation of the opposition that led to his being crucified.

4 A much shorter version appears in the Gospel of Mark 1.12–13.

5 B. Babington and P. W. Evans, *Biblical Epics: Sacred Narrative in the Hollywood Cinema*, Manchester: Manchester University Press 1993, 98.

6 Review of the film, 21 April 1989 (www.rogerebert.com).

7 'As for mortals, their days are like grass; they flourish like a flower of the field; for the wind passes over it, and it is gone, and its place knows it no more' (Psalm 103.15–16). The Psalm goes on to contrast transient humanity with the 'steadfast love of the Lord', but there is no clue in this Psalm that the Lord's steadfast love means that people survive beyond death.

8 'Arguable' because even in Paul there is great concern for the individual (see, e.g., Romans 7.7–25), a concern which proved very influential on twentieth-century Christian existentialists such as Rudolf Bultmann.

9 As Roger Ebert rightly notes: 'The movie sensibly never tries to make the slightest explanation for the strange events that happen after the diamond is constructed' (www.rogerebert.com).

10 And, interestingly, Jungian interpretations of the film and its effectiveness have been offered.

11 See further, e.g., R. S. Barbour (ed.), *The Kingdom of God and Human Society*, Edinburgh: T. & T. Clark 1993.

12 It should be stressed immediately that theological references to the 'elect' or 'the chosen' in Judaism and Christianity are not immediately to be linked with Gnosticism.

13 http:/www.fieldofdreamsmoviesite.com/.

14 http:/www.fieldofdreamsmoviesite.com/shoot.html.

11 A Christological postscript

1 I have argued this point myself in *Christ in Focus: Radical Christocentrism in Christian Theology*, London: SCM Press 2005.

2 I am aware that this could be said of any theme in theology i.e. all theological themes should be treated not only christologically, but also trinitarianly, eschatologically, pneumatologically, and so on. My point, however, is that Christian theology undoubtedly privileges Christology in this respect.

3 Pasolini's *The Gospel According to St. Matthew* is a notable exception.

12 Theology and life

1 I want to stress here that 'escape' can only be positive in the sense that many activities (prayer, sport, dog-walking, holidays, kite-flying) are both valuable in themselves, but also function recreatively as 'time apart' from life's main routines. The basis on which such activities function recreatively can, of course, prove very diverse.

2 For introductions to theories of religion, see, e.g., D. Pals, *Seven Theories of Religion*, Oxford: Oxford University Press 1996 (new edn: *Eight Theories of Religion*, Oxford: Oxford University Press 2006) and J. Thrower, *Religion: The Classical Theories*, Edinburgh: Edinburgh University Press 1999.

3 Naturally, from a theological perspective, such questions *do* need answering theologically. My point is that the need for theological responses cannot be presupposed for all.

4 It is at this point that there is intriguing convergence between what is happening in psychology (a shift from psychoanalytical methods to cognitive approaches) and in film studies (from screen theory to audience-response approaches in which cognitive psychology plays a part). My contention is simply that religious and theological studies should also be part of this mix. Failure to recognize the pertinence of religion and theology at this point would perpetuate a blind-spot which has long been present in film and cultural studies. Openness, in discussion about what films are doing, to what religions achieve could be very fruitful indeed. Religious studies could, in turn, benefit.

5 The background work for this conclusion was contained in my *Cinema and Sentiment*, Milton Keynes: Paternoster Press 2004.

6 For readers interested in following this up, the opening chapters (by Hiltner, Patton and Ballard) in J. Woodward and S. Pattison (eds), *The Blackwell Reader in Pastoral and Practical Theology*, Oxford: Blackwell 2000, are a useful starting point.

13 Theology and God

1 Richard Dawkins, who holds the Charles Simonyi of the Public Understanding of Science at the University of Oxford, is one of the most prominent contemporary exponents of this view. See his collection of essays *A Devil's Chaplain*, London: Weidenfeld and Nicolson 2003.

2 Don Cupitt, *Taking Leave of God*, London: SCM Press 1980 is a seminal text. Useful collections of essays on the debate include: J. Runzo (ed.), *Is God Real?*, Basingstoke: Macmillan 1993, C. Crowder (ed.), *God and Reality: Essays on Christian Non-Realism*, London: Mowbray 1997, and the opening essays in G. Hyman (ed.), *New Directions in Philosophical Theology*, Aldershot and Burlington, VT: Ashgate 2004.

3 Feuerbach was writing in the light of the philosophy of Immanuel Kant (1724–1804), whose work had made use of a basic distinction between the phenomenal world as we experience it and things as they are in themselves. His philosophy revolves around the fact that we cannot strictly know things in themselves and must work more on the extent to which we can order and shape what we experience. Kant's philosophy had a profound effect on all Western thought that followed him. Theology after Kant would always have to deal with the human subject, the believer, and struggled to keep its

focus on God, the object of belief, because of the attention given to the one who believes. Feuerbach appeared on the scene in the middle of that Kantian turn, and in his *The Essence of Christianity* (1841) took what was for him the logical step of concluding that God did indeed not exist. It was not simply that we could not know whether or not God existed. God did not exist and therefore what human beings were doing with the concept of God was projecting the highest aspirations of human consciousness onto an imagined being.

Feuerbach is therefore in a clear sense the first genuine non-realist because of the clarity with which he laid out his position. His position is a form of reductionism in that it explains theism in terms different from what theism had thus far claimed to be doing (i.e. talking about a reality 'God'). But it does not explain theism away. Feuerbach is describing what he thinks theology actually is and has been doing, whilst still acknowledging the value of religion. What he has done, however, has turned theology into an elaborate form of anthropology.

4   Tillich used the phrase 'ground of all being' in *The Shaking of the Foundations* (1949). He also speaks of 'the God above the God of theism', in *The Courage to Be* (1952; see the extract in Peter C. Hodgson and Robert H. King (eds), *Readings in Christian Theology*, Philadelphia: Fortress Press 1985, pp. 81–7) as a way of distinguishing the reality of God from human ideas about God.

5   Some would say that in prayer or in some forms of religious or mystical experience we do experience direct access.

6   See, e.g., J. Hick, *An Interpretation of Religion*, London: Macmillan 1988.

7   I am adopting the term and definition from John Hick, 'Religious Realism and Non-Realism: Defining the Issue' in Runzo (ed.), *Is God Real?*, pp. 3–16.

INDEX

Abelard, Peter 58
aesthetics 26, 57, 64, 67, 90
Alda, Alan 95
Allen, Woody 95–6, 103
Amadeus 80–1
Andersson, Harriet 97
Aniston, Jennifer 54
Anselm, Saint 58
Aquinas, Thomas 139
Athanasius, Saint 107–8
atheism 24, 47, 79, 173–4
atonement 55, 93
Auden, W.H. 65
Augustine, Saint 71–2, 77, 92, 106, 108
Axel, Gabriel 113

Babette's Feast 110, 112–13, 115, 117,120
baptism 109, 111, 115–16, 118–19
Barth, Karl 59
'base group' 134–5, 137–8
Basil of Caesarea 92
Bauckham, Richard 156
Bergman, Ingmar 97, 101

Blixen, Karen 113, 116
Bluteau, Lothaire 142
Body of Christ 37, 106, 157
'Born-again Christians' 28–30
Brassed Off 126, 128–30, 133, 135–6
Bruce Almighty 49–52, 54–6
Brunner, Emil 78
Buddhism 12

Callow, Simon 62
Calvin, John 58, 78
capitalism 16, 88
Carrey, Jim 49–50, 61
Cassian, John 92
Christ (inc. 'Jesus Christ' and 'Jesus of
    Nazareth') 12, 35, 48–52, 55, 72, 74–
    5, 88–90, 93, 95, 97, 99–100, 104–7,
    119–20, 124, 131, 142–4, 149–50,
    154–5, 157–8, 167
Christianity 12, 16, 18–20, 26, 28, 33, 35,
    39, 55, 69–70, 73–4, 93–4, 97, 163,
    165
Christie, Julie 112

church 12, 28–9, 31–2, 34, 39, 70–1, 74, 76, 87, 109, 124–5, 127, 129–38, 157, 164
cognition 26, 31, 37, 64, 82–3, 89–90, 105, 163–4
communities of practice 34
community 14, 23, 25–6, 31–4, 37–9, 55–6, 67, 71, 95, 113, 118, 120–1, 129, 138
Cone, James 59
Conservative Government 126, 128
Costner, Kevin 142
creation 33, 60, 67–8, 79, 90, 93, 122, 125, 155, 164
Cries and Whispers 97–8, 101, 105
Crimes and Misdemeanors 95–6, 98–9, 103
culture, cultures 12–15, 17, 21, 23–5, 27–31, 38, 53, 61, 64–5, 94–5, 132, 166–8
Curtis, Richard 62, 65, 75

Dafoe, Willem 101
Davies, Matthew 81
Dawkins, Richard 174
death 142–3, 145, 147–9, 151, 154
deism 79
Dogma 48
'Dogmatists' 29–30
Don't Look Now 11–14, 116–17, 121
Do the Right Thing 61–2, 64–5, 68–70, 73
Duff, Anne-Marie 126
Duffy, Dorothy 126–7

Eat Drink Man Woman 125–7, 133, 137
Ebert, Roger 65, 82, 145
Edwards, Jonathan 92
emotion, emotions 26, 36, 57, 63–4, 68, 71, 82–3, 85, 90, 99, 112, 127, 133, 143
Enlightenment 16, 148
entertainment 27
eschatology 141, 147, 149–52, 157
Eternal Sunshine of the Spotless Mind 61, 64, 71–3
ethics 26, 33, 57, 63, 90, 147, 149–51, 155
ethnicity 61–2, 64–5, 68, 70–1, 73, 76
Europe 18
Evangelicals 29

family 16–17, 33, 71, 76, 127, 133–5
Farrow, Mia 95

Feuerbach, Ludwig 172
Field of Dreams 142–5, 151
Fitzgerald, Michael 63
Fitzgerald, Tara 126
Florence, Council of 123
forgiveness 121, 152
Four Weddings and a Funeral 62, 65
Fox, George 140
Francis of Assisi 156
freedom 57, 79
Freeman, Morgan 49–50
friendship 33, 37, 71, 73, 76, 136–7
fundamentalism 36

Gibson, Mel 13, 49, 55, 167
gift 67–8, 84–5, 101
Glass, Philip 61
globalization 17
Gnosticism 54, 153–4
God 11–14, 34–5, 47–59, 67–9, 72–7, 79, 84–91, 93–4, 99–101, 104–5, 117–18, 121–2, 124–5, 131–2, 136, 147, 154–5, 157–8, 164, 170–6
Grant, Hugh 62–3
Gregory of Nyssa 156
Grimké, Sarah M. 78
guilt 82, 99, 103–4

Hampson, Daphne 108
Hannah, John 63
Harris, Ed 50
Hegel, G.W.F. 59
hell 149, 151
Hick, John 175
Hinduism 12
holiness 131
Holy Communion 24, 72, 109, 11, 113, 115–16, 118, 120–1, 134, 157
Holy Spirit 74, 87, 91, 131 see also Spirit
Hoover, Stewart 22–5, 28, 30–1
hope 152
Hugh of St Victor 116
human being 48, 60–77, 79–80, 87, 132, 155, 158, 163–4
Hunter, Holly 110
Huston, Angelica 95

incarnation 48
Irenaeus of Lyon 139, 155–6
Islam 12, 19

Jackson, Samuel 70
Jesus of Montreal 142–4, 149, 151, 157
Jesus of Nazareth *see* Christ
Jones, James Earl 143
Judaism 12, 19, 54, 73
judgment 149, 151

Kant, Immanuel 108
Kaufman, Charlie 61
Kazantzakis, Nikos 97, 100, 106
Kelsey, David 94–5
King, Martin Luther 61
kingdom of God 33, 70, 88, 90–1, 136–8,
    146, 149, 152, 154–5, 157
Koyaanisqatsi 60–1, 63, 67–8
Kundun 13

Lancaster, Burt 143
Landau, Martin 95
The Last Temptation of Christ 96–7, 100, 106,
    157–8
Lee, Ang 125, 127
Lee, Spike 61, 65, 70–1
Legally Blonde 80–3, 164
leisure 16–17, 34
Leo the Great 139
liberation 52, 93, 98, 110
Linney, Laura 50, 63
liturgy 24, 26
Lombard, Peter 117
love 62, 75–6, 118–19, 122, 157, 164
Love Actually 62–3, 66
Lung, Sihung 125
Luther, Martin 123, 139

Macquarrie, John 140
McInnerny, Tim 63
McKee, Gina 63
The Magdalene Sisters 125, 126–7, 129–30,
    132, 136
'Mainstream believers' 29–30
Maitland, Sara 78
Malcolm X 61

Maloney, Michael 142
Maris, Stella 149
Mbiti, John 78
meaning-making 22–4, 32
media 14, 16–17, 21–6, 29–31, 124
memory 71–2
'Metaphysical believers' 29–30
The Mission 127
Moltmann Jürgen 59, 156
Mozart, Wolfgang Amadeus 80–3, 85 88
Muentzer, Thomas 156
Mullan, Peter 126, 136, 138
music 63, 81–2, 112, 137
myth 24, 35–6, 39

narrative 35
Nicaea, Second Council of 123
Niebuhr, Reinhold 78
non-realism 171–4
Noone, Bernadette 126
Notting Hill 62–3, 65, 75
Nyman, Michael 112

Oh, God 48
omnipotence 56–7
Orange, Second Council of 108
Orthodox Church, Greek 117, 134, 149

Paquin, Anna 110
The Passion of the Christ 13, 49–51, 55–6, 96,
    157–8, 167
patriarchy 134
Pelletier, Gilles 142
Penn, Sean 96, 99
philosophy 12, 17, 25, 72, 132, 172
physical impairment 89
The Piano 110, 112, 115, 117–18
pluralism 16–17, 36, 55, 153–4
politics 16–17, 33–4, 39, 68, 128
postmodernism 15–16, 144, 151, 162
practical theology 168–9
prayer 24–5, 39, 87
Protestants 29, 121
providence 79
psychology 39, 133, 162, 164

Radbertus 123

Ratramnus 123
Rauschenbusch, Walter 156
realism (in theology) 171–5
redemption 33, 48, 93–107, 109, 125, 157
Reformation 148
Reggio, Godfrey 67
Renaissance 148
resurrection 105, 144–6, 148, 151
Rickman, Alan 63, 141
ritual 13, 22, 36–7, 39, 57, 77
Roberts, Julia 63
Roman Catholic, Roman Catholicism 29,
    117, 127, 129, 132, 142
Roof, Wade Clark 28, 31

sacraments, sacramentality 77, 111, 115–
    18, 120–1, 125, 157
Salieri, Antonio 80–1, 85, 88–9
salvation 67, 74, 98
Savage, John 64
Schleiermacher, F.D.E. 140, 168
Scorsese, Martin 13, 98, 100–1
scripture 13, 26
'Secularists' 29–30
'Seekers' 29
sex 16, 63, 75, 112
Shaffer, Peter 80
The Shawshank Redemption 101
Simpson, Joe 80–1, 83, 86–7, 89, 91
sin 69–70, 77, 105–6
spirit 80, 83–91, 119, 125, 148
spirituality 29, 38–9
sport 16, 27
Stevenson, Juliet 141
Sutherland, Donald 112
Swinburne, R. 78
systematic theology 57, 163–6

Temple, William 121
The Ten Commandments 48
Tertullian 122
therapy 15, 73
Thompson, Emma 63, 66
Thulin, Ingrid 97
Tillich, Paul 172
Tompkinson, Stephen 126
Touching the Void 80–2, 86, 89
transcendence 12, 38
Trinity, doctrine of 72, 74, 118
Truly Madly Deeply 141–3, 148–9
The Truman Show 49–52, 56
truth 162
21 Grams 96, 98–100

Ullmann, Liv 97
USA 18, 29

Vatican (Second Vatican Council) 140
violence 62, 68, 114

Wang, Yu-Wen 125
Waterston, Sam 99
Watts, Naomi 96, 99
Westhelle, Vitor 78
Westminster Shorter Catechism 74
Whaley, Frank 143
Winslet, Kate 61
Witherspoon, Reese 81
work 16, 33, 88
worship 25–6, 29, 85, 132, 134
Wu, Chien-Lien 125

Yang, Kuei-Mei 125
Yates, Simon 80–1, 86

Related titles from Routledge

THE FILM AND RELIGION READER
Edited by Jolyon Mitchell and S. Brent Plate

Edited by leading experts in the field, this is the first comprehensive reader to offer a survey of the subject to date. Film is now widely studied and researched in theology and religious studies departments; *The Film and Religion Reader* explores key topics including:

- early responses to film
- directors
- films and audiences
- cultural and social contexts
- Biblical connections
- theological approaches
- religious studies perspectives.

The *Reader* brings together a huge amount of material in a student-friendly format and will be an invaluable resource for courses within both theology and religious studies.

ISBN10: 0-415-40494-0 (hbk)
ISBN10: 0-415-40495-9 (pbk)

ISBN13: 978-0-415-40494-5 (hbk)
ISBN13: 978-0-415-40495-2 (pbk)

Available at all good bookshops
For ordering and further information please visit:
www.routledge.com

Related titles from Routledge

RELIGION IN THE MEDIA AGE

Stewart M. Hoover

Looking at the everyday interaction of religion and media in our cultural lives, *Religion in the Media Age* is an exciting new assessment of the state of modern religiosity. Recent years have produced a marked turn away from institutionalized religions towards more autonomous, individual forms of the search for spiritual meaning. Film, television, the music industry and the internet are central to this process, cutting through the monolithic assertions of world religions and giving access to more diverse and fragmented ideals. While the sheer volume and variety of information travelling through global media changes modes of religious thought and commitment, the human desire for spirituality also invigorates popular culture itself, recreating commodities – film blockbusters, world sport, popular music – as contexts for religious meaning.

Drawing on fascinating research into household media consumption Stewart M. Hoover charts the way in which media and religion intermingle and collide in the cultural experience of media audiences. The result will be essential reading for everyone interested in how today's mass media relate to contemporary religious and spiritual life.

Religion, Media and Culture Series
Edited by Stewart M. Hoover, Jolyon Mitchell, and David Morgan

ISBN10: 0-415-31422-4 (hbk)
ISBN10: 0-415-31423-2 (pbk)

ISBN13: 978-0-145-31422-0 (hbk)
ISBN13: 978-0-145-31423-7 (pbk)

Available at all good bookshops
For ordering and further information please visit:
www.routledge.com

THE BIBLE IN WESTERN CULTURE

Dee Dyas and Esther Hughes

The influence of the Bible in Western culture is immeasurable. *The Bible in Western Culture* is the essential guide for those wishing to find out more about the Bible and its impact on the world around us.

It offers concise and accessible introductions to the Bible's most important characters, stories and themes, enabling better understanding, study and analysis of the Christian element in Western culture.

With no prior biblical knowledge required, the volume offers a framework of understanding for those studying Western literature, art, historical events, or for those just wanting to improve their general knowledge.

It provides:

* edited extracts from the Bible
* explanations of the context and beliefs of each passage
* links to related biblical texts
* examples of related key works of art and literature
* brief biographies of key figures
* a comprehensive glossary defining specialist terms
* chronology
* suggested further reading.

This book enables readers to encounter key Bible stories directly, while also providing background information on issues of content, context and influence.

ISBN10: 0-415-32617-6 (hbk)
ISBN10: 0-415-32618-4 (pbk)

ISBN13: 978-0-415-32617-9 (hbk)
ISBN13: 978-0-415-32618-6 (pbk)

Related titles from Routledge

FIFTY KEY CHRISTIAN THINKERS

Peter McEnhill and George Newlands

'An accessible and thought-provoking way into the work of some of the most influential Christian thinkers from the first century AD to the present day. Clearly written, it provides succinct and lively, but not oversimplified, accounts of the thinkers discussed.'

Rachel Muers, University of Exeter

Fifty Key Christian Thinkers provides both valuable information and stimulating debate on the lives and work of fifty of the most important Christian theologians. This guide provides an overview of Christian theology from the emergence of the faith 2000 years ago to the present day. Among the figures profiled in this accessible guide are:

- St Paul
- Barth
- Aquinas
- Boethius
- Niebuhr
- Calvin
- Luther
- Feuerbach
- Kierkegaard
- Origen

ISBN10: 0-415-17049-4 (hbk)
ISBN10: 0-415-17050-8 (pbk)

ISBN13: 978-0-415-17049-9 (hbk)
ISBN13: 978-0-415-17050-5 (pbk)

Available at all good bookshops
For ordering and further information please visit:
www.routledge.com

Related titles from Routledge

PHILOSOPHY GOES TO THE MOVIES
SECOND EDITION
Christopher Falzon

- What can we learn about the nature of knowledge from *Rear Window*?
- How can *Total Recall* help us understand personal identity?
- What does *High Noon* have to do with Kant?

From *Metropolis* to *The Matrix*, from *Gattaca* to *Groundhog Day*, films can help to illustrate and illuminate complex philosophical thought.

Philosophy Goes to the Movies is a new kind of introduction to philosophy that makes use of film to help us understand philosophical ideas and positions. Drawing on a wide range of films from around the world, and the ideas of a diverse selection of thinkers from Plato and Descartes to Marcuse and Foucault, Christopher Falzon introduces and discusses central areas of philo-sophical concern, including the theory of knowledge, the self and personal identity, ethics, social and political philosophy and critical thinking.

Ideal for beginners, this book guides the reader through philosophy using lively and illuminating cinematic examples including *A Clockwork Orange*, *Mulholland Drive*, *Bladerunner*, *Modern Times* and *Wings of Desire*.

ISBN10: 0-415-35725-X (hbk)
ISBN10: 0-415-35726-8 (pbk)

ISBN13: 978-0-415-35725-8 (hbk)
ISBN13: 978-0-415-35726-5 (pbk)